I0749260

A LOVE STORY

A BUSHMAN

A Love Story

A Bushman

PO Box 2211
Fairfield, IA 52556
www.1stworldlibrary.com
First Edition

LCCN: 2006907696

Softcover ISBN: 1-4218-2414-0
Hardcover ISBN: 1-4218-2314-4
eBook ISBN: 1-4218-2514-7

1st World Library Literary Society

Giving Back to the World

"If you want to work on the core problem, it's early school literacy."

- James Barksdale, former CEO of Netscape

"No skill is more crucial to the future of a child, or to a democratic and prosperous society, than literacy."

- Los Angeles Times

Literacy... means far more than learning how to read and write... The aim is to transmit... knowledge and promote social participation."

- UNESCO

"Literacy is not a luxury, it is a right and a responsibility. If our world is to meet the challenges of the twenty-first century we must harness the energy and creativity of all our citizens."

- President Bill Clinton

"Parents should be encouraged to read to their children, and teachers should be equipped with all available techniques for teaching literacy, so the varying needs and capacities of individual kids can be taken into account."

- Hugh Mackay

Vol. I

"My thoughts, like swallows, skim the main,
And bear my spirit back again
Over the earth, and through the air,
A wild bird and a wanderer."

To

Lady Gipps

This Work Is Respectfully Inscribed,

By A Grateful Friend.

PREFACE

The author of these pages considered that a lengthened explanation might be necessary to account for the present work.

He had therefore, at some length, detailed the motives that influenced him in its composition. He had shown that as a solitary companionless bushman, it had been a pleasure to him in his lone evenings

> "To create, and in creating live
> A being more intense."

He had expatiated on the love he bears his adopted country, and had stated that he was greatly influenced by the hope that although

> "Sparta hath many a worthier son than he,"

this work might be the humble cornerstone to some enduring and highly ornamented structure.

The author however fortunately remembered, that readers have but little sympathy with the motives of authors; but expect that their works should amuse or instruct them. He will therefore content himself, with giving a quotation from one of those old authors, whose "well of English undefined" shames our modern writers.

He intreats that the indulgence prayed for by the learned Cowell may be accorded to his humble efforts.

"My true end is the advancement of knowledge, and therefore have I published this poor work, not only to impart the good thereof, to those young ones that want it, but also to draw from the learned, the supply of my defects.

"Whosoever will charge these travails with many oversights, he shall need no solemn pains to prove them.

"And upon the view taken of this book sithence the impression, I dare assure them, that shall observe most faults therein, that I, by gleaning after him, will gather as many omitted by him, as he shall shew committed by me.

"What a man saith well is not, however, to be rejected, because he hath some errors; reprehend who will, in God's name, that is, with sweetness, and without reproach.

"So shall he reap hearty thanks at my hands, and thus more soundly help in a few months, than I by tossing and tumbling my books at home, could possibly have done in some years."

CHAPTER I

THE FAMILY

"It was a vast and venerable pile."

"Oh, may'st thou ever be as now thou art,
Nor unbeseem the promise of thy spring."

The mansion in which dwelt the Delmés was one of wide and extensive range. Its centre slightly receded, leaving a wing on either side. Fluted ledges, extending the whole length of the building, protruded above each story. These were supported by quaint heads of satyr, martyr, or laughing triton. The upper ledge, which concealed the roof from casual observers, was of considerably greater projection. Placed above it, at intervals, were balls of marble, which, once of pure white, had now caught the time-worn hue of the edifice itself. At each corner of the front and wings, the balls were surmounted by the family device - the eagle with extended wing. One claw closed over the stone, and the bird rode it proudly an' it had been the globe. The portico, of a pointed Gothic, would have seemed heavy, had it not been lightened by glass doors, the vivid colours of which were not of modern date. These admitted to a capacious hall, where, reposing on the wide-spreading antlers of some pristine tenant of the park, gleamed many a piece of armour that in days of yore had not been worn ingloriously.

The Delmé family was an old Norman one, on whose

antiquity a peerage could have conferred no new lustre. At the period when the aristocracy of Great Britain lent themselves to their own diminution of importance, by the prevalent system of rejecting the poorer class of tenantry, in many instances the most attached, - the consequence was foreseen by the then proprietor of Delmé Park, who, spurning the advice of some interested few around him, continued to foster those whose ancestors had served his. The Delmés were thus enabled to retain - and they deserved it - that fair homage which rank and property should ever command. As a family they were popular, and as individuals universally beloved.

At the period we speak of, the Delmé family consisted but of three members: the baronet, Sir Henry Delmé; his brother George, some ten years his junior, a lieutenant in a light infantry regiment at Malta; and one sister, Emily, Emily Delmé was the youngest child; her mother dying shortly after her birth. The father, Sir Reginald Delmé, a man of strong feelings and social habits, never recovered this blow. Henry Delmé was barely fifteen when he was called to the baronetcy and to the possession of the Delmé estates. It was found that Sir Reginald had been more generous than the world had given him credit for, and that his estates were much encumbered. The trustees were disposed to rest contented with paying off the strictly legal claims during Sir Henry's minority. This the young heir would not accede to. He waited on his most influential guardian - told him he was aware his father, from hospitality and good nature, had incurred obligations which the law did not compel his son to pay; but which he could not but think that equity and good feeling did. He begged that these might be added to the other claims, and that the trustees would endeavour to procure him a commission in the army. He was gazetted to a cornetcy; and entered life at an age when, if the manlier traits are ready to be developed, the worthless ones are equally sure to unfold themselves. Few of us that have not found the first draught of life intoxicate! Few of us that have not then run wild, as colts that have slipped their bridle! Experience - that mystic word - is wanting; the retrospect of past years wakes no sigh; expectant youth looks forward to future ones without a shade of distrust. The mind is elastic - the body vigorous and free from pain; and it is then youth inwardly feels, although not daring to avow it, the almost total impossibility that the mind should wax less vigorous, or the body grow helpless, and decay.

But Sir Henry was cast in a finer mould, nor did his conduct at this dangerous period detract from this his trait of boyhood. He joined his regiment when before the enemy, and, until he came of age, never drew on his guardians for a shilling. Delmé's firmness of purpose, and his after prudence, met with their due reward. The family estates became wholly unencumbered, and Sir Henry was enabled to add to the too scanty provision of his sister, as well as to make up to George, on his entering the army, a sum more than adequate to all his wants. These circumstances were enough to endear him to his family; and, in truth, amidst all its members, there prevailed a confidence and an unanimity which were never for an instant impaired. There was one consequence, however, of Sir Henry Delmé's conduct that *he*, at the least, foresaw not, but which was gradually and unconsciously developed. In pursuing the line of duty he had marked out - in acting up to what he knew was right - his mind became *too* deeply impressed with the circumstances which had given rise to his determination. It overstepped its object. The train of thought, to which necessity gave birth, continued to pervade when that necessity no longer existed. His wish to re-establish his house grew into an ardent desire to aggrandize it. His ambition appeared a legitimate one. It grew with his years, and increased with his strength.

Many a time, on the lone bivouac, when home presents itself in its fairest colours to the soldier's mind, would Delmé's prayer be embodied, that his house might again be elevated, and that his descendants might know *him* as the one to whom they were indebted for its rise. Delmé's ambitious thoughts were created amidst dangers and toil, in a foreign land, and far from those who shared his name. But his heart swelled high with them as he again trod his native soil in peace - as he gazed on the home of his fathers, and communed with those nearest and dearest to him on earth. Sir Henry considered it incumbent on him to exert every means that lay in his power to promote his grand object. A connection that promised rank and honours, seemed to him an absolute essential that was worth any sacrifice. Sir Henry never allowed himself to look for, or give way to, those sacred sympathies, which the God of nature hath implanted in the breasts of all of us. Delmé had arrived at middle age ere a feeling incompatible with his views arose. But his had been a dangerous experiment. Our hearts or minds, or whatever it may be that takes the impression, resemble some crystalline lake that mirrors the smallest object, and heightens its beauty; but if it once gets muddied or ruffled, the most lovely object ceases to be reflected in its waters. By the time that lake is clear again, the fairy form that ere while lingered on its bosom is fled for ever.

Thus much in introducing the head of the family. Let us now attempt to sketch the gentle Emily.

Emily Delmé was not an ordinary being. To uncommon talents, and a mind of most refined order, she united great feminine propriety, and a total absence of those arts which sometimes characterise those to whom the accident of birth has given importance. With unerring discrimination, she drew the exact line between vivacity and satire, true religion and its semblance. She saw through and pitied those who, pluming themselves on the faults of others, and imparting to the outward man the ascetic inflexibility of the inner one, would fain propagate on all sides their rigid creed, forbidding the more favoured commoners of nature even to sip joy's chalice. If not a saint, however, but a fair, confiding, and romantic girl, she was good without misanthropy, pure without pretension, and joyous, as youth and hopes not crushed might make her. She was one of those of whom society might justly be proud. She obeyed its dictates without question, but her feelings underwent no debasement from the contact. If not a child of nature, she was by no means the slave of art.

Emily Delmé was more beautiful than striking. She impressed

more than she exacted. Her violet eye gleamed with feeling; her smile few could gaze on without sympathy - happy he who might revel in its brightness! If aught gave a peculiar tinge to her character, it was the pride she felt in the name she bore, - this she might have caught from Sir Henry, - the interest she took in the legends connected with that name, and the gratification which the thought gave her, that by her ancestors, its character had been but rarely sullied, and never disgraced.

These things, it may be, she had accustomed herself to look on in a light too glowing: for these things and all mundane ones are vain; but her character did not consequently suffer. Her lip curled not with hauteur, nor was her brow raised one shadow the more. The remembrance of the old Baronetcy were on the ensanguined plain, - of the matchless loyalty of a father and five valiant sons in the cause of the Royal Charles, - the pondering over tomes, which in language obsolete, but true, spoke of the grandeur - the deserved grandeur of her house; these might be recollections and pursuits, followed with an ardour too enthusiastic, but they stayed not the hand of charity, nor could they check pity's tear. If her eye flashed as she gazed on the ancient device of her family, reposing on its time worn pedestal, it could melt to the tale of the houseless wanderer, and sympathise with the sorrows of the fatherless.

CHAPTER II

THE ALBUM

"Oh that the desert were my dwelling place,
With one fair spirit for my minister;
That I might all forget the human race,
And, hating no one, love but only her."

A cheerful party were met in the drawing room of Delmé. Clarendon Gage, a neighbouring land proprietor, to whom Emily had for a twelvemonth been betrothed, had the night previous returned from a continental tour. In consequence, Emily looked especially radiant, Delmé much pleased, and Clarendon superlatively happy. Nor must we pass over Mrs. Glenallan, Miss Delmé's worthy aunt, who had supplied the place of a mother to Emily, and who now sat in her accustomed chair, with an almost sunny brow, quietly pursuing her monotonous tambouring. At times she turned to admire her niece, who occasionally walked to the glass window, to caress and feed an impudent white peacock; which one moment strutted on the wide terrace, and at another lustily tapped for his bread at ne of the lower panes.

"I am glad to see you looking so well, Clarendon!"

"And I can return the compliment, Delmé! Few, looking at you now, would take you for an old campaigner."

The style of feature in Delmé and Clarendon was very dissimilar. Sir Henry was many years Gage's senior; but his manly bearing, and dark decided features, would bear a contrast with even the tall and elegant, although slight form of Clarendon. The latter was very fair, and what we are accustomed to call English-looking. His hair almost, but not quite, flaxen, hung in thick curls over his forehead, and would have given an effeminate expression to the face, were it not for the peculiar flash of the clear blue eye.

"Come! Clarendon," said Emily, "I will impose a task. You have written twice in my album; once, years ago, and the second time on the eve of our parting. Come! you shall read us both effusions, and then write a sonnet to our happy meeting. Would that dear George were here now!"

Gage took up the book. It was a moderately-sized volume, bound in crimson velvet. It was the fashion to keep albums *then.* It glittered not in a binding of azure and gold, nor were its momentous secrets enclosed by one of Bramah's locks. The Spanish proverb says, "Tell me who you are with, and I will tell you what you are." Ours, in that album age, used to be, "Show me your scrap book, I will tell you your character." Emily's was not one commencing with -

"I never loved a dear gazelle!"

and ending with stanzas on the "Forget-me-not." It had not those hackneyed but beautiful lines addressed by Mr. Spencer to Lady Crewe -

> "I stay'd too late: forgive the crime!
> Unheeded flew the hours;
> For noiseless falls the foot of Time.
> That only treads on flowers."

Nor contained it those sublime, but yet more common ones, on Sir John Moore's death; which lines, by the bye, have suffered more from that mischief-making, laughter-loving creature, Parody, than any lines we know. It was not one of these books. Nor was it the splendid scrap book, replete with superb engravings and proof-impression prints; nor at all allied to the sentimental one of a garrison flirt, containing locks of hair of at least five gentlemen, three of whom are officers in the army. Nor, lastly, was it of that genus which has vulgarity in its very title-page, and is here and there interspersed with devilish imps, or caricatured likenesses of the little proprietress, all done in most infinite humour, and marking the familiar friendship, of some half-dozen whiskered cubs, having what is technically called the run of the house. No! it was a repository for feeling and for memory, and, in its fair pages, presented an image of Emily's heart. Many of these were marked, it is true; and what human being's character is unchequered? But it was blotless; and the virgin page looks not so white as when the contrast of the sable ink is there.

Clarendon read aloud his first contribution - who knows it not? The very words form a music, and that music is Metastasio's,

> "Placido zeffiretto,
> Se trovi il caro oggetto,
> Digli che sei sospiro
> Ma non gli dir di chi,
> Limpido ruscelletto,
> Se mai t'incontri in lei,
> Digli che pianto sei,
> Ma non le dir qual' eiglio
> Crescer ti fe cosi."

"And now, Emily! for my parting tribute - if I remember right, it was sorrowful enough."

Gage read, with tremulous voice, the following, which we will christen

THE FAREWELL.

I will not be the lightsome lark,
That carols to the rising morn, -
I'd rather be some plaintive bird
Lulling night's ear forlorn.

I will not be the green, green leaf,
Mingling 'midst thousand leaves and flowers
That shed their fairy charms around
To deck Spring's joyous bowers.

I'd rather be the one red leaf,
Waving 'midst Autumn's sombre groves: -
On the heart to breathe that sadness
Which contemplation loves.

I will not be the morning ray,
Dancing upon the river's crest,
All light, all motion, when the stream
Turns to the sun her breast.

I'd rather be the gentle shade,
Lengthening as eve comes stealing on,
And rest in pensive sadness there,
When those bright rays are gone.

I will not be a smile to play
Upon thy coral lip, and shed
Around it sweetness, like the sun
Risen from his crimson bed.

Oh, no! I'll be the tear that steals
In pity from that eye of blue,
Making the cheek more lovely red,
Like rose-leaf dipp'd in dew.

I will not be remember'd when
Mirth shall her pageant joys impart, -
A dream to sparkle in thine eye,
Yet vanish from thy heart.

But when pensive sadness clouds thee,
When thoughts, half pain, half pleasure, steal
Upon the heart, and memory doth
The shadowy past reveal.

When seems the bliss of former years, -
Too sweet, too pure, to feel again, -
And long lost hours, scenes, friends, return,
Remember me, love - then!

"Ah, Clarendon! how often have I read those lines, and thought - but I will not think now! Here come the letters! Henry will soon be busy - I shall finish my drawing - and aunt will finish - no! she never *can* finish her tambour work. Take my portfolio and give me another contribution!" Gage now wrote "The Return," which we insert for the reader's approval: -

THE RETURN.

When the blue-eyed morn doth peep
Over the soft hill's verdant steep,
Lighting up its shadows deep,
I'll think of thee, love, *then!*

When the lightsome lark doth sing
Her grateful song to Nature's King,
Making all the woodlands ring,
I'll think of thee, love, *then!*

Or when plaintive Philomel
Shall mourn her mate in some lone dell,
And to the night her sorrows tell,
I'll think of thee, love, *then!*

When the first green leaf of spring
Shall promise of the summer bring,
And all around its fragrance fling,
I'll think of thee, love, *then!*

Or when the last red leaf shall fall,
And winter spread its icy pall,
To mind me of the death of all,
I'll think of thee, love, *then!*

When the lively morning ray
Is dancing on the river's spray,
And sunshine gilds the joyous day,
I'll think of thee, love, *then*!

And when the shades of eve steal on,
Lengthening as life's sun goes down,
Like sweetest constancy alone,
I'll think of thee, love, *then*!

When I see a sweet smile play
On coral lips, like Phoebus' ray,
Making all look warm and gay,
I'll think of thee, love, *then*!

When steals the tear of pity, too,
O'er a cheek, whose crimson hue
Looks like rose-leaf dipp'd in dew,
I'll think of thee, love, *then*!

When mirth's pageant joys unbind
The gloomy spells that chain my mind,
And make me dream of all that's kind,
I'll think of thee, love, *then*!

And when pensive sadness clouds me,
When the host of memory crowds me,
When the shadowy past enshrouds me,
I'll think of thee, love, *then*!

When seems the bliss of former years, -
Too sweet, too pure, to feel again, -
And long lost hours, scenes, friends, return,
I'll think of thee, love, *then*!

CHAPTER III

THE DINNER

"Hues which have words, and speak to ye of heaven."

"Away! there need no words or terms precise,
The paltry jargon of the marble mart,
Where pedantry gulls folly: we have eyes."

We are told by the members of the silver-fork school, that no tale of fiction can be complete unless it embody the description of a dinner. Let us, therefore, shutting from our view that white-limbed gum-tree, and dismissing from our table tea and damper, [Footnote: *Damper*. Bushman's fare - unleavened bread] call on memory's fading powers, and feast once more with the rich, the munificent, the intellectual Belliston Græme.

Dinner! immortal faculty of eating! to what glorious sense or pre-eminent passion dost thou not contribute? Is not love half fed by thy attractions? Beams ever the eye of lover more bright than when, after gazing with enraptured glance at the coveted haunch, whose fat - a pure white; whose lean - a rich brown - invitingly await the assault. When doth lover's eye sparkle more, than when, at such a moment, it lights on the features of the loved fair one? Is not the supper quadrille the most dangerous and the dearest of all?

Cherished venison! delicate white soup! spare young susceptible bosoms! Again we ask, is not dinner the very aliment of friendship? the hinge on which it turns? Does a man's heart expand to you ere you have returned his dinner? It would be folly to assert it. Cabinet dinners – corporation dinners - election dinners - and vestry dinners - and rail-road dinners - we pass by these things, and triumphantly ask - does not *the* Ship par excellence - the Ship of Greenwich - annually assemble under its revered roof the luminaries of the nation? Oh, whitebait! called so early to your last account! a tear is all we give, but it flows spontaneously at the memory of your sorrows!

As Mr. Belliston Græme was much talked of in his day, it may not be amiss to say a few words regarding him. He was an only child, and at an early age lost his parents. The expense of his education was defrayed by a wealthy uncle, the second partner in a celebrated banking house. His tutor, with whom he may be said to have lived from boyhood - for his uncle had little communication with him, except to write to him one letter half-yearly, when he paid his school bill - was a shy retiring clergyman - a man of very extensive acquirements, and a first rate classical scholar. After a short time, the curate and young Græme became attached to each other. The tutor was a bachelor, and Græme was his only pupil. The latter was soon inoculated with the classical mania of his preceptor; and, as he grew up, it was quite a treat to hear the pair discourse of Greeks and Romans. A stranger who had *then* heard them would have imagined that Themistocles and Scipio Africanus were stars of the present generation. When Græme was nineteen, his uncle invited him to town for a month - a most unusual proceeding. During this period he studied closely his nephew's character. At the end of this term, Mr. Hargrave and his young charge were on their way to the classical regions, where their fancy had been so long straying. They explored France, and the northern parts of Italy - came on the shores of the Adriatic - resided and secretly made excavations near the amphitheatre of Polo - and finally reached the Morea. Not a crag, valley, or brook, that they were not conversant with before they left it. They at length tore themselves away; and found themselves at the ancient Parthenope. It was at Pompeii Mr. Græme first saw the beautiful Miss Vignoles, the Mrs. Glenallan of our story; and, in a strange adventure with some Neapolitan guides, was of some service to her party. They saw his designs of some tombs, and took the trouble of drawing him out. The young man now for the first time basked in the sweets of society; in a fortnight, to Mr. Hargrave's horror, was rolling in its vortex; in a couple of months found himself indulging in, and avowing, a hopeless passion; and in three, was once again in his native land, falsely deeming that his peace of mind had fled for ever. He was shortly, however, called upon to exert his energies. The death of his uncle suddenly made him, to his very great surprise, one of the wealthiest commoners of England. At this period he was quite unknown. In a short time Mr. Hargrave and himself were lodged luxuriously - were deep in the pursuit of science, literature, and the belle arte - and on terms of friendship with the cleverest and most original men of the day. Mr. Græme's occupations being sedentary, and his habits very regular, he shortly found that his great wealth enabled him, not only to indulge in every personal luxury at Rendlesham Park, but to patronise largely every literary work of merit. In him the needy man of genius found a friend, the man of wit a companion, and the publisher a generous customer. He became famous for his house, his library, his exclusive society. But he did not become spoilt by his prosperity, and never neglected his old tutor.

Our party from Delmé were ushered into a large drawing-room, the sole light of which was from an immense bow window, looking out on the extensive lawn. The panes were of enormous size, and beautiful specimens of classique plated glass. The only articles of furniture, were some crimson ottomans which served to set off the splendid paintings; and one table of the Florentine manufacture of pietra dura, on which stood a carved bijou of Benvenuto Cellini's. Our party were early. They were welcomed by Mr. Græme with great cordiality, and by Mr. Hargrave with some embarrassment, for the tutor was still the bashful man of former days. Mr. Græme's dress shamed these degenerate days of black stock and loose trowser. Diamond buckles adorned his knees, and fastened his shoes. His clear blue eye - the high polished forehead - the deep lines of the countenance - revealed the man of thought and intellect. The playful lip shewed he could yet appreciate a flash of wit or spark of humour.

"Miss Delmé, you are looking at my paintings; let me show you my late purchases. Observe this sweet Madonna, by Murillo! I prefer it to the one in the Munich Gallery. It may not boast Titian's glow of colour, or Raphael's grandeur of design, - in delicate angelic beauty, it may yield to the delightful efforts of Guido's or Correggio's pencil, - but surely no human conception can ever have more touchingly portrayed the beauteous resigned mother. The infant, too! how inimitably blended is the God-like serenity of the Saviour, with the fond and graceful witcheries of the loving child! How little we know of the beauties of the Spanish school! Would I could ransack their ancient monasteries, and bring a few of them to light!

"You are a chess player! Pass not by this check-mate of Caravaggio's. What undisguised triumph in one countenance! What a struggle to repress nature's feelings in the other! Here is a Guido! sweet, as his ever are! He may justly be styled the female laureat. What artist can compete with him in delineating the blooming expression, or the tender, but lighter, shades of female loveliness? who can pause between even the Fornarina, and that divine effort, the Beatrice Cenci of the Barberini?"

The party were by this time assembled. Besides our immediate friends, there was his Grace the Duke of Gatten, a good-natured fox-hunting nobleman, whose estate adjoined Mr. Græme's; there was the Viscount Chambéry, who had penned a pamphlet on finance - indited a folio on architecture - and astonished Europe with an elaborate dissertation on modern cookery; there was Charles Selby, the poet and essayist;

Daintrey, the sculptor - a wonderful Ornithologist - a deep read Historian - a learned Orientalist - and a novelist, from France; whose works exhibited such unheard of horrors, and made man and woman so irremediably vicious, as to make this young gentleman celebrated, even in Paris - that Babylonian sink of iniquity.

Dinner was announced, and our host, giving his arm very stoically to Mrs. Glenallan, his love of former days, led the way to the dining-room. Round the table were placed beautifully carved oaken fauteuils, of a very old pattern. The service of plate was extremely plain, but of massive gold. But the lamp! It was of magnificent dimensions! The light chains hanging from the frescoed ceiling, the links of which were hardly perceptible, were of silver, manufactured in Venice; the lower part was of opal-tinted glass, exactly portraying some voluptuous couch, on which the beautiful Amphitrite might have reclined, as she hastened through beds of coral to crystal grot, starred with transparent stalactites. In the centre of this shell, were sockets, whence verged small hollow golden tubes, resembling in shape and size the stalks of a flower. At the drooping ends of these, were lamps shaped and coloured to imitate the most beauteous flowers of the parterre. This bouquet of light had been designed by Mr. Græme. Few novelties had acquired greater celebrity than the Græme astrale. The room was warmed by heating the pedestals of the statues.

"Potage à la fantôme, and à l'ourika."

"I will trouble you, Græme," said my Lord Chambéry, "for the fantôme. I have dined on la pritannière for the last three months, and a novel soup is a novel pleasure."

Of the fish, the soles were à la Rowena, the salmon à l'amour. Emily flirted with the wing of a chicken sauté au suprême, coquetted with perdrix perdu masqué à la Montmorenci, and tasted a boudin à la Diebitsch. The wines were excellent - the Geisenheim delicious - the Champagne sparkling like a pun of Jekyll's. But nothing aroused the attention of the Viscount

Chambéry so much as a liqueur, which Mr. Græme assured him was new, and had just been sent him by the Conte de Desir. The dessert had been some time on the table, when the Viscount addressed his host.

"Græme! I am delighted to find that you at length agree with me as to the monstrous superiority of a French repast. Your omelette imaginaire was faultless, and as for your liqueur, I shall certainly order a supply on my return to Paris."

"That liqueur, my dear lord," replied Mr. Græme, "is good old cowslip mead, with a flask of Maraschino di Zara infused in it. For the rest, the dinner has been almost as imaginaire as the omelet. The greater part of the recipes are in an old English volume in my library, or perhaps some owe their origin to the fertile invention of my housekeeper. Let us style them à la Dorothée."

"Capital! I thank you, Græme!" said his Grace of Gatten, as he shook his host by the hand, till the tears stood in his eyes.

The prescient Chambéry had made a good dinner, and bore the joke philosophically. Coffee awaited the gentlemen in a small octagonal chamber, adjoining the music room. There stood Mr. Græme's three favourite modern statues: - a Venus, by Canova - a Discobole, by Thorwaldson - and a late acquisition - the Ariadne, of Dannecker.

"This is the work of an artist," said Mr. Græme, "little known in this country, but in Germany ranking quite as high as Thorwaldson. This is almost a duplicate of his Ariadne at Frankfort, but the marble is much more pure. How wonderfully fine the execution! Pray notice the bold profile of the face; how energetic her action as she sits on the panther!"

Mr. Græme touched the spring of a window frame. A curtain of crimson gauze fell over a globe lamp, and threw a rich shade on the marble. The features remained as finely chiselled, but their expression was totally changed.

They adjourned to the music-room, which deserved its title. Save some seats, which were artfully formed to resemble lyres, nothing broke the continuity of music's tones, which ascended majestically to the lofty dome, there to blend and wreath, and fall again. At one extremity of music's hall was an organ; at the other a grand piano, built by a German composer. Ranged on carved slabs, at intermediate distances, was placed almost every instrument that may claim a votary. Of viols, from the violin to the double bass, - of instruments of brass, from trombones and bass kettledrums even unto trumpet and cymbal, - of instruments of wood, from winding serpents to octave flute, - and of fiddles of parchment, from the grosse caisse to the tambourine. Nor were ancient instruments wanting. These were of quaint forms and diverse constructions. Mr. Græme would descant for hours on an antique species of spinnet, which he procured from the East, and which he vehemently averred, was the veritable dulcimer. He would display with great gusto, his specimens of harps of Israel; whose deep-toned chorus, had perchance thrilled through the breast of more than one of Judea's dark-haired daughters. Greece, too, had her representatives, to remind the spectators that there had been an Orpheus. There were flutes of the Doric and of the Phrygian mode, and - let us forget not - the Tyrrhenian trumpet, with its brazen-cleft pavilion. But by far the greater part of his musical relics he had acquired during his stay in Italy. He could show the litui with their carved clarions - the twisted cornua - the tuba, a trumpet so long and taper, - the concha wound by Tritons - and eke the buccina, a short and brattling horn.

Belliston Græme was an enthusiastic musician; and was in this peculiar, that he loved the science for its simplicity. Musicians are but too apt to give to music's detail and music's difficulties the homage that should be paid to music's self: in this resembling the habitual man of law, who occasionally forgetteth the great principles of jurisprudence, and invests with mysterious agency such words as latitat and certiorari. The soul of music may not have fled; - for we cultivate her assiduously, - worship Handel - and appreciate Mozart. But music *now* springs from the head, not the heart; is not for the mass, but for individuals. With our increased researches, and cares, and troubles, we have lost the faculty of being pleased. Past are those careless days, when the shrill musette, or plain cittern and virginals, could with their first strain give motion to the blythe foot of joy, or call from its cell the prompt tear of pity. Those days are gone! Music may affect some of us as deeply, but none as readily!

Mr. Græme had received from Paris an unpublished opera of Auber's.Emily seated herself at the piano - her host took the violin – Clarendon was an excellent flute player - and the tinkle of the Viscount's guitar came in very harmoniously. By the time refreshments were introduced, Charles Selby too was in his glory. He had already nearly convulsed the Orientalist by a theory which he said he had formed, of a gradual metempsychosis, or, at all events, perceptible amalgamation, of the yellow Qui Hi to the darker Hindoo; which said theory he supported by the most ingenious arguments.

"How did you like your stay in Scotland, Mr. Selby?" said Sir Henry Delmé.

"I am a terrible Cockney, Sir Henry, - found it very cold, and was very sulky. The only man I cared to see in Scotland was at the Lakes; but I kept a register of events, which is now on the table in my dressing-room. If Græme will read it, for I am but a stammerer, it is at your service."

The paper was soon produced, and Mr. Græme read the following: -

"THE BRAHMIN.

"A stranger arrived from a far and foreign country. His was a mind peculiarly humble, tremblingly alive to its own deficiencies. Yet, endowed with this mistrust, he sighed for information, and his soul thirsted in the pursuit of knowledge.

Thus constituted, he sought the city he had long dreamingly looked up to as the site of truth - Scotia's capital, the modern Athens. In endeavouring to explore the mazes of literature, he by no means expected to discover novel paths, but sought to traverse beauteous ones; feeling he could rest content, could he meet with but one flower, which some bolder and more experienced adventurer might have allowed to escape him. He arrived, and cast around an anxious eye. He found himself involved in an apparent chaos - the whirl of distraction - imbedded amidst a ceaseless turmoil of would-be knowing students, endeavouring to catch the aroma of the pharmacopaeia, or dive to the deep recesses of Scotch law. He sought and cultivated the friendship of the literati; and anticipated a perpetual feast of soul, from a banquet to which one of the most distinguished members of a learned body had invited him. He went with his mind braced up for the subtleties of argument - with hopes excited, heart elate. He deemed that the authenticity of Champolion's hieroglyphics might now be permanently established, or a doubt thrown on them which would for ever extinguish curiosity. He heard a doubt raised as to the probability of Dr. Knox's connection with Burke's murders! Disappointed and annoyed, he returned to his hotel, determined to seek other means of improvement; and to carefully observe the manners, customs, and habits of the beings he was among. He enquired first as to their habits, and was presented with scones, kippered salmon, and a gallon of Glenlivet; as to their manners and ancient costume, and was pointed out a short fat man, the head of his clan, who promenaded the streets without trousers. Neither did he find the delineation of their customs more satisfactory. He was made nearly tipsy at a funeral - was shown how to carve haggis - and a fit of bile was the consequence, of his too plentifully partaking of a superabundantly rich currant bun. He mused over these defeats of his object, and, unwilling to relinquish his hitherto fruitless search, - reluctant to despair, - he bent his steps to that city, where utility preponderates over ornament; that city which so early encouraged that most glorious of inventions, by the aid of which he hoped, that the diminutive barks of his countrymen might yet be propelled, thus superseding the ponderous paddle of teak, He here expected to be involved in an intricate labyrinth of mechanical inventions, - in a stormy discussion on the comparative merits of rival machinery, - to be immersed in speculative but gigantic theories. He was elected an honorary member of a news-room; had his coat whitened with cotton; and was obliged to confess that he knew of no beverage that could equal their superb cold punch. Our philosopher now gave himself up to despair; but before returning to his own warm clime, he sought to discover the reason of his finding the flesh creep, where he had deemed the spirit would soar. He at length came to the conclusion that we are all slaves to the world and to circumstances; and as, with his peculiar belief, he could look on our sacred volume with the eye of a philosopher, felt impressed with the conviction that the history of Babel's tower is but an allegory, which says to the pride of man,

"'Thus far shall ye go, and no farther.'"

The Brahmin's adventures elicited much amusement. In a short time, Selby was in a hot argument with the French novelist. Every now and then, as the Frenchman answered him, he stirred his negus, and hummed a translation of

"I'd be a butterfly."

"Erim papilio,
Natus in flosculo."

CHAPTER IV

THE POSTMAN

"Not in those visions, to the heart displaying
Forms which it sighs but to have only dream'd,
Hath aught like thee in truth or fancy seem'd;
Or, having seen thee, shall I vainly seek
To paint those charms which, imaged as they beam'd,
To such as see thee not, my words were weak;
To those who gaze on thee, what language could they speak?"

Delmé had long designed some internal improvements in the mansion; and as workmen would necessarily be employed, had proposed that our family party should pass a few weeks at a watering place, until these were completed. They were not without hopes, that George might there join them, as Emily had written to Malta, pressing him to be present at her wedding.

We have elsewhere said, that Sir Henry had arrived at middle age, before one feeling incompatible with his ambitious thoughts arose. It was at Leamington this feeling had imperceptibly sprung up; and to Leamington they were now going.

Is there an electric chain binding hearts predestined to love?

Hath Providence ordained, that on our first interview with that being, framed to meet our wishes and our desires - the rainbow to our cloud, and the sun to our noon-day - hath it ordained that there should also be given us some undefinable token - some unconscious whispering from the heart's inmost spirit?

Who may fathom these inscrutable mysteries?

Sir Henry had been visiting an old schoolfellow, who had a country seat near Leamington. He was riding homewards, through a sequestered and wooded part of the park, when he was aware of the presence of two ladies, evidently a mother and daughter. They sate on one side of the rude path, on an old prostrate beech tree. The daughter, who was very beautiful, was sketching a piece of fern for a foreground: the mother was looking over the drawing. Neither saw the equestrian.

It was a fair sight to regard the young artist, with her fine profile and drooping eyelid, bending over the drawing, like a Grecian statue; then to note the calm features upturn, and forget the statue in the breathing woman. At intervals, her auburn tresses would fall on the paper, and sweep the pencil's efforts. At such times, she would remove them with her small hand, with such a soft smile, and gentle grace, that the very action seemed to speak volumes for her feminine sympathies. Delmé disturbed them not, but making a tour through the grove of beech trees, reached Leamington in thoughtful mood.

It was not long before he met them in society. The mother was a Mrs. Vernon, a widow, with a large family and small means. Of that family Julia was the fairest flower. As Sir Henry made her acquaintance, and her character unfolded itself, he acknowledged that few could study it without deriving advantage; few without loving her to adoration. That character it would be hard to describe without our description appearing high-flown and exaggerated. It bore an impress of loftiness, totally removed from pride; a moral superiority, which impressed all. With this was united an innate purity, that seemed her birthright; a purity that could not for an instant be doubted. If the libertine gazed on her features, it awoke in him recollections that had long slumbered; of the time when his heart beat but for one. If, in her immediate sphere, any littleness of feeling was brought to her notice, it was met with an intuitive doubt, followed by painful surprise, that such feeling, foreign as she felt it to be to her own nature, could really have existence in that of another.

Thank God! she had seen few of the trickeries of this restless world, in which most of us are struggling against our neighbours; and, if we could look forward with certainty, to the nature of the world beyond this, it is most likely that we should breathe a fervent prayer that she should never witness more.

Her person was a fit receptacle for such a mind. A face all softness, seemed and *was* the index to a heart all pity. Taller than her compeers, - in all she said or did, a native dignity and a witching grace were exquisitely blended. She was one not easily seen without admiration; but when known, clung Cydippe-like to the heart's mirror, an image over which neither time nor absence possessed controul.

The Delmés resided at Leamington the remainder of the winter, which passed fleetly and happily. Emily, for the first time, gave way to that one feeling, which, to a woman, is the all-important and engrossing one, enjoying her happiness in that full spirit of content, which basking in present joys, attempts not to mar them by ideal disquietudes. The Delmés cultivated the society of the Vernons; Emily and Julia became great friends; and Sir Henry, with all his stoicism, was nourishing an attachment, whose force, had he been aware of it, he would have been at some pains to repress. As it was, he totally overlooked the possibility of his trifling with the feelings of another. He had a number of sage aphorisms to urge against his own entanglement, and, with a moral perverseness, from which the best of us are not free, chose to forget that it was possible his convincing arguments, might neither be known to, nor appreciated by one, on whom their effect might be far from unimportant.

At this stage, Clarendon thought it his duty to warn Delmé; and, to his credit be it said, shrunk not from it.

"Excuse me, Delmé," said he, "will you allow me to say one word to you on a subject that nearly concerns yourself?"

Sir Henry briefly assented.

"You see a great deal of Miss Vernon. She is a very fascinating and a very amiable person; but from something you once said to me, it has struck me that in some respects she might not suit you."

"I like her society," replied his friend; "but you are right. She would *not* suit me. *You* know me pretty well. My hope has ever been to increase, and not diminish the importance of my house. It once stood higher both in wealth and consideration. I see many families springing up around me, that can hardly lay claim to a descent so unblemished I speak not in a spirit of intolerance, nor found my family claim solely on its pedigree; but my ancestors have done good in their generation, and it is a proud thing to be 'the scion of a noble race!'"

"It may be;" said Clarendon quietly, "but I cannot help thinking, that with your affluence, you have every right to follow your own inclination. I know that few of my acquaintances are so independent of the world."

Sir Henry shook his head.

"The day is not very distant, Gage, when a Dacre would hardly have returned two members for my county, if a Delmé had willed it otherwise. But there is little occasion for me to have said thus much. Miss Vernon, I trust, has other plans; and I believe my own feelings are not enlisted deep enough, to make me forget the hopes and purposes of half a life-time."

It was some few days after this, when Emily had almost given up looking with interest to the postman's visit, that a letter at last came, directed to Sir Henry; not indeed in George's handwriting, but with the Malta post mark. Delmé read it over thoughtfully, and, assuring Emily that there was nothing to alarm her, left the room to consider its contents.

By the way, we have thought over heartless professions, and cannot help conceiving that of a postman, (it may be conceit!) the most callous and unfeeling of all. He is waited for with more anxiety than any guest of the morning; for his visits invariably convey something new to the mind. He is not love! but he bears it in his pocket; he cannot be friendship! but he daily hawks about its assurances. With all this, knowing his importance, aware of the sensation his appearance calls forth, his very knock is heartless - the tones of his voice cold. Feeling seems denied him; his head is a debtor and creditor account, his departure the receipt, and time alone can say, whether your bargain has been a good or a bad one. He has certainly no assumption - it is one of his few good traits; he walks with his arms in motion, but attempts not a swagger; his knock is unassuming, and his words, though much attended to, are few, and to the point. Why, then, abuse him? We know not, but believe it originates in fear. An intuitive feeling of dread - a rushing presentiment of evil - crosses our mind, as our eye dwells on his thread-bare coat, with its capacious pockets. News of a death - or a marriage - the tender valentine - the remorseless dun - your having been left an estate, or cut off with a shilling - fortune, and misfortune - he quietly dispenses, as if totally unconscious. Surely such a man - his round performed - cannot quietly sink to the private individual. Can such a man caress his wife, or kiss his child, when he knows not how many hearts are bursting with joy, or breaking with sorrow, from the tidings *he* has conveyed? To our mind, a postman should be an abstracted visionary being, endowed with a peculiar countenance, betraying the unnatural sparkle of the opium-eater, and evincing intense anxiety at the delivery of each sheet. But these, - they wait not to hear the joyful shout, or heart-rending moan - to know if hope deferred be at length joyful certainty, or bitter only half-expected woe. We dread a postman. Our hand shook, as we last year paid the man of many destinies his demanded Christmas box.

The amount was double that we gave to the minister of our corporeal necessities - the butcher's boy - not from a conviction of the superior services or merit of the former, but from an uneasy desire to bribe, if we could, that Mercury of fate.

The letter to Sir Henry, was from the surgeon of George's regiment. It stated that George had been severely ill, and that connected with his illness, were symptoms which made it imperative on the medical adviser, to recommend the immediate presence of his nearest male relative. Apologies were made for the apparent mystery of the communication, with a promise that this would be at once cleared up, if Sir Henry would but consent to make the voyage; which would not only enable him to be of essential service to his brother, but also to acquire much information regarding him, which could only be obtained on the spot. A note from George was enclosed in this letter. It was written with an unsteady hand, and made no mention of his illness. He earnestly begged his brother to come to Malta, if he could possibly so arrange it, and transmitted his kindest love and blessing to Emily.

Sir Henry at once made up his mind, to leave Leamington for town on the morrow, trusting that he might there meet with information which would be more satisfactory. He concealed for the time the true state of the case from all but Clarendon; nor did he even allude to his proposed departure.

It was Emily's birth-day, and Gage had arranged that the whole party should attend a little fête on that night. Sir Henry could not find it in his heart to disturb his sister's dream of happiness.

CHAPTER V

THE FÊTE

"Ye stars! which are the poetry of heaven!
If, in your bright leaves, we would read the fate
Of men and empires, - 'tis to be forgiven,
That, in our aspirations to be great,
Our destinies o'erleap their mortal state,
And claim a kindred with you."

The night came on with its crescent moon and its myriads of stars: just such a night as might have been wished for such a fête. It was in the month of April. April dews, in Britain's variable clime; are not the most salubrious, and April's night air is too often keen and piercing; but the season was an unusually mild one; and the ladies, with their cloaks and their furs, promenaded the well-lighted walks, determined to be pleased and happy.

The giver of the fête was an enterprising Italian. Winter's amusements were over, or neglected - summer's delights were not arrived; and Signor Pacini conceived, that during the dull and monotonous interval, a speculation of his own might prove welcome to the public and beneficial to himself. To do the little man justice, he was indefatigable in his exertions. From door to door he wended his smiling way, - here praising the mother's French, there the daughter's Italian. He gained hosts of partisans. "Of course you patronise Pacini!" was in every one's mouth. The Signor's prospectus stated, that "through the kindness of the steward of an influential nobleman, who was now on the continent, he was enabled to give his fete in the grounds of the Earl of W - ; where a full quadrille band would be in attendance, a pavilion pitched on the smooth lawn facing the river, and a comfortable ball room thrown open to a fashionable and enlightened public. The performance would be most various, novel, and exciting. Brilliant fireworks from Vauxhall would delight the eye, and shed a charm on the fairy scene; whilst the car would be regaled with the unequalled harmony of the Styrian brethren, Messrs. Schezer, Lobau, and Berdan, who had very kindly deferred their proposed return to Styria, in order to honour the fete of Signor Pacini."

As night drew on, the mimic thunder of carriages hastening to the scene of action, bespoke the Signor's success. After the ninth hour, his numbers swelled rapidly. Pacini assumed an amusing importance, and his very myrmidons gave out their brass tickets with an air. At ten, a rocket was fired. At this preconcerted signal, the pavilion, hitherto purposely concealed, blazed in a flood of light. On its balcony stood the three Styrian brethren, - although, by the way, they were not brethren at all, - and, striking their harmonious guitars, wooed attention to their strains. The crowd hurried down the walk, and formed round the pavilion. Our party suddenly found themselves near the Vernons. As the gentlemen endeavoured to obtain chairs for the ladies, a crush took place, and Sir Henry was obliged to offer his arm to Julia, who happened to be the nearest of her party. It was with pain Miss Vernon noted his clouded brow, and look of abstraction; but hardly one word of recognition had passed, before the deep voices of the Styrians silenced all. After singing some effective songs, accompanied by a zither, and performing a melodious symphony on a variety of Jew's-harps; Pacini, the manager, advanced to address his auditors, with that air of smiling confidence which no one can assume with better grace than a clever Italian. His dark eye flashed, and his whole features irradiated, as he delivered the following harangue.

"Ladies and gentlemen! me trust you well satisfied wid de former musical entertainment; but, if you permit, me mention one leetle circonstance. Monsieur Schezer propose to give de song; but it require much vat you call stage management: all must be silent as de grave. It ver pretty morceau."

The applause at the end of this speech was very great. Signor Pacini bowed, till his face rivalled, in its hue, the rosy under-waistcoat in which he rejoiced.

Schezer stepped forward. He was attired as a mountaineer. His hat tapered to the top, and was crowned by a single heron feather. Hussars might have envied him his moustaches. From his right side protruded a couteau de chasse; and his legs were not a little set off by the tight-laced boots, which, coming up some way beyond the ancle, displayed his calf to the very best advantage.

The singer's voice was a fine manly tenor, and did ample justice to the words, of which the following may be taken as a free version.

"Mountains! dear mountains! on you have I passed my green youth; to me your breeze has been fragrant from childhood. When may I see the chamois bounding o'er your toppling crags? When, oh when, may I see my fair-haired Mary?"

The minstrel paused - a sound was heard from behind the pavilion. It was the mountain's echo. It continued the air - then died away in the softest harmony. All were charmed. Again the singer stepped forward - the utmost silence prevailed - his tones became more impassioned - they breathed of love.

"Thanks! thanks to thee, gentle echo! Oft hast thou responded to the strains of love my soul poured to - ah me! how beautiful was the fair-haired Mary!"

Again the echo spoke - again all were hushed. The minstrel's voice rose again; but its tones were not akin to joy.

"Why remember this, deceitful echo? War's blast hath blown, and hushed are the notes of love. The foe hath polluted my hearth - I wander an exile. Where, where is Mary?"

The echo faintly but plaintively replied. There were some imagined that a tear really started to the eye of the singer. He struck the guitar wildly - his voice became more agitated - he advanced to the extremity of the balcony.

"My sword! my sword! May my right hand be withered ere it forget to grasp its hilt! One blow for freedom. Freedom - sweet as was the lip - Yes! I'll revenge my Mary!"

Schezer paused, apparently overcome by his emotion. The echo wildly replied, as if registering the patriot's vow. For a moment all was still! A thundering burst of applause ensued.

The mountain music was succeeded by a sweep of guitars, accompanying a Venetian serenade, whose burthen was the apostrophising the cruelty of "la cara Nina."

It was near midnight, when all eyes were directed to a ball of fire, which, rising majestically upward, soared amid the tall elm trees. For a moment, the balloon became entangled in the boughs, revealing by its transparent light the green buds of spring, which variegated and cheered the scathed bark. It broke loose from their embrace - hovered irresolutely above them - then swept rapidly before the wind, rising till it became as a speck in the firmament.

This was the signal for Mr. Robinson's fireworks, which did not shame Vauxhall's reputation. At one moment, a salamander courted notice; at another, a train of fiery honours, festooned round four wooden pillars, was fired at different places, by as many doves practised to the task. Here, an imitation of a jet d'eau elicited applause - there, the gyrations of a Catherine's wheel were suddenly interrupted by the rapid ascent of a Roman candle.

Directly after the ascent of the balloon, Emily and Clarendon had turned towards the ball room. Julia's sisters had a group of laughing beaux round their chairs, - Mrs. Glenallan and Mrs. Vernon were discussing bygone days, - and no one seemed disposed to leave the pavilion. Sir Henry, in his silent mood, was glad to escape from the party; and engaging Julia in a search for Emily, made his way to the crowded ball room. He there found his sister spinning round with Clarendon to one of Strauss's waltzes; and Sir Henry and his partner seated themselves on one of the benches, watching the smiling faces as they whirled past them. It was a melancholy thought to Delmé, how soon Emily's brow would be clouded, were he to breathe one word of George's illness and despondency. The waltz concluded, a quadrille was quickly formed. Miss Vernon declined dancing, and they rose to join Emily and Clarendon; but the lovers were flown. The ball room became still more thronged; and Delmé was glad to turn once more towards the pavilion. The party they had left there had also vanished, and strangers usurped their seats. In this dilemma, Miss Vernon proposed seeking their party in the long walk. They took one or two turns down this, but saw not those for whom they were in search.

"If you do not dislike leaving this busy scene," said Sir Henry, "I think we shall have a better chance of meeting Emily and Clarendon, if we turn down one of these winding paths."

They turned to their left, and walked on. How beautiful was that night! Its calm tranquillity, as they receded from the giddy throng, could not but subdue them. We have said that the moon was not riding the heavens in her full robe of majesty, nor was there a sombre darkness. The purple vault was spangled thick with stars; and there reigned that dubious, glimmering light, by which you can note a face, but not mark its blush. The walks wound fantastically. They were lit by festoons of coloured lamps, attached to the neighbouring trees, so as to resemble the pendent grape-clusters, that the traveller meets with just previous to the Bolognese vintage. Occasionally, a path would be encountered where no light met the eye save that of the prying stars overhead. In the distant vista, might be seen a part of the crowded promenade, where music held its court; whilst at intervals, a voice's swell or guitar's tinkle would be borne on the ear. There was the hum of men, too - the laugh of the idlers without the sanctum, as they indulged in the delights of the mischievous fire-ball - and the sudden whizz, followed by an upward glare of light, as a rocket shot into the air. But the hour, and the nameless feeling that hour invoked, brought with them a subduing influence, which overpowered these intruding sounds, attuning the heart to love and praise. They paced the walk in mutual and embarrassed silence. Sir Henry's thoughts would at one time revert to his brother, and at another to that parting, which the morrow would assuredly bring with it. He was lost in reverie, and almost forgot who it was that leant thus heavily upon his arm. Julia had loved but once. She saw his abstraction, and knew not the cause; and her timid heart beat quicker than was its wont, as undefined images of coming evil and sorrow, chased each other through her excited fancy. At length she essayed to speak, although conscious that her voice faltered.

"What a lovely night! Are you a believer in the language of the stars?"

This was said with such simplicity of manner, that Delmé, as he turned to answer her, felt truly for the first time the full force of his attachment. He felt it the more strongly, that his mind previously had been wandering more than it had done for years.

There are times and seasons when we are engrossed in a train of deep and unconscious thought. Suddenly recalled to ourselves, we start from our mental aberration, and a clearer insight into the immediate purposes and machinery of our lives, is afforded us. We seem endowed with a more accurate knowledge of self; the inmost workings of our souls are abruptly revealed - feeling's mysteries stand developed - our weaknesses stare us in the face - and our vices appear to gnaw the very vitals of our hope. The veil was indeed withdrawn, -

and Delmé's heart acknowledged, that the fair being who leant on him for support, was dearer - far dearer, than all beside. But he saw too, ambition in that heart's deep recess, and knew that its dictates, unopposed for years, were totally incompatible with such a love. He saw and trembled.

Julia's question was repeated, before Sir Henry could reply.

"A soldier, Miss Vernon, is particularly susceptible of visionary ideas. On the lone bivouac, or remote piquet, duty must frequently chase sleep from his eyelids. At such times, I have, I confess, indulged in wild speculations, on their possible influence on our wayward destinies. I was then a youth, and should not now, I much fear me, pursue with such unchecked ardour, the dreams of romance in which I could then unrestrainedly revel. Perhaps I should not think it wise to do so, even had not sober reality stolen from imagination her brightest pinion."

"I would fain hope, Sir Henry," replied Julia, "that all your mind's elasticity is not thus flown. Why blame such fanciful theories? I cannot think them wrong, and I have often passed happy hours in forming them."

"Simply because they remove us too much from our natural sphere of usefulness. They may impart us pleasure; but I question whether, by dulling our mundane delights, they do not steal pleasure quite equivalent. Besides, they cannot assist us in conferring happiness on others, or in gleaning improvement for ourselves. I am not quite certain, enviable as appears the distinction, whether the *too* feelingly appreciating even nature's beauties, does not bear with it its own retribution."

"Ah! do not say so! I cannot think that it *should* be so with minds properly regulated. I cannot think that *such* can ever gaze on the wonders revealed us, without these imparting their lesson of gratitude and adoration. If, full of hope, our eye turns to some glorious planet, and we fondly deem that *there,* may our dreams of happiness *here,* be perpetuated; surely in such poetical fancy, there is little to condemn, and much that may wean us from folly's idle cravings.

"If in melancholy's hour, we mourn for one who hath been dear, and sorrow for the perishable nature of all that may here claim our earthly affections; is it not sweet to think that in another world - perhaps in some bright star - we may again commune with what we have *so* loved - once more be united in those kindly bonds - and in a kingdom where those bonds may not thus lightly be severed?"

Julia's voice failed her; for she thought of one who had preceded her to "the last sad bourne."

Delmé was much affected. He turned towards her, and his hand touched hers.

"Angelic being!"

As he spoke, darker, more worldly thoughts arose. A fearful struggle, which convulsed his features, ensued. The world triumphed.

Julia Vernon saw much of this, and maiden delicacy told her it was not meet they should be alone.

"Let us join the crowd!" said she. "We shall probably meet our party in the long walk: if not, we will try the ball room."

Poor Julia! little was her heart in unison with that joyous scene!

By the eve of the morrow, Delmé was many leagues from her and his family.

Restless man, with travel, ambition, and excitement, can woo and almost win oblivion; - but poor, weak, confiding woman - what is left to her?

In secret to mourn, and in secret still to love.

CHAPTER VI

THE JOURNEY

"Adieu! adieu! My native land
Fades o'er the ocean blue;
The night winds sigh - the breakers roar -
 And shrieks the wild sea mew.
Yon sun that sets upon the sea,
We follow in his flight:
Farewell awhile to him and thee!
My native land! good night!"

We have rapidly sketched the dénouement of the preceding chapter; but it must not be forgotten, that Delmé had been residing some months at Leamington, and that Emily and Julia were friends. In his own familiar circle - a severe but true test - Sir Henry had every opportunity of becoming acquainted with Miss Vernon's sweetness of disposition, and of appreciating the many excellencies of her character. For the rest, their intercourse had been of that nature, that it need excite no surprise, that a walk on a gala night, had the power of extracting an avowal, which, crude, undigested, and hastily withdrawn as it was, was certainly more the effusion of the heart - more consonant with Sir Henry's original nature - than the sage reasonings on his part, which preceded and followed that event.

On Delmé's arrival in town, he prosecuted with energy his

enquiries as to his brother. He called on the regimental agents, who could give him no information. George's military friends had lost sight of him since he had sailed for the Mediterranean; and of the few persons, whom he could hear of, who had lately left Malta; some were passing travellers, who had made no acquaintances there, others, English merchants, who had met George at the Opera and in the streets, but nowhere else. It is true, there was an exception to this, in the case of a hair-brained young midshipman; who stated that he had dined at George's regimental mess, and had there heard that George "had fallen in love with some young lady, and had fought with her brother or uncle, or a soldier-officer, he did not know which."

Meagre as all this information was, it decided Sir Henry Delmé.

He wrote a long letter to Emily, in which he expressed a hope that both George and himself would soon be with her, and immediately prepared for his departure.

Ere we follow him on his lonely journey, let us turn to those he left behind. Mrs. Glenallan and Emily decided on at once leaving Leamington for their own home. The marriage of the latter was deferred; and as Clarendon confessed that his period of probation was a very happy one, he acquiesced cheerfully in the arrangement. Emily called on the Vernons, and finding that Julia was not at home, wrote her a kind farewell; secretly hoping that at some future period they might be more nearly related. The sun was sinking, as the travellers neared Delmé. The old mansion looked as calm as ever. The blue smoke curled above its sombre roof; and the rooks sailed over the chimneys, flapping their wings, and cawing rejoicefully, as they caught the first glimpse of their lofty homes. Emily let down the carriage window, and with sunshiny tear, looked out on the home of her ancestors.

There let us leave her; and turn to bid adieu for a season, to one, who for many a weary day, was doomed to undergo the pangs of blighted affection. Such pangs are but too poignant and enduring, let the worldly man say what he may. Could we but read the history of the snarling cynic, blind to this world's good - of him, who from being the deceived, has become the deceiver - of the rash sensualist, who plunging into vice, thinks he can forget; - could we but know the train of events, that have brought the stamping madman to his bars - and his cell - and his realms of phantasy; - or search the breast of her, who lets concealment "feed on her damask cheek" - who prays blessings on him, who hath wasted her youthful charms - then mounts with virgin soul to heaven: - we, in our turn, might sneer at the worldling, and pin our fate on the tale of the peasant girl, who discourses so glibly of crossed love and broken hearts.

Sir Henry Delmé left England with very unenviable sensations. A cloud seemed to hang over the fate of his brother, which no speculations of his could pierce. Numberless were the conjectures he formed, as to the real causes of George's sickness and mental depression. It was in vain he re-read the letters, and varied his comments on their contents. It was evident, that nothing but his actual presence in Malta, could unravel the mystery. Sir Henry had *one* consolation; how great, let those judge who have had aught dear placed in circumstances at all similar. He had a confidence in George's character, which entirely relieved him from any fear that the slightest taint could have infected it. But an act of imprudence might have destroyed his peace of mind - sickness have wasted his body. Nor was his uncertainty regarding George, Delmé's only cause of disquiet. When he thought of Julia Vernon, there was a consequent internal emotion, that he could not subdue. He endeavoured to forget her - her image haunted him. He meditated on his past conduct; and at times it occurred to him, that the resolutions he had formed, were not the result of reason, but were based on pride and prejudice. He thought of her as he had last seen her. *Now* she spoke with enthusiasm of the bright stars of heaven; anon, her eye glistened with piety, as she showed how the feeling these created, was but subservient to a nobler one still. Again, he was beside her in the moment of maiden agony; when low accents faltered from her quivering lip, and the hand that rested on his arm, trembled from her heart's emotion.

Such were the bitter fancies that assailed him, as he left his own, and reached a foreign land. They cast a shadow on his brow, which change of scene possessed no charm to dispel. He hurried on to France's capital, and only delaying till he could get his passports signed, hastened from Paris to Marseilles.

On his arrival at the latter place, his first enquiries were, as to the earliest period that a vessel would sail for Malta. He was pointed out a small yacht in the harbour, which belonging to the British government, had lately brought over a staff officer with despatches.

A courier from England had that morning arrived - the vessel was about to return - her canvas was already loosened - the blue Peter streaming in the wind. Delmé hesitated not an instant, but threw himself into a boat, and was rowed alongside. The yacht's commander was a lieutenant in our service, although a Maltese by birth. He at once entered into Sir Henry's views, and felt delighted at the prospect of a companion in his voyage. A short time elapsed - the anchor was up - the white sails began to fill - Sir Henry was once more on the wide sea.

What a feeling of loneliness, almost of despair, infects the landsman's mind, as he recedes from an unfamiliar port - sees crowds watching listlessly his vessel's departure - crowds, of whom not one feels an interest in *his* fate; and then, turning to the little world within, beholds but faces he knows not, persons he wots not of!

But to one whose home is the ocean, such are not the emotions which its expanse of broad waters calls forth. To such an one, each plank seems a friend; the vessel, a refuge from the world and its cares. Trusting himself to its guidance, deceit wounds him no more - hollow-hearted friendship proffers not its hand to sting - love exercises not its fatal sorcery - foes are afar - and his heart, if not the waves, is comparatively at peace. And oh! the wonders of the deep! Ocean! tame is the soul that loves not thee! grovelling the mind that scorns the joys thou impartest! To lean our head on the vessel's side, and in idleness of spirit ponder on bygone scene, that has brought us anything but happiness, - to gaze on the curling waves, as impelled by the boisterous wind, we ride o'er the angry waters, lashed by the sable keel to a yeasty madness, - to look afar upon the disturbed billow, presenting its crested head like the curved neck of the war horse, - *then* to mark the screaming sea bird, as, his bright eye scanning the waters, he soars above the stormy main - its wide tumult his delight - the roaring of the winds his melody - the shrieks of the drowned an harmonious symphony to the hoarse diapason of the deep! All these things may awake reflections, which are alike futile and transitory; but they are accompanied by a mental excitement, which land scenes, however glorious, always fail to impart.

Delmé's voyage was not unpropitious, although the yacht was frequently baffled by contrary winds, which prevented the passage being very speedy. During the day, the weather was ordinarily blustering, at times stormy; but with the setting sun, it seemed that tranquillity came; for during the nights, which were uncommonly fine, gentle breezes continued to fill the sails, and their vessel made tardy but sure progress. Henry would sit on deck till a late hour, lost in reverie. *There* would he remain, until each idle mariner was sunk to rest; and nothing but the distant tread of the wakeful watch, or the short cough of the helmsman, bespoke a sentinel over the habitation on the waters. How would the recollections of his life crowd upon him! - the loss of his parent - the world's first opening - bitter partings - painful misgivings - the lone bivouac - the marshalling of squadrons - the fierce charge - the excitement of victory, whose charm was all but flown, for where were the comrades who had fought beside him? These things were recalled, and brought with them alternate pain and pleasure. And a less remote era of his life would be presented him; when he tasted the welcome of home - saw hands uplifted in gratitude - was cheered by a brother's greeting, and subdued by a sister's kiss. But there *was* a thought, which let him dwell as he might on others, remained the uppermost of all. It was of Julia Vernon, and met him as a reproach. If his feelings were not of that enthusiastic nature, which they might have been were he now in his green youth, they were not on this account the less intense. They were coloured by the energy of manhood. He had lost a portion of his self-respect: for he knew that his conduct had been vacillating with regard to one, whom each traversed league, each fleeting hour, proved to be yet dearer than he had deemed her.

In the first few days of their passage, the winds shaped their vessel's course towards the Genoese gulf. They then took a direction nearly south, steering between Corsica and Sardinia on the one hand - Italy on the other.

Delmé had an opportunity of noting the outward aspect of Napoleon's birth-place; and still more nearly, that of its opposite island, which also forms so memorable a link in the history of that demi-god of modern times. How could weaker spirits deem that *there*, invested with monarchy's semblance, the ruler of the petty isle could forget that he had been master of the world?

How think that diplomacy's cobweb fibre could hold the eagle, panting for an upward flight?

They fearfully misjudged! What a transcendent light did his star give, as it shot through the appalled heavens, ere it sunk for ever in endless night!

The commander of the yacht pointed out the rock, which is traditionally said to be the one, on which Napoleon has been represented - his arms folded - watching intently the ocean - and ambition's votary gleaning his moral from the stormy waves below. As they advanced farther in their course, other associations were not wanting; and Delmé, whose mind, like that of most Englishmen, was deeply tinctured with classic lore, was not insensible to their charms. They swept by the Latian coast. Every creek and promontory, attested the fidelity of the poet's description, by vividly recalling it to the mind. On the seventh day, they doubled Cape Maritime, on the western coast of Sicily; and two days afterwards, the vessel neared what has been styled the abode of Calypso, the island of Gozzo. As they continued to advance, picturesque trading boats, with awnings and numerous rowers, became more frequent - the low land appeared - they were signalled from the palace - the point of St. Elmo was turned - and a wide forest of masts met the gaze. The vessel took up her moorings; and in the novelty of the scene, and surrounding bustle, Sir Henry for a time rested from misgivings, and forgot his real causes for melancholy. The harbour of Malta is not easily forgotten. The sun was just sinking, tinging with hues of amber, the usually purple waters of the harbour, and bronzing with its fiery orb, the batteries and lofty Baraca, where lie entombed the remains of Sir Thomas Maitland. Between the Baraca's pillars, might be discerned many a faldette, with pretty face beneath, peering over to mark the little yacht, as she took her station, amidst the more gigantic line of battle ships.

The native boatmen, in their gilded barks with high prows, were seen surrounding the vessel; and as they exerted themselves in passing each other, their dress and action had the most picturesque appearance. Their language, a corrupted Arabic, is not unpleasing to the ear; and their costume is remarkably graceful. A red turban hangs droopingly on one side, and their waistcoats are loaded with large silver buttons, the only remains of their uncommon wealth during the war, when this little island was endowed with a fictitious importance, it can never hope to resume. Just as the yacht cast anchor, a gun from the saluting battery was fired. It was the signal for sunset, and every flag was lowered. Down came in most seaman-like style the proud flag of merry England - the *then* spotless banner of France - and the great cross, hanging ungracefully, over the stout, but clumsy, Russian man of war. All these flags were then in the harbour of Valletta, although it was not at that eventful time when - the Moslem humbled -

they met with the cordiality of colleagues in victory.

The harbour was full of vessels. Every nation had its representative. The intermediate spaces were studded by Maltese boats, crowded with passengers indiscriminately mingled. The careless English soldier, with scarlet coat and pipe-clayed belt - priests and friars - Maltese women in national costume sat side by side. Occasionally, a gig, pulled by man of war's men, might be seen making towards the town, with one or more officers astern, whose glittering epaulettes announced them as either diners out, or amateurs of the opera. The scene to Delmé was entirely novel; although it had previously been his lot to scan more than one foreign country.

The arrival of the health officers was the first circumstance that diverted his mind from the surrounding scene. There had been an epidemic disease at Marseilles, and there appeared to be some doubts, whether, as a precaution, some quarantine would not be imposed. The superintendent of quarantine was rowed alongside, chiefly for the purpose of regulating this. The spirited little commander of the yacht, however, was not at all desirous of any such arrangement; and after some energetic appeals on his part, met by cautious remonstrances on the part of the other, their pratique was duly accorded.

During the discussion with the superintendent, Sir Henry had enquired from the health officer, as to where he should find George, and was informed that his regiment was quartered at Floriana, one of Valletta's suburbs. In a short time a boat from the yacht was lowered, and the commander prepared to accompany the government courier with his dispatches to the palace.

Previous to leaving the deck, he hailed a boat alongside - addressed the boatmen in their native language - and consigned Sir Henry to their charge. Twilight was deepening into night as Delmé left the vessel. The harbour had lost much of its bustle; lights were already gleaming from the town, and as seen in some of the loftiest houses, looked as if suspended in the air above. Our traveller folded his cloak around him, and was rowed swiftly towards the shore.

CHAPTER VII

THE YOUNG GREEK

"But not in silence pass Calypso's isles,
The sister tenants of the middle deep."

* * * * *

"Her reign is past, her gentle glories gone,
But trust not this; too easy youth, beware!
A mortal sovereign holds her dangerous throne.
And thou mayst find a new Calypso there."

Night had set in before Sir Henry reached the shore. The boatmen, in broken, but intelligible English, took the trouble of explaining, that they must row him to a point higher up the harbour, than the landing place towards which the commander's gig was directing its course, on account of his brother's regiment being quartered at Floriana. Landing on the quay, they took charge of Delmé's portmanteau, and conducted him through an ascending road, which seemed to form a part of the fortifications, till they arrived in front of a closed gate. They were challenged by the sentinel, and obliged to explain their business to a non-commissioned officer, before they were admitted.

This form having been gone through, a narrow wicket was opened for their passage. They crossed a species of common, and, after a few minutes' walk, found themselves in front of the barrack. This was a plain stone building, enclosing a small court, in the centre of which stood a marble bason. The taste of some of the officers had peopled this with golden fish; whilst on the bason's brim were placed stands for exotics, whose fragrance charmed our sea-worn traveller, so lately emancipated from those sad drawbacks to a voyage, the odours of tar and bilge water.

On either side, were staircases leading to the rooms above. A sentry was slowly pacing the court, and gave Delmé the necessary directions for finding George's room. Delmé's hand was on the latch, but he paused for a moment ere he pressed it, for he pictured to himself his brother lying on the bed of sickness. This temporary irresolution soon gave way to the impulse of affection, and he hastily entered the chamber. George was reading, and had his back turned towards him. As he heard the footsteps, he half turned round; an enquiry was on his lip, when his eye caught Henry's figure - a hectic flush suffused his cheek - he rose eagerly, and threw himself into his brother's arms.

Ah! sweet is fraternal affection! As boys, we own its just, its proper influence; but as men - how few of us can lay our hands on our hearts, and in the time of manhood feel, that the thought of a brother, still calls up the kindly glow which it did in earlier years. Delmé strained his brother to his heart, whilst poor George's tears flowed like a woman's.

"Ah, how," he exclaimed, "can I ever repay you for this?"

The first burst of joyful meeting over - Sir Henry scanned his brother's features, and was shocked at the apparent havoc a few short years had wrought. It was not that the cheek - whose carnation tint had once drawn a comment from all who saw it - it was not that the cheek was bronzed by an eastern sun. The alabaster forehead, showed that this was the natural result, of exposure to climate. But the wan, the sunken features - the unnatural brilliancy of the eye - the almost impetuous agitation of manner - all these bespoke that more than even sickness had produced the change: - that the mind, as well as body, must have had its sufferings.

"My dear, dear brother," said Henry, "tell me, I implore you, the meaning of this. You look ill and distressed, and yet from you I did not hear of sickness, nor do I know any reason for grief." George smiled evasively; then, as if recollecting himself, struck his forehead. He pressed his brother's arm, and led him towards a room adjoining the one in which they were.

"It were in vain to tell you now, Henry, the eventful history of the last few months; but see!" said he, as they together entered, "the innocent cause of much that I have gone through."

Sir Henry Delmé started at the sight that greeted him. The room was dimly lighted by a lamp, but the moon was up, and shed her full light through part of the chamber. On a small French bed, whose silken linings threw their rosy hue on the face of its fair occupant, lay as lovely a girl as ever eye reposed on.

The heat had already commenced to become oppressive; the jalousies and windows were thrown open. As the night breeze swept over the curtains, and the tint these gave, trembled on that youthful beauty; Delmé might well be forgiven, for deeming it was very long since he had seen a countenance so exquisitely lovely. The face did indeed bear the stamp of youth. Delmé would have guessed that the being before him, had barely attained her fifteenth year, but that her bosom heaved like playful billows, as she breathed her sighs in a profound slumber. Her style of beauty for a girl was most rare. It had an almost infantine simplicity of character, which in sleep was still more remarkable; for awake, those eyes, now so still, did not throw unmeaning glances.

Such as these must Guarini have apostrophised, as he looked at his slumbering love.

"Occhi! stelle mortale!
Ministri de miei mali!
Se chiusi m'uccidete,
Aperti, - che farete?"

Or, as Clarendon Gage translated it.

"Ye mortal stars! ye eyes that, e'en in sleep,
Can thus my senses chain'd in wonder keep,
Say, if when closed, your beauties thus I feel,
Oh, what when open, would ye not reveal?"

Her beauty owed not its peculiar charm to any regularity of feature; but to an ineffable sweetness of expression, and to youth's freshest bloom. Hafiz would have compared that smooth cheek to the tulip's flower. Her eye-lashes, of the deepest jet, and silken gloss, were of uncommon length. Her lips were apart, and disclosed small but exquisitely formed teeth. Their hue was not that of ivory, but the more delicate though more transient one of the pearl. One arm supported her head - its hand tangled in the raven tresses - of the other, the snowy rounded elbow was alone visible.

She met the eye, like a vision conjured up by fervid youth; when, ere our waking thoughts dare to run riot in beauty's contemplation - sleep, the tempter, gives to our disordered imaginations, forms and scenes, which in after life we pant for, but meet them - never!

George put his finger to his lips, as Delmé regarded her - kissed her silken cheek, and whispered,

"Acmé, carissima mia!"

The slumberer started - the envious eye-lid shrouded no more its lustrous jewel - the wondering eyes dilated, as they met her lover's - and she murmured something with that sweet Venetian lisp, in which the Greek women breathe their Italian. But, as she saw the stranger, her face and neck became suffused with crimson, and her small hand wrapped the snowy sheet round her beauteous form.

Sir Henry, who felt equally embarrassed, returned to the room theyhad left; whilst George lingered by the bedside of his mistress, and told her it was his brother. Once more together, Sir Henry turned towards George.

"For God's sake," said he, "unravel this mystery! Who is this young creature?"

"Not now!" said his brother, "let us reserve it for to-morrow, and talk only of home. Acmé has retired earlier than usual - she has been complaining." And he commenced with a flushed brow and rapid voice, to ask after those he loved.

"And so, dearest Emily will soon be married. I am glad of it; you speak so well of Gage! I wish I had stayed three weeks longer in England, and I should have seen him. We shall miss her in the flower garden, Henry! Yes! and every where else! And how is my kind aunt? I forgot to thank her when I last wrote to Delmé, for making Fidèle a parlour inmate! - and I don't think she likes dogs generally either! - And Mrs. Wilcox! As demure as ever? - Do you recollect the trick I played her the last April I was at home? - And my favourite pony! does *he* still adorn the paddock, or is he gone at last? Emily wrote me he could hardly support himself out of the shed. And the old oak - have you railed it round as I advised? And the deer - Is my aunt still as tenacious of killing them? I suppose Emily's pet fawn is a fine antlered gentleman by this time. And your charger, Henry - how is he? And Mr. Sims? and the new green house? Does the aviary succeed? did you get my slips of the blood orange? Have the Zante melon seeds answered? And the daisy of Delmé, Fanny Porter - is she married? I stole a kiss the day I left. And so the coachman is dead? and you have given the reins to Jenkins, and have taken my little fellow on your own establishment? And Ponto? and Ranger? and my friend Guess?"

Here George paused, quite out of breath; and his brother, viewing with some alarm his nervous agitation, attempted to answer his many queries; determined in his own mind, not to seek the explanation he so much longed for, until a more favourable period for demanding it arrived. The brothers continued conversing on English topics till a late hour, when Henry rose to retire.

"I cannot," said George, "give you a bed here to-night; but my servant shall show you the way to an hotel; and in the course of to-morrow, we will take care to have a room provided for you. You must feel harassed: will nine be too early an hour for breakfast?"

It was a beautiful night, still and starry. Till they arrived in the busy street, no sound could be heard, but the cautious opening of the lattice, answering the signal of the guitar. Escorted by his guide, Delmé entered Valletta, which is bustling always, even at night; but was more than usually so, as there happened to be a fête at the palace. As they passed through the Strado Teatro, the soldier pointed out the Opera-house; although from the lateness of the hour, Rossini's melodies were hushed. From a neighbouring café, however, festive sounds proceeded; and Delmé, catching the words of an unfamiliar language, paused before the door to recognise the singer. The table at which he sat, was so densely enveloped in smoke, that it was some time before he could make out the forms of the party, which consisted of some jovial British midshipmen, and some Tartar-looking Russians. One of the Russian officers was charming his audience with a chanson à boire, acquired on the banks of the Vistula, His compatriots were yelling the chorus most unmercifully. A few calèche drivers, waiting for their fares, and two or three idle Maltese, were pacing outside the cafe, and appeared to regard the scene as one of frequent occurrence, and calculated to excite but little interest. His guide showed Delmé the hotel, and was dismissed; and Sir Henry, preceded by an obsequious waiter, was introduced to a spacious apartment facing the street.

It was long ere sleep visited him. He had many subjects on which to ruminate; there were many points which the morrow would clear up. His mind was too busy to permit him to rest.

When he did, however, close his eyes; he slept soundly, and did not awake till the broad glare of day, penetrating through the Venetian blinds, disclosed to him the unfamiliar apartment at Beverley's.

CHAPTER VIII

THE INVALID

"'Mid many things most new to ear and eye,
The pilgrim rested here his weary feet."

As Sir Henry Delmé stepped from the hotel into the street, the sun's rays commenced to be oppressive, and, although it was only entering the month of May, served to remind him that he was in a warmer clime. The scene was already a bustling one. The shopkeepers were throwing water on the hot flag stones, and erecting canvas awnings in front of their doors. In the various cafés might be seen the subservient waiters, handing round the small gilded cup, which contained thick Turkish coffee, or carrying to some old smoker the little pipkin, whence he was to light his genial cigar. In front of one of these cafés, some English officers were collected, sipping ices, and criticising the relieving of the guard. Turning a corner of the principal street, a group of half black and three-parts naked children assaulted our traveller, and vociferously invoked carità. They accompanied this demand by the corrupted cry of "nix munjay" - nothing to eat, - which they enforced by most expressive gestures, extending their mouths, and exhibiting rows of ravenous-looking teeth. The calèche drivers, too, were on the alert, and respectfully taking off their turbans, proffered their services to convey the Signore to Floriana. Delmé declined their offers, and, passing a draw-bridge which divides Valletta from the country, made his way through an embrasure, and descending some half worn stone steps - during which operation he was again surrounded by beggars - he found himself within sight of the barracks. Acmé and George were ready to receive him. The latter's eye lit, as it was wont to do, on seeing his brother, whilst the young Greek appeared in doubt, whether to rejoice at what gave him pleasure, or to stand in awe of a relation, whose influence over George might shake her own. This did not, however, prevent her offering Delmé her hand, with an air of great frankness and grace. Nor was he less struck with her peculiar beauty than he had been on the night previous. Her dress was well adapted to exhibit her charms to the greatest advantage. Her hair was parted in front, and smoothly combed over her neck and shoulders, descending to her waist. Over her bosom, and fastened by a chased silver clasp, was one of the saffron handkerchiefs worn by the Parganot women. A jacket of purple velvet, embroidered with gold, fitted closely to her figure. Round her waist was a crimson girdle, fastened by another enormous broach, or rather embossed plate of silver. A Maltese gold rose chain of exquisite workmanship was flung round her neck, to which depended a locket, one side of which held, encased in glass, George's hair braided with her own; the other had a cameo, representing the death of the patriot Marco Bozzaris.

"Giorgio tells me," said she, "that you speak Italian, at which I am very glad; for his efforts to teach me English have quite failed. Do you know you quite alarmed me last night, and I really think it was too bad of George introducing you when he did;" and she placed her hand on her lover's shoulder, and looked in his face confidingly. In spite of the substance of her speech, and the circumstances under which Delmé saw her, he could not avoid feeling an involuntary prepossession in her favour. Her manner had little of the polish of art, but much of nature's witching simplicity; and Sir Henry felt surprised at the ease and animation of the whole party. Acmé presided at the breakfast table, with a grace which many a modern lady of fashion might envy; and during the meal, her conversation, far from being dull or listless, showed that she had much talent, and that to a quick perception of nature's charms, she united great enthusiasm in their pursuit. The meal was over, when the surgeon of the regiment was announced, and introduced by George to Sir Henry. After making a few inquiries as to the invalid's state of health, he proposed to Delmé, taking a turn in the botanical garden, which was immediately in front of their windows.

Sir Henry eagerly grasped at the proposition; anxious, as he felt himself, to ascertain the real circumstances connected with his brother's indisposition. They strolled through the garden, which was almost deserted - for none but dogs and Englishmen, to use the expression of the natives, court the Maltese noon-day sun, - and the surgeon at once entered into George's history. He was a man of most refined manners, and a cultivated intellect, and his professional familiarity with horrors, had not diminished his natural delicacy of feeling. His narrative was briefly thus: -

George Delmé's bosom companion had been an officer of his own age and standing in the service, with whom he had embarked when leaving England. Their intercourse had ripened into the closest friendship. George had met Acmé, although the surgeon knew not the particulars of the rencontre, - had confided to his friend the acquaintance he had made - and had himself introduced Delancey at the house where Acmé resided. Whether her charms really tempted the friend to endeavour to supplant George, or whether he considered the latter's attentions to the young Greek to be without definite object, and undertaken in a spirit of indifference, the narrator could not explain; but it was not long before Delancey considered himself as a principal in the transaction. Acmé, whose knowledge of the world was slight, and whose previous seclusion from society, had rendered her timidity excessive, considered that her best mode of avoiding importunities she disliked, and attentions that were painful to her, would be to speak to George himself on the subject.

By this time, the latter, quite fascinated by her beauty and simplicity, and deeming, as was indeed the fact, that his love was returned, needed not other inquietudes than those his attachment gave him. The pride of ancestry and station on the one hand - on the other, a deep affection, and a wish to act nobly by Acmé - caused an internal struggle which made him open to any excitement, nervously alive to any wrong. He sought his friend, and used reproaches, which rendered it imperative that they should meet as foes. Delancey was wounded; and as *he* thought - and it was long doubtful whether it *were* so - *mortally*. He beckoned George Delmé to his bedside - begged him to forgive him - told him that his friendship had been the greatest source of delight to him - a friendship which in his dying moments he begged to renew - that far from feeling pain at his approaching dissolution, he conceived that he had merited all, and only waited his full and entire forgiveness to die happy. George Delmé wrung his hands in the bitterness of despair - prayed him to live for his sake - told him, that did he not, his own life hereafter would be one of the deepest misery, - that the horrors of remorse would weigh him down to his grave. The surgeon was the first to terminate a scene, which he assured Delmé was one of the most painful it had ever been his lot to witness. This meeting, though of so agitating a nature, seemed to have a beneficial effect on the wounded man. He sunk into a sweet sleep; and on awaking, his pulse was lower, and his symptoms less critical. He improved gradually, and was now convalescent. But it was otherwise with George Delmé. He sought the solitude of his chamber, a prey to the agonies of a self-reproaching spirit. He considered himself instrumental in taking the life of his best friend - of one, richly endowed with the loftiest feelings humanity can boast. His nerves previously had been unstrung; body and mind sank under the picture his imagination had conjured up. His servant was alarmed by startling screams, entered his room, and found his master in fearful convulsions. A fever ensued, during which George's life hung by a thread. To this succeeded a long state of unconsciousness, occasionally broken by wild delirium.

During his illness, there was one who never left him - who

smoothed his pillow - who supported his head on her breast - who watched him as a mother watches her first-born. It was the youthful Greek, Acmé Frascati. The instant she heard of his danger, she left her home to tend him. No entreaties could influence her, no arguments persuade. She would sit by his bedside for hours, his feverish hand locked in hers, and implore him to recover, to bless one who loved him so dearly. They could not part them; for George, even in his delirious state, seemed to be conscious that some one was near him, and, did she leave his side, would rise in his bed, and look around him as if missing some accustomed object. In his wilder flights, he would call passionately upon her, and beg her to save his friend, who was lying so dead and still.

For a length of time, neither care nor professional skill availed. Fearful was the struggle, between his disease, and a naturally hardy constitution. Reason at last resumed her dominion. "I know not," said the surgeon, "the particulars of the first dawning of consciousness. It appears that Acmé was alone with him, and that it was at night. I found him on my professional visit one morning, clear and collected, and his mistress sobbing her thanks. I need perhaps hardly inform you," said the narrator, "that George's gratitude to Acmé was vividly expressed. It was in vain I urged on her the propriety of now leaving her lover. This was met on both sides by an equal disinclination, and indeed obstinate refusal; and I feared the responsibility I should incur, by enforcing a separation which might have proved of dangerous consequence to my patient. Alas! for human nature, Sir Henry! need it surprise you that the consequences were what they are? Loving him with the fervency of one born under an eastern sun - with the warm devotion of woman's first love - with slender ideas of Christian morality - and with a mind accustomed to obey its every impulse - need it, I say, surprise you, that the one fell, and that remorse visited the other? To that remorse, do I attribute what my previous communication may not have sufficiently prepared you for; namely, the little dependence to be placed on the tone of the invalid's mind. Reason is but as a glimmering in a socket; and painful as my professional opinion may be to you, it is my duty to avow it; and I frankly confess, that I entertain serious apprehensions, as to the stability of his mind's restoration. It is on this account, that I have felt so anxious that one of his relations should be near him. Change of scene is absolutely necessary, as soon as change of scene can be safely adopted. Every distracting thought must be avoided, and the utmost care taken that no agitating topic is discussed in his presence. These precautions may do much; but should they have no effect, which I think possible; as a medical man, I should then recommend, what as a member of his family may startle you. My advice would be, that if it be ultimately found, that his feelings as regard this young girl, are such as are likely to prevent or impede his mind's recovery; why I would then at once allow him to make her any reparation he may think just.

"To what do you allude?" enquired Sir Henry.

"Why," continued the surgeon, "that if his feelings appear deeply enlisted on that side of the question, and all our other modes have failed in obtaining their object; that he should be permitted to marry her as soon as he pleases. I see you look grave. I am not surprised you should do so; but life is worth preserving, and Acmé, if not entirely to our notions, is a good, a very good girl - warm-hearted and affectionate; and it is not fair to judge her by our English standard. You will however have time and scope, to watch yourself the progress and extent of his disorder. I fear this is more serious than you are at present aware of; but from your own observations, would I recommend and wish your future line of conduct to be formed. May I trust my frankness has not offended you?"

Sir Henry assured him, that far from this being the case, he owed him many thanks for being thus explicit. Shaking him by the hand, he returned to George's room with a clouded brow; perplexed how to act, or how best discuss with his brother, the points connected with his history.

CHAPTER IX

THE NARRATIVE

"The seal Love's dimpling finger hath impress'd,
Denotes how soft that chin which bears his touch,
Her lips whose kisses pout to leave their nest,
Bid man be valiant ere he merit such;
Her glance how wildly beautiful - how much
Hath Phoebus woo'd in vain to spoil her cheek,
Which grows yet smoother from his amorous clutch,
Who round the north for paler dames would seek?
How poor their forms appear! how languid, wan,
and weak."

Love! Heavenly love! by Plato's mind conceived, and Sicyon's artist chiselled! not thou! night's offspring, springing on golden wing from the dark bosom of Erebus! the first created, and the first creating: but thou! immaculate deity; effluence of unspotted thought, and child of a chaster age! where, oh where is now thy resting place?

Pensile in mid-heaven, gazest thou yet with seraphic sorrow on this, the guilty abode of guilty man? - with pity's tear still mournest thou, as yoked to the car of young desire, we bow the neck in degrading and slavish bondage? Or dost thou, the habitant of some bright star, where frailty such as ours is yet unknown, lend to lovers a rapture unalloyed by passion's grosser sense; as, symphonious with the tremulous zephyr, chastened vows of constancy are there exchanged? Ah! vainly does one solitary enthusiast, in his balmy youth, for a moment conceive he really grasps thee! 'tis but a fleeting phantasy, doomed to fade at the first sneer of derision - and for ever vanish, as a false and fascinating world stamps its dogmas on his heart! Celestial love! oh where may he yet find thee? and a clear voice whispers, ETERNITY!

Hope! guide the fainting pilgrim! undying soul! shield him from the world's venomed darts, as he painfully wends his toilsome way!

When Delmé returned to his brother, he found the latter anxiously expecting him, and desirous of ascertaining the impression, which his conversation with the surgeon had created.

But Delmé thought it more prudent, to defer the discussion of those points, till he had heard from George himself, as to many circumstances connected with Acmé's history, and had been able to form some personal opinion regarding the health of the invalid. He therefore begged George, if he felt equal to the task, to avail himself of the opportunity of Acmé's absence, to tell him how he had first met her. To this George willingly assented; and as there is ever a peculiarity in foreign scenes and habits, which awakens interest, we give his story in his own language.

"There are some old families here, Henry," began the invalid, "whose names are connected with some of the proudest, which the annals of the Knights of St. John of Jerusalem can boast. They are for the most part sunk in poverty, and possess but little of the outward trappings of rank. But their pride is not therefore the less; and rather than have it wounded, by being put in collision with those with whom in worldly wealth they are unable to compete, they prefer the privacy of retirement; and are rarely seen, and more rarely known, by any of the English residents, whom they distrust and dislike. It is true, there are a few families, some of the male members of which have accepted subordinate situations under government: and these have become habituated to English society, and meet on terms of tolerable cordiality, the English whose acquaintance they have thus made. But there are others, as I have said, whose existence is hardly recognised, and who vegetate in some lone palazzo; brooding over the decay of their fortunes - never crossing the threshold of their mansions - except when religious feelings command them to attend a mass, or public procession. Of such a family was Acmé a member. By birth a Greek, she was a witness to many of the bloody scenes which took place at the commencement of the struggle for Grecian freedom. She was herself present at the murder of both her parents. Her beauty alone saved her from sharing their fate. One of the Turks, struck with, her expression of childish sorrow, interfered in her behalf, and permitted a friend and neighbour to save her life and his own, by taking shipping for one of the islands in our possession. After residing in Corfu for some months, she received an invitation from her father's brother-in-law, a member of an ancient Maltese family; and for the last few years has spent a life, if not gay, at least free from a repetition of those sanguinary scenes, which have lent their impress to a sensitive mind, and at moments impart a melancholy tinge, to a disposition by nature unusually joyous. It was on a festa day, dedicated to the patron saint of the island, when no Maltese not absolutely bed-ridden, but would deem it a duty, to witness the solemn and lengthy procession which such a day calls forth; that I first met Acmé Frascati.

"I was alone in the Strada Reale, and strolling towards the Piazza, when my attention was directed to what struck me as the loveliest face I had ever seen.

"Acmé, for it was her, was drest in the costume of the island; and, although a faldette is not the best dress for exhibiting a figure, there was a grace and lightness in her carriage, that would have arrested my attention, even had I not been riveted by her countenance. She was on the opposite side of the street to myself, and was attended by an old Moorish woman, who carried an illumined missal. Of these women, several may yet be seen in Malta, looking very Oriental and duenna-like. As I stopped to admire her, she suddenly attempted to cross to the side of the street where I stood. At the same moment, I observed a horse attached to a calèche galloping furiously towards her. It was almost upon her ere Acmé saw her danger. The driver, anxious to pass before the procession formed, had whipped his horse till it became unmanageable, and it was now in vain that he tried to arrest its progress. A natural impulse induced me to rush forward, and endeavour to save her. She was pale and trembling, as I caught her and placed her out of the reach of danger; but before I could touch the pavement, I felt myself struck by the wheel of the carriage, was thrown down, and taken up insensible. When consciousness returned, I found they had conveyed me to a neighbouring shop, and that medical attendance had been procured. But more than all, I noticed the solicitude of Acmé. Until the surgeon had given a favourable report, she could not address me, but when this had been pronounced, she overwhelmed me with thanks, begged to know where I would wish to be taken, and rested not until her own family calèche came up, and she saw me, attended by the Moorish woman, on the road to Floriana.

"My accident, though not a very serious one, proved of sufficient consequence, to confine me to my room for some time; and during that period, not a day passed, that did not give me proof of the anxiety of the young Greek for my restoration. I need not say that one of my first visits was to her. Her family received me as they would an absent brother. The obligations they considered I had conferred, outweighed all prejudices which they might have imbibed against my nation. On *my* part, charmed with my adventure, delighted with Acmé, and gratified by the kindness of her relations, I endeavoured to increase their favourable opinion by all the means in my power. Acmé and myself were soon more than friends, and I found my visits gave and imparted pleasure.

"I now arrive at the unhappy part of my narrative. How do I wish it were effaced from my memory. You may remember how, in all my letters to Delmé, I made mention of my dear friend Delancey. We were indeed dear friends. We joined at the same time, lived together in England, embarked together, and when, one dreadful night off the African coast, the captain of the transport thought we must inevitably drift on the lee shore, we solaced each other, and agreed that, if it came to the worst, on one plank would we embark our fortunes. On our landing in Malta, we were inseparable, and my first impulse was to inform Delancey of all that had occurred, and to introduce him to a house where I felt so happy. I must here do him the justice to state, that whether I was partly unaware of the extent of my own feelings towards Acmé, or whether I felt a morbid sense of delicacy, in alluding to what I knew to be the first attachment I had ever formed, I am unable to inform you! but the only circumstance I concealed from my friend was my attachment to the young Greek. Perhaps to this may be mainly attributed what happened. God, who knows all secrets, knows this; but I may now aver, that my friend, with many faults, has proved himself to have as frank and ingenuous a spirit, as noble ideas of friendship, as can exist in the human breast. For some time, matters continued thus. We were both constant visitors at Acmé's house. With unparalleled blindness, I never mistrusted the feelings of my friend. I never contemplated that *he* also might become entangled with the young beauty. I considered her as my own prize, and was more engaged in analysing my own sensations, and in vainly struggling against a passion, which I was certain could not meet my family's approval, than at all suspicious that fresh causes of uneasiness might arise in another quarter. As Acmé's heart opened to mine, I found her with feelings guileless and unsuspecting as a child's; although these were warm, and their expression but little restrained. There was a confiding simplicity in her manner, that threw an air over all she said or did, which quite forbade censure, and excited admiration. My passion became a violent and an all-absorbing one. I had made up my mind, to throw myself on the kindness of my family, and endeavour to obtain all your consents. Thus was I situated, when one day Acmé came up to me with frankness of manner, but a tremulous voice, to beg I would use my interest with my friend, to prevent his coming to see her.

"'Indeed, indeed,' said she, 'I have tried to love him as a friend, as the friend of my life's preserver, but ever since he has spoken as he now does, his visits are quite unpleasant. My family begged me to tell you. They would have asked him to come no more, but were afraid you might be angry. Will you still come to us, and love us all, if they tell him this? If you will not, he shall still come; for indeed we could not offend one to whom we owe so much.'

"'*I*, too,' said I to Acmé, '*I*, too, dearest, ought perhaps to leave you, *I*, too' -

"'Oh, never! never!' said she, as she turned to me her dark eyes, bright with humid radiance. 'We cannot thus part!'

"She *did*, then, love me! I clasped her to my arms - our lips clung together in one rapturous intoxicating embrace.

"Yet, even in that moment of delirium, Henry, I told her of you, and of the many obstacles which still presented themselves to retard or even prevent our union. I sought my friend Delancey, and remonstrated with him. He appeared to doubt my right to question his motives. Success made me feel still more injured. I showered down reproaches. He could not have acted differently. We met! and I saw him fall! Till then, I had considered myself as the injured man; but as I heard him on the ground name his mother, and one dearer still - as he took from his breast the last gift *she* had made him - as he begged of *me* to be its bearer; I then first felt remorse. He was taken to his room. Even the surgeon entertained no hopes. He again called me to his side; I heard his noble acknowledgment, his reiterated vows of friendship, the mournful tones of his farewell. I entered this room a heart-broken man. I felt my pulse throb fearfully, a gasping sensation was in my throat, my head swam round, and I clung to the wall for support. The next thing of which I have any recollection, was the dawn of reason breaking through my troubled dreams. It was midnight - all was still. The fitful lamp shone dimly through my chamber. I turned on my side - and, oh! by its light, I saw the face I most loved - that face, whose gentle lineaments, were each deeply and separately engraven on my heart. I saw her bending over me with a maiden's love and a mother's solicitude. As I essayed to speak - as my conscious eye met her's - as the soft words of affection were involuntarily breathed by my feeble lips - how her features lit up with joy! Oh, say not, Henry, till you have experienced such a moment of transport, say not that the lips which then vowed eternal fidelity, that the young hearts which *then* plighted their truth, and vowed to love for ever - oh call not these guilty!

"Since that time my health has been extremely precarious. Whether the events crowded too thickly on me, or that I have not fully recovered my health, or - which I confess I think is the case - that my compunctions for my conduct to Acmé weigh me down, I know not; but it is not always, my dear Henry, that I can thus address you. There are hours when I am hardly sensible of what I do, when my brain reels from its oppression. At such times, Acmé is my guardian angel - my tender nurse - my affectionate attendant! In my lucid intervals, she is what you see her - the gentle companion - the confiding friend. I love her, Henry, more than I can tell you! I shall never be able to leave her! From Acmé you may learn more of those dreary hours, which appear to me like waste dreams in my existence. She has watched by my bed of sickness, till she knows every turn of the disorder. From her, Henry, may you learn all."

Thus did George conclude his tale of passion; which Delmé mused over, but refrained from commenting on.

Soon afterwards, George's calèche, in which he daily took exercise, was announced as being at the door. The brothers entered, and left Floriana.

CHAPTER X

THE CALÈCHE

"The car rattling through the stony street."

For an easy conveyance, commend us to a Maltese calèche! Many a time, assaulted by the blue devils, have we taken refuge in its solacing interior - have pulled down its silken blinds, and unseeing and unseen, the motion, like that of the rocking-cradle to the petulant child of less mature growth, has restored complacency, and lulled us to good humour. The calèche, the real calèche, is, we believe, peculiar to Malta. It is the carriage of the rich and poor - Lady Woodford may be seen employing it, to visit her gardens at St. Antonio; and in the service of the humblest of her subjects, will it be enlisted, as they wend their way to a picnic in the campagna. Every variety of steed is put in requisition for its draught.

We may see the barb, with nostril of fire, and mane playing with the wind, perform a curvet, as he draws our aristocratic countrywoman - aristocratic and haughty at least in Malta, although, in England, perhaps a star of much less magnitude.

We may view too the over-burthened donkey, as he drags along some aged vehicle, in which four fat smiling women, and one lean weeping child, look forward to his emaciated carcase, and yet blame him for being slow.

And thou! patient and suffering animal, whose name has passed into a proverb, until each vulgar wight looks on thee as the emblem of obstinacy, - maligned mule! when dost thou appear to more advantage, more joyous, or more self-satisfied, than when yoked to the Maltese calèche? Who that has witnessed thee, taking the scanty meal from the hand of thine accustomed driver, with whinnying voice, waving tail, thy long ears pricked upwards, and thy head rubbing his breast, who that has seen thee thus, will deny thee the spirit of gratitude?

Most injured of quadrupeds! if we ascend the rugged mountain's path, where on either side, precipices frown, and the pines wave far - far beneath - when one false step would plunge us, with our hopes, our fears, and our vices, into the abyss of eternity; is it not to thee we trust?

Calumniated mule! go on thy way.

This world's standard is but little to be relied on, whether it be for good, or whether it be for evil.

The motion of a calèche, such as we patronised, is an easy and luxurious one - the pace, a fast trot or smooth canter, of seven miles an hour - and with the blinds down, we have communed with ourselves, with as great freedom, and as little fear of interruption, as if we had been crossing the Zahara. The calèche men too are a peculiar and happy race - attentive to their fares - masters of their profession - and with a cigar in their cheek dexter, will troll you Maltese ditties till your head aches. Their costume is striking. Their long red caps are thrown back over their necks - their black curls hang down on each side of the face - and a crimson, many-folded sash, girds in a waist usually extremely small. Their neck, face, and breast, from continued exposure to the sun, are a red copper colour. They are always without shoes and stockings; and even our countrywomen, who pay much attention to the costume of their drivers, have not yet ventured to encase their brawny feet in the mysteries of leather. They run by the side of their calèches, the reins in one hand - the whip in the other -

cheering on their animals by a constant succession of epithets, oaths, and invocations to their favourite saint.

They are rarely fatigued, and may be seen beside their vehicles, urging the horses, with the thermometer at 110°, and perhaps a stout-looking Englishman inside, with white kerchief to his face, the image of languor and lassitude.

Their horses gallop down steeps, which no English Jehu dare attempt; and ascend and descend with safety and hardihood, stone steps which occur in many parts of Valletta; and which would certainly present an insurmountable obstacle to our steeds at home.

The proper period, however, to see a calèche man in his glory, is during the carnival. Every calèche is in employ; and many a one which has reposed for the twelvemonth previous, is at that time wheeled from its accustomed shed, and put in requisition for some of pleasure's votaries. Long lines of them continue to pass and repass in the principal street. Their inmates are almost universally of the fair sex, and of the best part of it, the young and beautiful. Cavaliers, with silken bags, containing bon-bons, slung on their left arm, stand at intervals, ready to discharge the harmless missiles, at those whom their taste approves worthy of the compliment. Happy the young beauty, who, returning homewards, sees the carpet of her calèche thickly strewn with these dulcet favours! The driver is now in his element! He ducks his head, as the misdirected sweetmeat approaches; he has an apt remark prompt for the occasion. As he nears too the favoured inamorato, for whom he well knows his mistress' sweetest smile is reserved - who already with his right hand grasping the sugared favours, is prepared to lavish his whole store on this one venture - how arch his look - how roguish his eye - as he turns towards his donna, and speaks as plainly as words could do, "See! there he is, he whom you love best!"

Ah! well may we delight to recal once more those minute details! ah! well may we remember how - when our brow was smoothed with youth, as it is now furrowed with care - when our eye sparkled from pleasure, as it is now dimmed from time, or mayhap, tears - well may we love to remember, how our whole hearts were engrossed in that mimic warfare. How impatiently did we watch for *one*, amidst that crowded throng, for one - whose beauty haunted us by day, and whose smile we dreamt over by night. Well do we recal with what unexampled ingenuity, we laboured to befit the snow white egg for a rare tenant - attar-gul. Well do we remember how that face, usually so cloudless, became darkened almost to a frown, as our heart's mistress saw the missile approach her. What a radiant smile bewitched us, as it burst on her lap, and filled the air with its fragrance! Truly we had our reward!

Delmé and George took a quiet drive, and enjoyed that sweet interchange of ideas, that characterises the meeting of two brothers long absent from each other.

They went in the direction of St. Julian's, a drive all our Maltese friends will be familiar with. The road lay almost wholly by the sea side. A gentle breeze was crisping the waters, and served to allay the heat, which, at a more advanced period of the season, is by no means an enviable one. Sun-shine seemed to beam on George's mind, as he once more spoke of home ties, to one to whom those home ties were equally dear. And gratefully did he bask in its rays! Long used to the verdant but tame, beautiful but romantic landscapes, which the part of England he resided in presented; the scenery around him, novel and picturesque, struck Sir Henry forcibly. To one who has resided long in Malta, its scenes may wear an aspect somewhat different. The limited country - the ceaseless glare - the dust, or rather the pulverised rock - the ever-present lizard, wary and quick, peeping out at each crevice - the buzzing mosquito, inviting the moody philosopher to smite his own cheek, - these things may come to be regarded as real grievances.

But Delmé, as a visitor, was pleased with what he saw. The promising vineyards - the orange groves, with their glowing fruit and ample foliage, "looking like golden lamps" in a dark night of leaves - the thick leaves of the prickly pear - the purple sky above him, lending its rich hue to the sea beside - the architectural beauties of the cottages - the wide portico of the mansions - the flat terrace with its balustrade, over which might be seen a fair face, half concealed by the faldette, smilingly peering, and through whose pillars might be noted a pretty ancle, and siesta-looking slipper - these were novelties, and pleasing ones! Their drive over, Delmé felt more tranquil as to George's state of mind, and more inclined to look on the bright side, as to his future fortunes.

Acmé was waiting to receive them, and as she scanned George's features, Delmé could not but observe the affectionate solicitude that marked her glance and manner.

Let it not be thought we would make vice seductive!

Fair above all things is the pure affection of woman! happy he who may regard it his! he may bask without a shade of distrust in its glorious splendour, and permanently adore its holy beauty.

While, fascinating though be the concentred love of woman, whether struggling in its passion - enraptured in its madness - or clinging and loving on in its guilt: Man - that more selfish wanderer from virtue's pale, that destroyer of his own best sympathies - will find too late that a day of bitterest regret must arrive: a day when love shall exist no more, or, linked with remorse, shall tear - a fierce vulture - at his very heart strings.

CHAPTER XI

THE COLONEL

"Not such as prate of war, but skulk in peace."

Delmé strolled out half an hour before his brother's dinner hour, with the intention of paying a visit of ceremony to the Colonel of George's regiment. His house was not far distant. It had been the palazzo of one of the redoubted Knights of St. John; and the massive gate at which Sir Henry knocked for admittance, seemed an earnest, that the family, who had owned the mansion, had been a powerful and important one. The door was opened, and the servant informed Delmé, that Colonel Vavasour was on the terrace.

The court yard through which they passed was extensive; and a spring

"Of living water from its centre rose,
Whose bubbling did a genial softness fling."

Ascending a lofty marble staircase, along which were placed a few bronzed urns, Delmé crossed a suite of apartments - thrown open in the Italian mode - and passing through a glass door, found himself on a wide stone terrace, edged by pillars.

Immediately beneath this, was an orange grove, whose odours perfumed the air. Colonel Vavasour was employed in reading a

German treatise on light infantry tactics. He received Sir Henry with great cordiality, and proposed adjourning to the library. Delmé was pleased to observe, for it corresponded with what he had heard of the man; that, with the exception of the chef d'oeuvres of the English and German poets, the Colonel's library, which was an extensive one, almost wholly consisted of such books as immediately related to military subjects, or might be able to bear on some branch of science connected with military warfare. Pagan, and his follower Vauban, and the more matured treatises of Cormontaigne, were backed by the works of that boast of the Low Countries, Coehorn; and by the ingenious theories, as yet *but* theories, of Napoleon's minister of war, Carnot.

Military historians, too, crowded the shelves. *There* might be noted the veracious Polybius - the classic Xenophon - the scientific Cæsar - the amusing Froissart, with his quaint designs, and quainter discourses - and many an author unknown to fame, who in lengthy quarto, luxuriated on the lengthy campaigns of Marlborough or Eugene; those wise commanders, who flourished in an era, when war was a well debated scientific game of chess; when the rival opponents took their time, before making their moves; and the loss of a pawn was followed by the loss of a kingdom. *There* might you be enamoured with even a soldier's hardships, as your eye glanced on the glowing circumstantial details of Kincaid; - or you might glory in your country's Thucydides, as you read the nervous impassioned language of a Napier. *Thou*, too, Trant! our friend! wert there! Ah, why cut off in thy prime? Did not thy spirit glow with martial fire? Did not thy conduct give promise, that not in vain were those talents accorded thee? What hadst *thou* done, to sink thus early to a premature inglorious grave? Nor were our friends Folard and Jomini absent; nor eke the minute essays of a Jarry, who taught the aspiring youths of Great Britain all the arts of castrametation. With what gusto does he show how to attack Reading; or how, with the greatest chance of success, to defend the tranquil town of Egham. *Here* would he sink trous de loup on the ancient Runnimede, whereby the advance of the enemy's cavalry would be frustrated; *there* would he cut down an abattis, or plant chevaux de frise. At *this* winding of England's noblest river, would he establish a pontoon bridge; the approaches to which he would enfilade, by a battery placed on yonder height.

Before relating the conversation between Delmé and Colonel Vavasour, it may not be improper to say a few words as to the character of the latter. When we say that he was looked up to as an officer, and adored as a man, by the regiment he had commanded for years; we are not according light praise.

Those who have worn a coat of red, or been much conversant with military affairs, will appreciate the difficult, the ungrateful task, devolving on a commanding officer.

How few, how very few are those, who can command respect, and ensure love. How many, beloved as men, are imposed on, and disregarded as officers. How many are there, whose presence on the parade ground awes the most daring hearts, who are passed by in private life, with something like contumely, and of whom, in their private relations, few speak, and yet fewer are those who wish kindly. When deserving in each relation, how frequently do we see those who want the manner, the tact, to show themselves in their true colours. An ungracious refusal - ay! Or an ungraciously accorded favour! may raise a foe who will be a bar to a man's popularity for years: - whilst how many a free and independent spirit is there, who criticises with a keener eye than is his wont, the sayings and doings of his commanding officer, solely because he *is* such. How apt is such an one to misrepresent a word, or create a wrong motive for an action! how slow in giving praise, lest *he* should be deemed one of the servile train! Pass we over the host of petty intrigues - the myriads of conflicting interests: - show not how the partial report of a favourite, may make the one in authority unjust to him below him; or how the false tale-bearer may induce the one below to be unjust to his superior. Colonel Vavasour was not only considered in the field, as one of England's bravest soldiers; but was yet more remarkable for his gentlemanly deportment, and for the attention he ever paid to the interior economy of his corps. This gave a tone to the - mess, almost incredible to one, who has not witnessed, what the constant presence of a commanding officer, if he be a real gentleman, is enabled to effect. Colonel Vavasour had ideas on the duties of a soldier, which to many appeared original. We cannot but think, that the Colonel's ideas, in the main, were right. He disliked his officers marrying; often stating that he considered a sword and a wife as totally incompatible.

"Where," would he say, "is *then* that boasted readiness of purpose, that spirit of enterprise? Can an officer *then*, with half a dozen shirts in his portmanteau, and a moderate quantity of cigars, if he be a smoker, declare himself ready to sail over half the world?"

The Colonel would smile as he said this, but would continue with a graver tone.

"No, there is a choice, and I blame no one for making his election: - a soldier's hardships and a soldier's joys; - or domestic happiness, and an inglorious life: - but to attempt to blend the two, is, I think, injudicious."

On regimental subjects, he was what is technically called, a regulation man. No innovations ever crept into his regiment, wanting the sanction of the Horse Guards; whilst every order emanating from thence, was as scrupulously adopted and adhered to, as if his own taste had prompted the change. On parade, Colonel Vavasour was a strict disciplinarian; - but his sword in the scabbard, he dropped the officer in his manner, - it was impossible to do so in his appearance, - and no one ever heard him discuss military points in a place inappropriate. He knew well how to make the distinction between his public and his private duties. On an officer under his command, being guilty of any dereliction of duty, he would send for him, and reprimand him before the assembled corps, if he deemed that such reprimand would be productive of good effect to others; but - the parade dismissed - he would probably take this very officer's arm, or ask to accompany him in his country ride.

Colonel Vavasour had once a young and an only brother under his command. In no way did he relax discipline in his favour. Young Vavasour had committed a breach of military etiquette. He was immediately ordered by his brother to be placed in arrest, and would inevitably have been brought to a court martial, had not the commanding officer of the station interfered. During the whole of this time, the Colonel's manner towards him continued precisely the same. They lived together as usual; and no man, without a knowledge of the circumstance, could have been aware that any other but a fraternal tie bound them together. What was more extraordinary, the younger brother saw all this in its proper light; and whilst he clung to and loved his brother, looked up with awe and respect to his commanding officer.

As for Colonel Vavasour, no one who saw his convulsed features, as his brother fell heading a gallant charge of his company at Waterloo, could have doubted for a moment his deep-rooted affection. From that period, a gloomy melancholy hung about him, which, though shaken off in public, gave a shade to his brow, which was very perceptible.

In person, he was particularly neat; being always the best dressed officer in his regiment, "How can we expect the men to pay attention to *their* dress, when we give them reason to suppose we pay but little attention to our own?" was a constant remark of his. And here we may observe, that no class of men have a stricter idea of the propriety of dress, than private soldiers. To dress well is half a passport to a soldier's respect; whilst on the other hand, it requires many excellent qualities, to counterbalance in his mind a careless and slovenly exterior. Colonel Vavasour had an independent fortune, which he spent at the head of his regiment. Many a dinner party was given by him, for which the corps he commanded obtained the credit; many a young officer owed relief from pecuniary embarrassments, which might otherwise have overwhelmed him, to the generosity of his Colonel. He appeared not to have a wish, beyond the military circle around him, although those who knew him best, said he had greater talent, and possessed the art of fascinating in general society, more than most men.

"I am glad to see you here, Sir Henry," said he to Delmé, "although I cannot but wish that happier circumstances had brought you to us. I have a very great esteem for your brother, and am one of his warmest well wishers. But I must not neglect the duties of hospitality. You must allow me to present you to my officers at mess this evening. Our dinner hour is late; but were it otherwise, we should miss that delightful hour for our ride, when the sun's rays have no longer power to harm us, and the sea breezes waft us a freshness, which almost compensates for the languor attending the summer's heat."

Delmé declined his invitation, stating his wish to dine with his brother on that day; but expressed himself ready to accept his kind offer on the ensuing one.

"Thank you!" said Colonel Vavasour, "it is natural you should wish to see your brother; and it pains me to think that poor George cannot yet dine with his old friends. Have you seen Mr. Graham?"

Delmé replied in the affirmative; adding, that he could not but feel obliged to him for his frankness.

"I am glad you feel thus," said Vavasour, "it emboldens me to address you with equal candour; and, painful as our advice must be, I confess I am inclined to side with George's medical attendant. I have myself been witness to such lamentable proofs of George's state of mind - he has so often, with the tears in his eyes, spoken to me of his feelings with regard to Acmé Frascati, that I certainly consider these as in a great measure the cause, and his state of mind the effect. I speak to you, Sir Henry, without disguise. I had once a brother - the apple of my eye - I loved him as I shall never love human being more; and, as God is my witness, under similar circumstances, frankness is what I should have prayed for, - my first wish would have been at once to know the worst. Mr. Graham has told you of his long illness - his delirium - and has, I conclude, touched upon the present state of his patient. Shall I shock you, when I add that his lucid intervals are not to be depended upon; that occasionally the wildest ideas, the most extraordinary projects, are conceived by him? I wish you not, to act on any thing that Mr. Graham, or that I may tell you, but to judge for yourself. Without this, indeed, you would hardly understand the danger of these mental paroxysms. So fearful are they, that I confess I should be inclined to adopt any remedy, make any sacrifices which promised the remotest possibility of success."

"I trust," said Sir Henry, "there are no sacrifices I would not personally make for my only brother, were I once convinced these were for his real benefit."

"I frankly mean," said Vavasour, "that I think almost the only chance of restoring him, is by allowing him to marry Acmé Frascati."

Delmé's brow clouded.

"Think not," continued he, "that I am ignorant of what such a determination must cost you. *I*, too, Sir Henry," - and the old man drew his commanding form to its utmost height, - "*I* too, know what must be the feelings of a descendant of noble ancestors. I know them well; and in more youthful days, the blood boiled in my veins as I thought of the name they had left me. Thank heaven! I have never disgraced it. But were *I* situated as *you* are, and the dead Augustus Vavasour in the place of the living George Delmé, I would act as I am now advising you to do. I speak solely as to the expediency of the measure. From what I have stated - from my situation in life - from my character - you may easily imagine that all my prejudices are enlisted on the other side of the question. But I must here confess that I see something inexpressibly touching in the devotion which that young Greek girl displayed, during the whole of George's illness. But putting this on one side, and considering the affair as one of mere expediency, I think you will finally agree with me, that however desperate the remedy, some such must be applied. And now, let me assure you, that nothing could have induced me to obtrude thus, my feelings and opinions on a comparative stranger, were it not that that stranger is the brother of one in whose welfare I feel the liveliest interest."

Sir Henry Delmé expressed his thanks, and inwardly determined that he would form no opinion till he had himself been witness to some act of mental aberration. It is true, he had heard the medical attendant give a decided opinion, - from George's own lips he had an avowal of much that had been stated, - and now he had heard one, for whom he could not but feel great respect - one who had evidently no interest in the question - declare his sentiments as strongly. We are all sanguine as to what we wish. It may be, that a hope yet lurked in Delmé's breast, that these accounts might be unconsciously exaggerated, or that his brother's state of health was now more established than heretofore.

On returning to Floriana, Delmé found George and the blushing Acmé awaiting him. A delightful feeling is that, of again finding ourselves with those from whom we have long been parted, once more engaged in the same round of familiar avocations, once more re-acting the thousand little trifles of life which we have so often acted before, and that, too, in company with those who now sit beside us, as if to mock the lapse of intervening years. These meetings seem to steal a pinion from time's wing, and hard indeed were it if the sensations they called forth were not pleasurable ones; for oh! how rudely and frequently, on the other hand, are we reminded of the changes which the progress of years brings with it: the bereavement of loved ones - the prostration of what we revered - our buoyant elasticity of body and mind departed - all things changing and changed.

We sigh, and gaze back. How few are the scenes, which memory's kaleidoscope presents in their pristine bright colours, of that journey, performed so slowly, as it once appeared, but which, to the eye of retrospection, seems to have hurried to its end with the rapid wings of the wind!

Imbued with an association, what a trivial circumstance will please! As the brothers touched each other's glass; and drank to mutual happiness, what grateful recollections were called up by that act! How did these manifest their power, as they lighted up the wan features of George Delmé. Acmé looked on smilingly; her hair flowing about her neck - her dark eyes flashing with unusual brilliancy. Delmé felt it would be unsocial were he alone to look grave; and although many foreboding thoughts crowded on him, *he* too seemed to be happy. It was twilight when the dinner was over. The windows were open, and the party placed themselves near the jalousies. They here commanded a view of the public gardens, where groups of Maltese were enjoying the coolness of the hour, and the fragrance of the flowers. The walk had a roof of lattice work supported by wooden pillars; round which, an image of woman's love, the honeysuckle clingingly twined, diffusing sweets.

Immediately before them, the principal outlet of the town presented itself. Laughing parties of English sailors were passing, mounted on steeds of every size, which they were urging forward, in spite of the piteous remonstrances of the menials of their owners. The latter, for the most part, held by the tails of their animals, and uttered a jargon composed of English, Italian, and Maltese. The only words however, that met the unregarding ears of the sailors, were some such exclamations as these.

"Not you go so fast, Signore; he good horse, but much tire."

The riders sat in their saddles swinging from side to side, evidently thinking their tenure more precarious than that on the giddy mast; and wholly unmindful of the expressive gestures, and mournful ejaculations of the bare-legged pursuers. At another time, their antics and buffoonery, as they made unmerciful use of the short sticks with which they were armed, would have provoked a smile. *Now* our party gazed on these things as they move the wise. They felt calm and happy; and deceptive hope whispered they might yet remain so. Acmé took up her guitar, and throwing her fingers over it, as she gave a soft prelude, warbled that sweet although common song, "Buona notte, amato bene." She sung with great feeling, and feeling is the soul of music.

How plaintively! how tenderly did her lips breathe the

"ricordati! ricordati di me!"

There was something extremely witching in her precocious charms. She resembled some beauteous bud, just ready to burst into light and bloom. It is not yet the rose, - but a moment more may make it such. Her beauties were thus ripe for maturity. It seemed as if the sunshine of love were already upon them - they were basking in its rays. A brief space - and the girl shall no longer be such. What was promise shall be beauty. She shall meet the charmed eye a woman; rich in grace and loveliness. As Delmé marked her sympathising glance at George - her beaming features - her innocent simplicity; - as he thought of all she had lost, all she had suffered for his brother's sake, - as he thought of the scorn of the many - the pity of the few - the unwearied watching - the sleepless nights - the day of sorrow passed by the bed of sickness - all so cheerfully encountered for *him* - he could not reproach her. No! he took her hand, and the brothers whispered consolation to her, and to each other.

Late that evening, they were joined by Colonel Vavasour, and Mr. Graham. George's spirits rose hourly. Never had his Colonel appeared to such advantage - Acmé so lovely - or Henry so kind - as they did to George Delmé that night.

It was with a sigh at the past pleasures that George retired to his chamber.

CHAPTER XII

THE MESS

"Red coats and redder faces."

The following day, a room having been given up to Delmé, he discharged his bill at Beverley's; and moved to Floriana. He again accompanied George in his drive; and they had on this occasion, the advantage of Acmé's society, who amused them with her artless description of the manners of the lower orders of Maltese.

Pursuant to his promise, at the bugle's signal Delmé entered the mess room; and the Colonel immediately introduced him to the assembled officers. To his disappointment, for he felt curious to see one, who had exercised such an influence over his brother, Delancey was not amongst them. Sir Henry was much pleased with the feeling that appeared to exist, between Colonel Vavasour and his corps of officers: - respect on one side - and the utmost confidence on both. We think it is the talented author of Pelham, who describes a mess table as comprising "cold dishes and hot wines, where the conversation is of Johnson of ours and Thomson of jours."

This, though severe, is near the truth; and if, to this description, be added *lots* of plate of that pattern called the Queen's - ungainly servants in stiff mess liveries - and a perpetual recurrence to Mr. Vice; we have certainly caught the most glaring features of a commonplace regimental dinner. Vavasour was well aware of this, and had directed unremitting attention, to give a tone to the conversation at the mess table, more nearly approaching to that of private life; one which should embrace topics of general interest, and convey some general information. Even in *his* well ordered regiment, there were some, whose nature would have led them, to confine their attention to thoughts of the daily military routine. This inclination was repressed by the example of their Colonel; and these, if not debaters, were at least patient listeners, as the conversation dealt of matters, to them uncongenial, and the value of the discussion of which they could not themselves perceive. Not that military subjects were interdicted; the contrary was the case. But these subjects took a somewhat loftier tone, than the contemplation of an exchange of orderly duty, or an overslaugh of guard.

When dinner was announced, Colonel Vavasour placed his hand on the shoulder of a boy near him.

"Come, Cholmondeley!" said he, "sit near me, and give me an account of your match. You must not fail to write your Yorkshire friends every particular. Major Clifford, will you sit on the other side of Sir Henry? You are both Peninsula men, and will find, I doubt not, that you have many friends in common.

"There is something," said he to Delmé, as he took his seat, "revivifying to an old soldier, in noting the exhilaration of spirit of these boys. It reminds us of the zeal with which *we* too buckled on our coat of red. It is a great misfortune these youngsters labour under, that they have no outlet for their ambition, no scene on which they can display their talents. Never were youthful aspirants for service more worthy, or more zealous, and yet it is probable their country will not need them, until they arrive at an age, when neither body nor mind are attuned for *commencing* a life of hardship, however well adapted to *continue* in it. *We* have had the advantage there - *we* trod the soldier's proudest stage when our hopes and buoyancy of heart were at their highest; and for myself, I am satisfied that much of my present happiness, arises from the very different life of my earlier years."

The conversation took a military turn; and Delmé could not help observing the attention, with which the younger members of the corps heard the anecdotes, related by those who had been actually engaged. Occasionally, the superior reading of the juniors would peep out, and give them the advantage of knowledge, even with regard to circumstances, over those who had been personal actors in the affairs they spoke of. The most zealous of these detail narrators, were the quarter-master of the regiment, and Delmé's right-hand neighbour, Major Clifford. The former owed his appointment to his gallantry, in saving the colours of his regiment, when the ensign who bore them was killed, and the enemy's cavalry were making a sudden charge, before the regiment could form its square.

His was a bluff purple face, denoting the bon vivant. Indeed, it was with uncommon celerity, that his previous reputation of being the best maker of rum punch in the serjeants' mess, had changed into his present one of being the first concoctor of sangaree at the officers'.

Major Clifford merits more especial notice. He was a man hardly appreciated in his own profession; out of it, he was misrepresented, and voted a bore. He had spent all the years of his life, since the down mantled his upper lip, in the service of his country; and for *its* good, as he conceived it, he had sacrificed all his little fortune. It is true his liberality had not had a very comprehensive range: he had sunk his money in the improvement of the personal appearance of his company - in purchasing pompons - or new feathers - or whistles, when he was a voltigeur - in establishing his serjeants' mess on a more respectable footing - in giving his poor comrade a better coffin, or a richer pall: - these had been his foibles; and in indulging them, he had expended the wealth, that might have purchased him on to rank and honours. His eagle glance, his aquiline nose, and noble person, showed what he must have been in youth. His hair was now silvered, but his coat was as glossy as formerly - his zeal was unabated - his pride in his profession the same - and what he could spare, still went, to adorn the persons of the soldiers he still loved. He remained a captain, although his long standing in the army had brought him in for the last brevet. It is true every one had a word for poor Clifford. "Such a fine fellow! what a shame!" But *this* did not help him on. At the Horse Guards, too, his services were freely acknowledged. The Military Secretary had always a smile for him at his levee, and an assurance that "he had his eye on him" The Commander in Chief, too, the last time he had inspected the regiment, attracted by his Waterloo badge, and Portuguese cross, had stopped as he passed in front of the ranks, and conversed with him most affably, for nearly two minutes and a half; as his colour serjeant with some degree of pride used to tell the story. But yet, somehow or other, although Major Clifford was an universal favourite, they always forgot to reward him. A man of the world, would have deemed the Major's ideas to be rather contracted; and to confess the truth, there were two halcyon periods of his life, to which he was fond of recurring. The one was, when he commanded a light company, attached to General Crauford's light brigade; - the other, when he had the temporary command of the regimental depot, and at his own expense, had dressed out its little band, as it had never been dressed out before.

Do you sneer at the old soldier, courtly reader?

There breathes not a man who dare arraign that man's courage; - there is not one who knows him, who would not cheerfully stake his life as a gage for his stainless honour.

The soup and fish had been removed, when Delmé observed a young officer glide in, with that inexpressible air of fashion, which appears to shun notice, whilst it attracts it. His arm was in a sling, and his attenuated face seemed to bespeak ill health. Sir Henry addressed Colonel Vavasour, and begged to know if the person who had just entered the room was Delancey. He was answered in the affirmative; and he again turned to scrutinise his features. These rivetted attention; and were such as could not be seen once, without being gazed at again. His eyes were dark and large, and rested for minutes on one object, with an almost mournful expression; nor was it until they turned from its contemplation, that the discriminating observer might read in their momentary flash, that their possessor had passions deep and uncontrollable. His dark hair hung in profusion over his forehead, which it almost hid; though from the slight separation of a curl, the form of brow became visible; which was remarkable for its projection, and for its pallid hue, which offered a strong contrast to the swart and sunburnt face.

"Are you aware of his history?" said the Colonel.

"Not in the slightest," replied Delmé. "I felt curious to see him, on account of the way in which he has been mixed up with George's affair; and think his features extraordinary - very extraordinary ones."

"He is son," said Vavasour, "to the once celebrated Lady Harriet D - , who made a marriage so disgracefully low. He is the only child by that union. His parents lived for many years on the continent, in obscurity, and under an assumed name. They are both dead. It is possible Delancey may play a lofty role in the world, as he has only a stripling between him and the earldom of D - , which descends in the female line. I am sure he will not be a common character; but I have great fears about him. In the regiment he is considered proud and unsocial; and indeed it was your brother's friendship that appeared to retain him in our circle. He has great talents, and some good qualities; but from his uncommon impetuosity of temper, and his impatience of being thwarted, I should be inclined to predict, that the first check he receives in life, will either make him a misanthrope, or a pest to society."

At a later period of his life, Delmé again encountered Delancey; and this prophecy of the Colonel's was vividly recalled.

In the ensuing chapter, we purpose giving Oliver Delancey's history, as a not uninstructive episode; although we are aware that episodes are impatiently tolerated, and it is in nowise allied to the purpose of our story. But before doing so, we must detail a conversation which occurred between Delancey and Delmé, at the table of the - mess. The latter was scanning the features of the former, when their eyes met. A conviction seemed to flash on Delancey, that Delmé was George's brother; for the blood rushed to his cheek - his colour went and came - and as he turned away his head, he made a half involuntary bow. Delmé was struck with his manner, and apparent emotion; and in returning the salute, ventured "to hope he was somewhat recovered."

When Major Clifford left the table, Delancey took his vacant seat.

"Sir Henry Delmé," said he, "I have before this wished to see you, to implore the forgiveness of your family for the misery I have occasioned. How often have I cursed my folly! I acted on an impulse, which at the time I could not withstand. I had never serious views with regard to Acmé Frascati. Indeed, I may here tell you, - to no other man have I ever named it, - that I have ties in my own country far dearer, and more imperatively binding. I knew I had erred. The laws of society could alone have made me meet George Belmé as a foe; but even then - on the ground - God and my second know that my weapon was never directed at my friend. I am an unsocial being, Sir Henry, and, from my habits, not likely to be popular. Your brother knew this, and saved me from petty contentions and invidious calumnies. He was the best and only friend I possessed. I purpose soon to leave Malta and the army. The former is become painful to me, - for the latter I have a distaste, A feeling of delicacy to Acmé Frascati would prevent my seeing your brother, even if Mr. Graham had not forbidden the interview, as likely to harass his mind. Will you, then, assure him of my unabated attachment, and tell me that *you* forgive me for the part I have taken in this unhappy affair."

Delmé was much moved as he assured him he would do all he wished; that he could see little to blame him for - that George's excited feelings had brought on the present crisis, and that *he* had amply atoned for any share he might have had in the transaction. Delancey pressed his hand gratefully.

It was at a somewhat late hour that Delmé joined Acmé and his brother; declining the hearty invitation of the Quartermaster to come down to his quarters.

"He could give him a devilled turkey and a capital cigar."

CHAPTER XIII

OLIVER DELANCEY

> "Then the few, whose spirits float above the wreck of happiness,
> Are driven o'er the shoals of guilt, or ocean of excess;
> The magnet of their course is gone, or only points in vain
> The shore to which their shiver'd sail shall never reach again."

We have said that Delmé saw Delancey once more. It was at a later period of our story, when business had taken Sir Henry to Bath. He had been dining with Mr. Belliston Græme, who possessed a villa in the neighbourhood. Tempted by the beauty of the night, he dismissed his carriage, and, turning from the high road, took a by-path which led to the city. The air was serene and mild. The moon-light was sufficiently clear to chase away night's dank vapours. The ground had imperceptibly risen, until having ascended a grassy eminence, over which the path stretched, the well-lighted city burst upon the eye.

Immediately in front of the view, a principal street presented itself, the lamps on either side stretching in regular succession, until they gradually narrowed and joined in the perspective. Nearer to the spectator, the flickering lights of the detached villas, and the moving ones of the carriages in the public road, relieved the stillness of the scene. Delmé paused to regard it, with that subdued feeling with which men, arrived at a certain period of life, scan the aspect of nature. The moon at the moment was enveloped in light clouds. As it broke through them, its shimmering light revealed a face and form that Delmé at once recognised as Delancey's. It was with a consciousness of pain he did so, for it brought before him recollections of scenes, whose impressions had still power to subdue him. All emotions, however, soon became absorbed in that of curiosity, as he noted the still figure and agitated features before him. A block of granite lay near the path. Delancey leant back over it - his right hand nearly touched the ground - his hat lay beside him. The dark hair, wet with the dews of night, was blown back by the breeze. His high forehead was fully shewn. His vest and shirt were open, as he gazed with an air of fixedness on the city, and conversed to himself. His teeth were firmly clenched, and it seemed that the lips moved not, but the words were fearfully distinct. We often hear of these soliloquies, - they afford scope to the dramatist, food for the poet, a chapter for the narrator of fiction, - but we rarely witness them. When we do, they are eminently calculated to thrill and alarm. It was evident that Delancey saw him not; but had it been otherwise, Delmé's interest was so aroused that he could not have left the spot.

"Hail! sympathising night!" thus spoke the young man, "the calm of thy silent hour seems in unison with my lone heart - thy dewy breeze imparts a freshness to this languid and darkened spirit, Sweet night! how I love thee! And moon, too! fair moon! how abruptly! - how chastely! - how gloriously! - dost thou break through the variegated and fleecy clouds, which would impede thy progress, and deny me to gaze on thy white orb unshrouded. And thou, too! radiant star of eve! oh that woman's love but resembled thee! that it were gentle, constant, and pure as thy holy gleam. That *that* should dazzle to bring in its train - oh God! What misery." He raised his hand to his brow, as if a poignant thought had stung him.

Sir Henry Delmé stole away, and ruminated long that night, on the distress that could thus convulse those fine features. Afterwards, when Delancey's name was no longer the humble one he had first known it, but became bruited in loftier circles, - for Vavasour's prediction became realised, - Delmé heard it whispered, that his affections had suffered an early blight, from the infidelity of one to whom he had been affianced. We may relate the circumstances as they occurred. Blanche Allen was the daughter of a country gentleman of some wealth, whose estate joined that of the Earl of D - 's, where Delancey's boyhood had been spent. For years Blanche and Oliver considered themselves as more than friends. Each selected the other as the companion in the solitary walk, or partner in the joyous dance. Not a country girl but had her significant smile, as young Delancey's horse's head was turned towards Hatton Grange.

Delancey joined the army at an early age. Blanche was some eighteen months his junior. They parted with tears, and thus they continued to do for the two following years, during which Oliver frequently got leave to run down to his uncle's. This was while he was serving with part of the regiment at home. When it came to his turn to embark for foreign service, it was natural from this circumstance, as well as from their riper age, that their farewell should be of a more solemn nature. They bade adieu by the side of the streamlet that divided the two properties. It was where this made a small fall, down which it gushed in crystal brightness, and then meandered with gentle murmur through a succession of rich meadows. A narrow bridge was below the fall, while beside it, a rustic seat had been placed, on which the sobbing Blanche sat, with her lover's arm round her waist. For the first time he had talked seriously of their attachment, and it was with youthful earnestness, that they mutually plighted their troth. Nor did Blanche hesitate, though blushing deeply as she did so, to place in his hand a trivial gage d'amour, and that which has so long solaced absent lovers, a lock of her sunny hair. Blanche was very beautiful, but she had a character common to many English women - more so, we think, than to foreign ones.

As a girl, Blanche was nature's self, warm, gentle, confiding, - as an unmarried woman, she was a heartless coquette, - as a matron, an exemplary mother and an affectionate wife. During the time Delancey was abroad, he heard of Blanche but seldom, for the lovers were not of that age in which a correspondence would be tolerated by Blanche's family. She once managed to send him, by the hands of a young cousin, some trifling present, with a few lines accompanying it, informing him that she had not forgotten him. His uncle - his only correspondent in England - was not exactly the person to make a confidant of; but he would, in an occasional postscript, let him know that he had seen Blanche Allen lately - that "she was very gay, prettier than ever, and always blushing when spoken to of a certain person."

To do Oliver justice, he at all times thought of Blanche. We have seen him, with regard to Acme, apparently disregarding her, but in that affair he had been actuated by a mere spirit of adventure. His heart was but slightly enlisted, and his feelings partook of any thing but those of a serious attachment.

Oliver Delancey left Malta soon after his conversation with Delmé. Previous to doing so, he had forwarded his resignation to Colonel Vavasour.

He passed some time in Italy, and, as the season arrived, found himself a denizen in that gayest of cities, Vienna. Pleasure is truly there enshrouded in her liveliest robes. As regards Delancey, not in vain was she thus clothed. Just relieved from the dull monotony of a military life - dull as it ever must be without war's excitement, and peculiarly distasteful to one constituted like Delancey, who refused to make allowance for the commonplace uncongenial spirits with whom he found himself obliged to herd - he was quite prepared to embrace with avidity any life that promised an agreeable change. Austria's capital holds out many inducements to dissipation, and to none are these more freely tendered, than to young and handsome Englishmen. The women, over the dangerous sentimentality of their nation, throw such an air of ease and frankness, that their victims resemble the finny tribe in the famous tunny fishery. While they conceive the whole ocean is at their command - disport here and there in imagined freedom - they are already encased by the insidious nets; the harpoon is already pointed, which shall surely pierce them. Delancey plunged headlong into pleasure's vortex - touched each link between gaiety and crime. He wandered from the paths of virtue from the infatuation of folly, and continued to err from the fascinations of sin. He was suddenly recalled to himself, by one of those catastrophes often sent by Providence, to awaken us from intoxicating dreams. His companion, with whom he had resided during his stay in Vienna, lost his all at a gaming table. Although he had not the firmness of mind to face his misfortunes, yet had he the rashness to meet his God unbidden. Sobered and appalled, Oliver left Germany for England. There was a thought, which even in the height of his follies obtruded, and which now came on him with a force that surprised himself. That thought was of Blanche Allen. He turned from the image of his expiring friend to dwell unsated on hers. A new vista of life seemed to open - thoughts which had long slept came thronging on his mind - he was once more the love-sick boy. The more, too, he brooded over his late unworthiness, the more did his imagination ennoble the one he loved. He now looked to the moment of meeting her, as that whence he would date his moral regeneration. "Thank God!" thought he, "a sure haven is yet mine. There will I - my feelings steadied, my affections concentrated - enjoy a purified and unruffled peace. What a consolation to be loved by one so good and gentle!"

He hurried towards England, travelled day and night, and only wondered that he could have rested any where, while he had the power of flying to her he had loved from childhood. Occasionally a feeling of apprehension would cross him. It was many months since he had heard of her - she might be ill. His love was of that confiding nature, that he could not conceive her changed. As he came near his home, happier thoughts succeeded. In fancy, he again saw her enjoying the innocent pleasures in which he had been her constant companion, - health on her cheek - affection in her glance. He had to pass that well known lodge. His voice shook, as he told the driver to stop at its gate. As he drove through the avenue of elms, he threw himself back in the carriage, and every limb quivered from his agitation. He could hardly make himself understood to the domestic - he waited not an answer to his enquiry - but bounded up the stairs, and with faltering step entered the room. Blanche was there, and not alone but oh! how passing fair! Even Delancey had not dared to think, that the beauty of the girl could have been so eclipsed by the ripe graces of the woman. She recognised him, and rose to meet him with a burst of unfeigned surprise. She held out her hand with an air of winning frankness; and yet for an instant, - and his hand as it pressed hers, trembled with that thought, - he deemed there was a hesitating blush on her cheek, which should not have been there. But it passed away, and radiant with smiles, she turned to the one beside her.

"My dear," said she, as she gave him a confiding look, which haunts Delancey yet, "this is a great friend of Papa's, and an old playmate of mine - Mr. Delancey;" and as the stranger stepped forward to shake his hand, Blanche looked at her old lover, with a glance that seemed to say, "How foolish were we, to deem we were ever more than friends." Oliver Delancey turned deadly pale; but pride bade him scorn her, and his hand shook not, as it touched that of him, who had robbed him of a treasure, he would have died to have called his.

"And you have been to D - Castle, I suppose, and found your uncle had left it for Bath. Indeed, *we* only arrived the day before yesterday; but Papa wrote us, saying he had got one of his attacks of rheumatism, from the late fishing, and begged us to take this on our way to Habberton, Did you see my marriage in the papers, or did your uncle write you, Oliver?"

Delancey's lips quivered, but his countenance did not change, as he looked her in the face, and told her he had not known it until now.

And now her husband spoke: "It was very late, and he must want refreshment; and Mr. Allen intended to be wheeled to the dinner table; and they could so easily send up to D - Castle to tell them to get a bed aired; and he could dismiss the chaise now, and their carriage could take him there at night."

And Delancey *did* stay, although unable to analyse the feeling that made him do so.

And during dinner, *he* was the life of that little party. He spoke of foreign lands - related strange incidents of travel - dwelt with animation on his schoolboy exploits. The old man was delighted - the husband forgot his wife; - and she, the false one, sat silent, and for the moment disregarded. She gazed and gazed again on that familiar face - drank in the tones of that accustomed voice - and the chill of compunction crept over her frame.

But Delancey's brain was on fire; and in the solitude of his chamber - no! he was not calm there. He paced hurriedly across the oaken floor; and he opened wide his window, and looked out on the bright stars, spangling heaven's blue vault; and then beneath him, where the cypress trees bowed their heads to the wind, and the moon's light fell on the marble statues on the terrace.

And he turned to his bed-side, and hid his tearless face in his hands; and in the fulness of his despair, he knelt and prayed, that though he had long neglected his God, his God would not now forsake him. And, as if to mock his sufferings, sleep came; but it was short, very short; and a weight, a leaden weight, oppressed his eye-lids even in slumber. And he gave one start, and awoke a prey to mental agony. His despair flashed on him - he sprung up wildly in his bed. "Liar! liar!" said he, as with clenched teeth, and hand upraised, he recalled that fond look given to another. Drops of sweat started to his brow - his pulse beat quick and audibly - quicker - quicker yet. A feeling of suffocation came over him - and God forgive him! Oliver Delancey deemed that hour his last. He staggered blindly to the bell, and with fearful energy pulled its cord, till it fell clattering on the marble hearth stone. The domestics found him speechless and insensible on the floor - the blood oozing from his mouth and ears.

It may be said that this picture is overcharged; that no vitiated mind could have thus felt. But it is not so. In life's spring we all feel acutely: and to the effects of disappointed love, and wounded pride, there are few limits.

Woman! dearest woman! born to alleviate our sorrow, and soothe our anguish! who canst bid feeling's tear trickle down the obdurate cheek, or mould the iron heart, till it be pliable as a child's - why stain thy gentle dominion by inconstancy? why dismiss the first form that haunted thy maiden pillow, until - or that vision is a dear reality beside thee - or thou liest pale and hushed, on thy last couch of repose?

And then - shall not thy virgin spirit hail him? Why first fetter us, slaves to virtue and to thee; *then* become the malevolent Typhoon, on whose wings our good genius flies for ever? In this - far worse than the iconoclasts of yore art thou! *They* but disfigured images of man's rude fashioning: whilst *thou* wouldst injure the *once* loved form of God's high creation, - wouldst entail on the body a premature decay - and on that which dieth not, an irradicable blight.

"Then the mortal coldness of the soul, like death itself comes down; It cannot feel for others woes - it dares not dream its own. That heavy chill has frozen o'er the fountain of our tears; And though the eye may sparkle still, 'tis where the ice appears."

On such a character as was Delancey's, the blow did indeed fall heavy. Not that his paroxysms of grief were more lasting, or his pangs more acute, than is usual in similar cases; but to his moral worth it was death. An infliction of this nature, falling on a comparatively virtuous man, is productive of few evil consequences. It may give a holier turn to his thoughts - wean him from sublunary vanities - and purify his nature. On an utterly depraved man, its effects may be fleeting also; for few can *here* expect a moral regeneration. But falling on Delancey, it was not thus. The slender thread that bound him to virtue, was snapt asunder; the germ whence the good of his nature might have sprung, destroyed for ever. Such a man could not love purely again. To expect him to wander to another font, and imbibe from as clear a stream, would be madness. The love of a man of the world, let it be the first and best, is gross and earthly enough; but let him be betrayed in that love - let him see the staff on which he confidingly leant, break from under him - and he becomes from henceforth the deceiver - but never the deceived. When Delmé saw him, Delancey was writhing under his affliction. When he again entered the world, and it was soon, he regarded it as a wide mart, where he might gratify his appetites, and unrestrainedly indulge his evil propensities. He believed not that virtue and true nobility were there; could he but find them. He looked at the blow his happiness had sustained, and thought it afforded a fair sample of human nature. Oliver Delancey became a selfish and a profligate man.

He was to be pitied; and from his soul did Delmé pity him. He had been one of promise and of talent; but *now* his lot is cast on the die of apathy; - and it is to be feared - without a miracle intervene – and should his life be spared - that when the wavy locks of youth are changed to the silver hairs of age - that he will then be that thing of all others to be scoffed at - the hoary sensualist. Let us hope not! Let us hope that she who hath brought him to this, may rest her head on the bosom of her right lord, and forget the one, whose hand used to be locked in her own, for hours - hours which flew quick as summer's evening shadows! Let us trust that remorse may be absent from her; that she may never know that worst of reflections - the having injured one who had loved her, irremediably; that she may gaze on her fair-haired children, and her cheek blanch not as she recals another form than the father's; that her life may be irreproachable, her end calm and dignified; that dutiful children may attend the inanimate clay to its resting place; that filial tears may bedew her grave; and, when the immortal stands appalled before

its Judge, that the destruction of that soul may not be laid to her charge.

CHAPTER XIV

THE SPITFIRE

"And I have loved thee! Ocean! and my joy
Of youthful sports was on thy breast to be
Borne like thy bubbles onward."

* * * * *

"Pull away! yo ho! boys!"

Delmé continued to reside with his brother, whose health seemed to amend daily. George generally managed to accompany him in his sight-seeing, from which Henry derived great gratification.

He mused over the antique tombs of some of the departed knights; and admired the rich mosaics in that splendid church, dedicated to Saint John; than which the traveller may voyage long, and meet nothing worthier his notice. He visited the ancient armoury - dined at the palace, and at the different messes - inspected the laborious travailings of the silkworm at the boschetto - conversed with the original of Byron's Leila - a sweet creature she is! - looked with wondering eye on the ostrich of Fort Manuel - and heard the then commandant's wife relate her tale thereanent. He went to Gozz o too - shotrabbits - and crossed in a basket to the fungus rock. He saw a festa in the town, and a festa in the country - rode to St.

Antonio, and St. Paul's Bay - and was told he had seen the lions. Nor must we pass over that most interesting of spectacles; viz., some figures enveloped in monkish cowl, and placed in convenient niches; but beneath the close hood, the blood mounts not with devotion's glow, nor do eyes glare from sockets shrunk by abstinence. Skeletons alone are there!

These, curious reader, are the bodies of saintly Capuchins; thus exhibited - dried and baked - to excite beholders to a life of virtue!

One morning, George said he felt rather unwell, and would stay at home. An oar happened to be wanted in the regimental gig, which Sir Henry offered to take. He was soon accoutred in the dress of an absent member, and in a short time was discharging the duties of his office to the satisfaction of all; for he knew every secret of *feathering,* and had not *caught a crab* for years.

It was a beautifully calm day - not a speck in the azure heaven. It was hot too - but for this they cared not. They had porter; and on such occasions, what better beverage would you ask? Swiftly and gaily did the slim bark cleave through the glassy sea. Its hue was a dark crimson, with one black stripe - its nom de guerre, the Spitfire.

As the - regiment particularly prided itself on its aquatic costume, we shall describe it. Small chased pearl buttons on the blue jacket and white shirt; a black band round the neck, to match the one on the narrow-brimmed thick straw hat; white trousers; couleur de rose silk collar, fastened to the throat by a golden clasp; and stockings of the same colour. How joyously did the gig hold her course! What a thrilling sensation expanded the soul, as the steersman, a handsome little fellow with large black whiskers, gave the encouraging word, "Stroke! my good ones!" Then were exerted all the energies of the body - then was developed each straining muscle - then were the arms thrown back in sympathy, to give a long pull, and a strong pull - till the bark reeled beneath them, and shot through the wave.

The tall ship - the slender mole - the busy deck - the porticoed palace - the strong fort - the bristling battery - the astonished fisher's bark as it sluggishly crept on - were all cheeringly swept by, as the bending oars in perfect unison, kissed the erst slumbering water. What sensation can be more glorious? The only thing to compete with it, is the being in a crack coach on the western road; the opposition slightly in front - a knowing whip driving - when the horses are at their utmost speed - the traces tight as traces can be - the ladies inside pale and screaming - one little child cramming out her head, her mouth stuffed with Banbury cakes, adding her shrill affetuoso - whilst the odd-looking man in the white hat, seated behind, is blue from terror, and with chattering teeth, mumbles undistinguishable sentences of furious driving and prosecution. Surely such moments half redeem our miseries! What bitter thought can travel twelve miles an hour?

And ever and anon would the Spitfire dart into some little creek, and the thirsty rowers would rest on their oars, whose light drip fell on purple ocean, tinged by a purple sky. And now would the jovial steersman introduce the accommodating corkscrew, first into one bottle and then into another, as these were successively emptied, and thrown overboard, to give the finny philosophers somewhat to speculate on.

Delmé landed weary; but it was a beneficial weariness. He felt he had taken manly exercise, and that it would do him good. He was walking towards the barrack, with his jacket slung over his shoulder, when he was met by George's servant.

"Oh, Sir!" said the man, "I am so glad you are come. The Signora is terribly afraid for my young master. I fear, Sir, he is in one of his fits."

Delmé hurried forward, and entered his brother's room. George held a riding whip in his hand. He had thrown off his cravat - his throat was bare - his eyes glanced wildly.

"And who are you, Sir?" said he, as Henry entered.

"What! not know me, dearest George?" replied his brother, in agony.

"I do not understand your insolence, Sir; but if you are a dun, go to my servant. Thompson," continued he, "give me my spurs! I shall ride."

"Ride!" said Delmé.

Thompson made him a quiet sign. "I am very sorry, Sir," said he, "but the Arab is quite lame, and is not fit for the saddle."

"Give me a glass of sangaree then, you rascal! Port - do you hear?"

The glass was brought him. He drained its contents at a draught.

"Now, kick that scoundrel out of the room, Thompson, and let me sleep."

He threw himself listlessly on the sofa. Acmé was weeping bitterly, but he seemed not to notice her. It was late in the day. The surgeon had been sent for. He now arrived, and stated that nothing could be done; but recommended his being watched closely, and the removing all dangerous weapons. He begged Henry, however, to indulge him in all his caprices, in order that he might the better observe the state of his mind.

While George slept, Delmé entered another room, and ordering the servant to inform him when he awoke, he sat down to dinner alone and dispirited; for Acmé refused to leave George. It was indeed a sad, and to Sir Henry Delmé an unforeseen shock.

In a couple of hours, Thompson came with a message from Acmé. "Master is awake, Sir - knows the Signora - and seems much better. He has desired me to brush his cloak, as he intends going out. Shall I do so, Sir, or not?"

"Do so!" said Delmé, "but fail not to inform me when he is about to go; and be yourself in readiness. We will watch him."

CHAPTER XV

THE CHARNEL HOUSE

"And when at length the mind shall be all free,
From what it hates in this degraded form,
Reft of its carnal life, save what shall be
Existent happier in the fly or worm;
When elements to elements conform,
And dust is as it should be."

The last grey tinge of twilight, was fast giving place to the sombre hues of night, as a figure, enveloped in a military cloak, issued from the barrack at Floriana.

Henry at once recognised George; and only delaying till a short distance had intervened between his brother and himself, Delmé and Thompson followed his footsteps.

George Delmé walked swiftly, as if intent on some deep design. The long shadow thrown out by his figure, enabled his pursuers to distinguish him very clearly. He did not turn his head, but, with hurried step, strode the species of common which divides Floriana from La Valette. Crossing the drawbridge, and passing through the porch which guards the entrance to the town, he turned down an obscure street, and, folding his cloak closer around him, rapidly - yet with an appearance of caution - continued his route, diving from one street to another, till he entered a small court-yard, in which stood an isolated gloomy-looking house. No light appeared in the windows, and its exterior bespoke it uninhabited. Henry and the domestic paused, expecting George either to knock or return to the street. He walked on, however, and, turning to one side of the porch, descended a flight of stone steps, and entered the lower part of the house.

"Perhaps we had better not both follow him," said the servant.

"No, Thompson! do you remain here, only taking care that your master does not pass you: and I think you may as well go round the house, and see if there is any other way of leaving it."

Sir Henry descended the steps in silence. Arrived at the foot of the descent, a narrow passage, diverging to the left, presented itself. Beyond appeared a distant glimmering of light. Delmé groped along the passage, using the precaution to crouch as low as possible, until he came before a large comfortless room in the centre of which, was placed a brass lamp, whose light was what he had discerned at the extremity of the passage. He could distinctly observe the furniture and inmates of the room. Of the former, the only articles were a table - on which were placed the remains of a homely meal - an iron bedstead, and a barrel, turned upside down, which served as a substitute for a chair. The bedstead had no curtains, but in lieu of them, there were hangings around it, which struck Delmé as resembling mourning habiliments. Whilst the light operated thus favourably, in enabling Sir Henry to note the interior of the apartment, it was hardly possible, from its situation, that he himself could be observed. Its rays did not reach the passage; and he was also shrouded in some degree by a door, which was off its hinges, and which was placed against the wall. Fastened to the side of the room were two deep shelves - the lower one containing some bottles and plates; the upper, a number of human sculls. In a corner were some more of these, intermingled in a careless heap, with a few bleached bones.

George Delmé was standing opposite the door, conversing

earnestly with a Maltese, evidently of the lowest caste. The latter was seated on the barrel we have mentioned, and was listening with apparently a mixture of surprise and exultation to what George was saying. George's voice sunk to an inaudible whisper, as the conversation continued, and he was evidently trying to remove some scruples, which this man either affected to feel, or really felt. The man's answers were given in a gruff and loud tone of voice, but from the Maltese dialect of his Italian, Sir Henry could not understand what was said. His countenance was very peculiar. It was of that derisive character rarely met with in one of his class of life, except when called forth by peculiar habits, or extraordinary circumstances. His eyes were very small, but bright and deeply set. His lips wore a constant sarcastic smile, which gave him the air of a bold but cunning man. His throat and bosom were bare, and of a deep copper colour; and his muscular chest was covered with short curly hair. The conversation on George's part became more animated, and he at length made use of what seemed an unanswerable argument. Taking out a beaded purse, which Sir Henry knew well - it had been Emily's last present to George - he emptied the contents into the bronzed hand of his companion, who grasped the money with avidity. The Maltese *now* appeared to acquiesce in all George's wishes; and rising, went towards the bed, and selected some of the articles of wearing apparel Delmé had already noticed. He addressed some words to George, who sat on the bedside quiescently, while the man went to the table, and took up a knife that was upon it. For a moment, Delmé felt alarm lest his design might be a murderous one; but it was not so. He laughed savagely, as he made use of the knife, to cut off the luxuriant chestnut ringlets, which shaded George's eyes and forehead. He then applied to the face some darkening liquid, and commenced choosing a sable dress. George threw off his cloak, and was attired by the Maltese, in a long black cotton robe of the coarsest material, which, descending to the feet, came in a hood over his face, which it almost entirely concealed. During the whole of this scene, George Delmé's features wore an air of dogged apathy, which alarmed his brother, even more than his agitation in the earlier part of the day. After his being metamorphosed in the way we have described, it would have been next to an impossibility to have recognised him. His companion put on a dress of the same nature, and Sir Henry was preparing to make his retreat, presuming that they would now leave the building, when he was induced to stay for the purpose of remarking the conduct of the Maltese. He took up a scull, and placing his finger through an eyeless hole, whence *once* love beamed or hate flashed, he made some savage comment, which he accompanied by a long and malignant laugh. This would at another time have shocked Sir Henry, but there was another laugh, wilder and more discordant, that curdled the blood in Delmé's veins. It proceeded from his brother, the gay - the happy George Delmé; and as it re-echoed through the gloomy passage, it seemed that of a remorseless demon, gloating on the misfortunes of the human race. Delmé turned away in agony, and, unperceived, regained the anxious domestic. Screened by an angle of the building, they saw George and his companion ascend the stone steps, cross the yard, and turn into the street. They followed him cautiously - Delmé's ears ringing with that fiendish laugh. George's companion stopped for a moment, at a house in the street, where they were joined by a sallow-looking priest, apparently one of the most disgusting of his tribe. He was accompanied by a boy, also drest in sacerdotal robes, in one hand bearing a silver-ornamented staff, of the kind frequently used in processions, and in other observances of the Catholic religion; and in the other, a rude lanthorn, whose light enabled Delmé to note these particulars. As the four figures swept through the streets, the lower orders prostrated themselves, before the figure of the crucified and dying Saviour which surmounted the staff. They again stopped, and the priest entered a house alone. On coming back, he was followed by a coffin, borne on the shoulders of four of the lower order of Maltese. At the moment these were leaving the house, Henry heard a solitary scream, apparently of a woman. It was wild and thrilling; such an one as we hear from the hovering sea bird, as the tempest gathers to a head. To Delmé, coming as it did at that lone hour from one he saw not, it seemed superhuman. In the front of the house stood two calèches, the last of which, Sir Henry observed was without doors. At a sign from the Maltese, George and his strange companion entered it. They were followed by the coffin, which was placed lengthways, with the two ends projecting into the street. In the *leading* calèche were the priest and boy, the latter of whom thrust the figure of the bleeding Jesus out at the window, whilst with the other hand he held up the lanthorn. Twice more did the calèche stop - twice receive corpses. Another light was produced, and placed in the last conveyance, and Delmé took the opportunity of their arranging this, to pass by the calèche. The light that had been placed in it shone full on George. The coffins were on a level with the lower part of his face. Nothing of his body, which was jammed in between the seat and the coffins, could be seen. But the features, which glared over the pall, were indeed terrific; apathy no longer marked them. George seemed wound up to an extraordinary state of excitement. Gone was the glazed expression of his eye, which now gleamed like that of a famished eagle. The Maltese leant back in the carriage, with a sardonic smile, his dark face affording a strange contrast to the stained, but yet ghastly hue of George Delmé's.

"They intend to take them to the vault at Floriana, your honor," said the servant, "shall I call a calèche, and we can follow them?"

Without waiting a reply, for the man saw that Sir Henry's faculties, were totally absorbed in the strange scene he had witnessed; Thompson called a carriage, which passed the other two - now commencing at a funeral pace to proceed to the vault - and, taking the same direction which they had done on entering the town, a short time sufficed to put them down immediately opposite the church. They had time allowed them to dismiss their carriage, and screen themselves from observation, before the funeral procession arrived.

This stopped in front of the vault, and Delmé anxiously scrutinised the proceedings. Another man - probably the one whose place George had supplied - had joined them outside the town, and now walked by the side of the calèche. He assisted George's companion in bearing out the coffins. The huge door grated on its hinges, as they opened it. The coffins were borne in, and the whole party entered; the priest mumbling a short Latin prayer. In a short time, the priest alone returned; and looking cautiously around, and seeing no one, struck a light from a tinder box, and lighted his cigar. The other two men brought back the coffins, evidently relieved of their weight; and the priest - the boy - with the man who had last joined them, and who had also lit his cigar - entered the first calèche, after exchanging some jokes with George's companion, and returned at a rapid pace towards the town. During this time, George Delmé had been left alone in the vault. His companion returned to him, after taking the precaution to fasten its doors inside.

Sir Henry was now at a loss what plan to adopt; but Thompson, after a moment's hesitation, suggested one.

"There is an iron grating, Sir, over part of the vault, through which, when a bar was loose, I know one of our soldiers went down. Shall I get a cord?"

The man ran towards his barrack, and returned with it. To wrench by their united efforts, one bar from its place, and to fasten the rope to another, was the work of an instant. Space was just left them to creep through the aperture. Sir Henry was the first to breathe the confined air of the sepulchre. A voice warned him in what direction to proceed; and not waiting for the domestic, he groped his way forward through a narrow passage. At first, Delmé thought there was a wall on either side him; but as he made a false step, and the bones crumbled beneath, he knew that it was a wall, formed of the bleached remains of the bygone dead. As he drew nearer the voice, he was guided by the lanthorn brought by George's companion; and towards this he proceeded, almost overpowered by the horrible stench of the charnel house, As he drew near enough to distinguish objects, what a scene presented itself! In one corner of the vault, lay a quantity of lime used to consume the bodies, whilst nearer the light, lay corpses in every stage of putrefaction. In some, the lime had but half accomplished its purpose; and while in parts of the body, the bones lay bare and exposed; in others, corruption in its most loathsome form prevailed. Here the meaner reptiles - active and prolific - might be seen busily at work, battening on human decay. Sir Henry stepped over a dead body, and started, as a rat, scared from its prey, rustled through a wreath of withered flowers, and hid itself amid a mouldering heap of bones. But there were some forms lovely still! In them the pulse of life had that day ceased to beat. The rigidity of Death - his impressive stillness was there - but he had not yet "swept the lines where beauty lingers."

The Maltese stood with folded arms, closely regarding George Delmé.

George leant against a pillar, with one knee bent. Over it was stretched the corpse of a girl, with the face horribly decomposed. The dull and flagging winds of the vault moved her dank and matted hair.

"Acmé," said he, as he parted the dry hair from the blackened brow, "*do* but speak to your own George! Be not angry with me, dearest!" He held the disgusting object to his lips, and lavished endearments on the putrid corpse.

Delmé staggered - and Thompson supported him - as he gasped for breath in the extremity of his agony. At this moment his eye caught the face of the Maltese. He had advanced towards George - his arms were still folded - his eyes were sparkling with joy - and his features wore the malignant expression of gratified revenge. Sir Henry sprang to his feet and rushed forward.

"George! my brother! my brother!"

The maniac raised his pallid brow - his eye flashed consciousness - the blue veins in his forehead swelled almost to bursting - he tossed his arms wildly - and sunk powerless on the corpses around - his convulsive shrieks re-echoing in that lonely vault. Thompson seized the Maltese, and making him unlock the door, bore the brothers into the open air; for Henry, at the time, was as much overpowered as George himself.

A clear solution to that curious scene was never given, for George could not give the clue to his train of mental aberration.

With regard to his companion's share in the transaction, the man was closely questioned, and other means of information resorted to, but the only facts elicited were these:

His son had been executed some years before for a desperate attempt to assassinate a British soldier, with whom he had had an altercation during the carnival.

The man himself said, that he had no recollection of ever having seen George before, but that he certainly *did* remember some officers questioning him on two occasions somewhat minutely as to his mode of life.

This part of his story was confirmed by another officer of the regiment, who remembered George and Delancey being with him on one occasion, when the latter had taken much interest in the questioning of this man. The Maltese declared, that on the night in question he was taken entirely by surprise - that George entered the room abruptly - offered him money to be allowed to accompany him to the vault - and told him that he had just placed a young lady there whom he wished to see.

Colonel Vavasour, who took some trouble in arriving at the truth, was satisfied that the man was well aware of George's insanity, but that he felt too happy in being able to wreak an ignoble revenge on a British officer.

CHAPTER XVI

THE MARRIAGE

"The child of love, though born in bitterness,
And nurtured in convulsion."

For many days, George Delmé lay on his couch unconscious and immoveable. If his eye looked calm, it was the tranquillity of apathetic ignorance, the fixedness of idiotcy. He spoke if he was addressed, but recognised no one, and his answers were not to the purpose. He took his food, and would then turn on his side, and close his eyes as if in sleep. In vain did Acmé watch over him - in vain did her tears bedew his couch - in vain did Delmé take his hand, and endeavour to draw his attention to passing objects.

George had never been so long without a lucid interval. The surgeon's voice grew less cheering every day, as he saw the little amendment in his patient, and remarked that the pulse was gradually sinking. Colonel Vavasour never allowed a day to elapse without visiting the invalid; and in the regiment, his illness excited great commiseration, and drew forth many expressions of kindness.

"Oh God! oh God!" said Delmé, "he must not sink thus. Just as I am with him - just as - oh, poor Emily! what will *she* feel? Can nothing he done, Mr. Graham?"

"Nothing! Sir: we must now put our whole trust in an all-seeing Providence. *My* skill can neither foresee nor hasten the result."

One soft summer's evening, when the wind blew in the scent of flowers from the opposite gardens - and the ceaseless hum of the insects - those twilight revellers - sounded happily on the ear, Acmé started from the couch as a thought crossed her.

"We have never tried music," said she, "I have been too unhappy to think of it."

Her tears fell fast on the guitar, as she tuned its strings. She sung a plaintive Greek air. It was the first George ever heard her sing, and was the favourite. He heard it, when watching; lover-like beneath her balcony during the first vernal days of their attachment. The song was gone through sadly, and without hope. George's face was from her, and she laid down the guitar, weary of life.

George gently turned his head. His eyes wore a subdued melancholy expression, bespeaking consciousness. Down his cheek one big drop was trickling.

"Acmé!" said he, "dearest Acmé!"

Delmé, who had left the room, was recalled by the hysterical sobs of the poor girl, as she fell back on the chair, her hands clasped in joyful gratitude.

The surgeon, who had immediately been sent for, ordered that George should converse as little as possible.

What he did say was rational. What a solace was that to Henry and Acmé! The invalid too appeared well aware of his previous illness, although he alluded to it but seldom. To those about him, his manner was femininely soft, as he whispered his thanks, and sense of their kindness.

Immediately after the horrible scene he had witnessed, Sir Henry's mind had been made up, as to the line of conduct he ought to pursue. The affectionate solicitude of the young Greek, during George's illness, gave him no reason to regret his determination.

"Now," said Mr. Graham, one day as George was rapidly recovering, "now, Sir Henry, I would recommend you to break all you have to say to George. For God's sake, let them be married; and although, mark me! I by no means assert that it will quite re-establish George's health, yet I think such a measure *may* effectually do so, and at all events will calm him for the present; which, after all, is the great object we have in view."

The same day, Delmé went to his brother's bed-side. "George," said he, "let me take the present opportunity of Acmé's absence, to tell you what I had only deferred till you were somewhat stronger. She is a good girl, George, a very good girl. I wish she had been English - it would have been better! - but this we cannot help. You must marry her, George! I will be a kind brother-in-law, and Emily shall love her for your sake."

The invalid sat up in his bed - his eyes swam in tears. He twice essayed to speak, ere he could express his gratitude.

"Thank you! a thousand times thank you! my kind brother! Even *you* cannot tell the weight of suffering, you have this day taken from my mind. My conduct towards Acmé has been bowing me to the earth; and yet I feared your consent would never be obtained. I feared that coldness from you and Emily would have met her; and that I should have had but *her* smile to comfort me for the loss of what I so value. God bless you for this!"

Delmé was much affected.

To complete his good work, he waited till Acmé had returned

from a visit she had just made to her relations; and taking her aside, told her his wishes, and detailed his late conversation with George.

"Never! never!" said the young Greek, "I am too happy as I am. I have heard you all make better lovers than husbands. I cannot be happier! No! no! I will never consent to it."

All remonstrances were fruitless - no arguments could affect her - no entreaties persuade.

Delmé, quite perplexed at finding such a difficulty, where he had so little expected to find one, - pitying her simplicity, but admiring her disinterestedness, - went to George, and told him Acmé's objections.

"I feared it," said his brother, "but perhaps I may induce her to think differently. Were I to take advantage of her unsophisticated feelings, and want of knowledge of the world, I should indeed be a villain."

Acmé was sent for, and came weeping in - took Georg's hand - and gazed earnestly in his face as he addressed her.

"You must change your mind, dearest," said he. And he told her of the world's opinion - the contumely she might have to endure - the slights to which she would be subjected. Still she heeded not.

"Why mention these things?" said she. "Who would insult me, were *you* near? or if they did, should I regard them while *you* were kind?"

And her lover's words took a loftier tone; and he spoke of religion, and of the duties it imposes; of the feelings of his countrywomen; and the all-seeing eye of their God. Still the fond girl wept bitterly, but spoke not.

"My own Acmé! consider *my* health too, dearest! Were you

now to consent, I might never again be ill. It would be cruelty to me to refuse. Say you consent for *my* sake, sweet!"

"For your sake, then!" said Acme, as she twined her snowy arms round his neck, "for *your* sake, Giorgio, I do so! But oh! when I am yours for ever by that tie; when - if this be possible - our present raptures are less fervent - our mutual affections less devoted - do not, dearest George - do not, I implore you - treat me with coldness. It would break my heart, indeed it would."

They were married according to the rites of both the Protestant and Catholic Church. Few were present. George had been lifted to the sofa, and sat up during the ceremony; and although his features were pale and emaciated, they brightened with internal satisfaction, as he heard those words pronounced, which made his love a legitimate one. Acmé was silent and thoughtful; and tears quenched the fire of her usually sparkling eye. George Delmé's recovery from this date became more rapid.

He was able to resume his wonted exercise - his step faltered less - his eye became clearer. His convalescence was so decided, that the surgeon recommended his at once travelling, and for the present relinquishing the army.

"Perhaps the excessive heat may not be beneficial. I would, if possible, get him to Switzerland for the summer months. I will enquire what outward-bound vessels there are. If there is one for Leghorn, so much the better. But the sooner he tries change of scene, the more advantageous it is likely to be; and after all, the climate is but a secondary consideration."

An American vessel bound to Palermo, happened to be the only one in the harbour, whose destination would serve their purpose; and determined not to postpone George's removal, Sir Henry at once engaged its cabin. Colonel Vavasour obtained George leave for the present, and promised to arrange as to his exchanging from full pay. He likewise enabled him, which George felt as a great boon, to take his old and attached servant with him; with the promise that he would use all his interest to have the man's discharge forwarded him, before the expiration of his leave.

"He may be useful to you, my dear boy, if you get ill again, which God forbid! He is an old soldier, and a good man - well deserving the indulgence. And remember! if you should be better, and feel a returning penchant for the red coat, write to me - we will do our best to work an exchange for you."

CHAPTER XVII

THE DEPARTURE

> "Farewell! a word that must be, and hath been,
> A sound that makes us linger, yet farewell."

The day of departure at length arrived. Thompson had been busy the greater part of the night in getting every thing ready for the voyage. It was a lovely morning, and the wind, although light, was propitious.

Acmé had parted with her relations and friends the day previous.

She was henceforward to share the destiny of one, who was to supply the place of both to her. Attached to them as she was, and grateful as she felt for their kindness in the hour of need, there was nothing in that parting to throw a permanent gloom on the hopes of the youthful bride.

Her love, and the feelings it engendered, were of that confiding nature, that she could have followed George anywhere, and been happy still. As it was, her lot seemed cast "in pleasant places," and no foreboding of evil, except indeed for George, ever marred the waking dreams of Acmé. Her simple heart had already learnt, to look up with respect and affection to Sir Henry, and yearned with fond longing for the period when she should return a sister's love.

She had that lively talent too, which, miniatured as it was, allowed of her fully appreciating the superiority of the English she had lately met, to the general run of those with whom she had hitherto associated. An English home had none but charms for her.

"Come Acmé," said George, as he assisted her in adjusting the first bonnet that had ever confined her wavy curls, "wish good bye to your ring-dove, dear! Mrs. Graham will take good care of it; and Thompson has just finished the packing."

The boat which was to convey them to the vessel was so near, that they had agreed to walk down to the place of embarkation.

As George left the room, a tall figure presented itself on the staircase.

"Ah, Clark!" said George, "my good fellow! I am very sorry to part with you. I do not know what I shall do without my pay serjeant!" and he held out his hand.

It was grasped gratefully.

"Thank you, your honour!"

The old soldier stood erect, and put his hand to his cap.

"God bless you! Mr. Delmé. I have served under many officers, but never under a kinder. May the Almighty bless you, Sir, in all your wanderings."

The soldier turned away - one large drop burst o'er the lid, and trickled down his sun-burnt cheek.

With the back of his hand, he brushed it off indignantly.

His converse may be rough - his manner rude - his hand ever ready for quarrel; - but, believe us! ye who deem the soldier beneath his fellow-men, - that the life of change - of chance - of hardship - and of danger - which is his, freezes not the kindlier emotions of the soul, if it sweep away its sicklier refinements. Beneath the red vest, beat hearts as warm and true, as ever throbbed beneath operative apron, or swelled under softest robe of ermine.

George was moved by the man's evidently sincere grief. He reached the bottom of the stairs. The company to which he belonged was drawn up in the court yard.

In front of it, the four tallest men supported a chair, and almost before George Delmé was aware of their purpose, bore him to it, and lifted him on their shoulders, amidst the huzzas of their comrades. The band, too, which had voluntarily attended, now struck up the march which George delighted to hear; and, followed by his company, he was carried triumphantly towards the mole.

George's heart was full.

Sir Henry felt deeply interested in the scene; and poor Acmé leant on his arm, and wept with joy.

Yes! there are moments in life, and this was one, when the approval of our inferiors awakens a degree of pride and mental satisfaction, that no panegyric of our superiors, no expressions of esteem from our equals, could have ever called forth. Such approval meets us, as the spontaneous effusion of hearts that have looked up to ours, and have *not* been deceived.

This pride was it that flushed George's cheek, and illumed with brightness his swimming eye. He was thus carried till he arrived at the spot where his boat should have been. It was already, with Thompson and their baggage, half way towards the vessel. In its place was the regimental gig, manned by George's best friends. Its steersman was Colonel Vavasour, drest in the fanciful aquatic costume his regiment had adopted.

Trifling as this may appear, this act of his Colonel, seemed to George the very highest compliment that had ever been paid him.

George Delmé turned to his company, and with choking voice thanked them for this last mark of attention. We are very certain that a shake of the hand from a prince, would not have delighted him as much, as did the hearty farewell greeting of his rough comrades.

Even Acmé blushingly went up to the chair-supporters, and, with a winning smile, extended her small hand. Vavasour assisted her into the gig, and it was with a bounding elasticity of spirit, to which he had long been a stranger, that George followed. As the boat cut through the water, they were greeted with a last and deafening huzza.

In a short time they were alongside the vessel. The captain was pacing the deck, and marking the signs of the wind, with the keen eye of the sailor. A chair was lowered for Acmé. She shook hands with the rowers. George parted from them as if they had been brothers, and from Colonel Vavasour last of all.

"Take care of yourself, my dear boy," said the latter, "do not forget to write us; we shall all be anxious to know how you have stood the voyage."

As the gig once more shot its way homewards, and many a friendly handkerchief waved its adieu, George felt, that sad as the parting was, he should have felt it more *bitterly* if they had loved him less.

To divert their minds from thoughts of a melancholy nature, Sir Henry, as the boat made a turn of the land, and was no longer visible, proposed exploring the cabin. This they found small, but cleanly. Some hampers of fruit, and a quantity of ice, exhibited agreable proofs of the attention of Acmé's relations. We may, by the way, observe, that rarely does the sense of the palate assert its supremacy with greater force than on board-ship. There will the *thought* - much more the *reality* of a mellow pine - or juicy pomegranate - cause the mouth to water for the best part of a long summer's day. On their ascending the deck, the captain approached Sir Henry.

"No offence! Sir; but I guess the wind is fair. If you want nothing ashore, we will off, Sir, *now*! if you please."

Delmé acquiesced.

How disagreable is the act of leaving harbour in a merchant ship!

Even sailors dislike it, and growl between their teeth, like captive bears. The chains of the anchor clank gratingly on the ear. The very chorus of the seamen smacks of the land, and wants the rich and free tone that characterises it in mid-sea. Hoarse are the mandates of the boat-swain! his whistle painfully shrill! The captain walks the deck thoughtfully, and frowningly ruminates on his bill of lading - or on some over-charge in the dock duties - or, it may be, on his dispute on shore with a part owner of the vessel.

And anon, he shakes off these thoughts, and looks on the weather-side - then upwards at the the masts - and, as he notes the proceedings, his orders are delivered fiercely, and his passions seem ungovernable.

The vessel, too, seems to share the general feeling - is loath to leave the port.

She unsteadily answers the call of her canvas - her rigging creaks - and her strong sides groan - as she begins lazily and slowly to make her way.

Glad to turn their attention to anything rather than the scene around, George began conversing on the effect the attentions of his company and brother officers had had on him.

"Their kindness," said George, "was wholly unexpected by me, and I felt it very deeply. An hour before, I fancied that Acmé and my own family monopolised every sympathy I possessed. But, thank God! the heart has many hidden channels through which kindness may steal, and infuse its genial balm."

"*I* felt it, too, George!" said his brother, "and was anxious as to the effect the scene might have on you. I am glad it *was* unexpected. We are sometimes better enabled to enact our parts improvising them, than when we have schooled ourselves, and braced all our energies to the one particular purpose.

"Acmé, how did you like the way George's men behaved?"

"It made me weep with joy," replied the young Greek, "for I love all who love my Giorgio."

CHAPTER XVIII

THE ADIEU

"Adieu! the joys of La Valette."

* * * * *

"No more! no more! No! never more on me
The freshness of the heart shall fall like dew."

* * * * *

"Absence makes the heart grow fonder,
Isle of Beauty! fare thee well."

Malta! the snowy sail shivers in the wind - the waves, chafed by our intruding keel, are proudly foaming - sea birds soar, screaming their farewell aloft - as we wave our hand to thee for ever! What is our feeling, as we see thee diminish hourly?

Regret! unfeigned regret!

Albeit we speed to our native land, on the wing of a bark as fleet as ever - but it matters not - *thou* hast seen the best of our days.

Visions conjured up by thee, have the unusual power, to banish anticipations of Almack's glories, and of home flirtations.

We are recalling balls enjoyed in thee, loved island! the valse spun round with the darling fleet-footed Maltese, who during its pauses leant back on our arm, against which her spangled zone throbbed, from the pulsations of her heart.

Dreams of turtle and of grand master - the *fish*, not the *official* - and of consecutive iced champagne, mock our sight! But more - yes! far more than all, are we reminded of thy abode – thou dispenser of cheering liquids! thou promoter of convivial happiness! meek Saverio! How swiftly glided the mirth-loving nights as - the enchanting strains of the prima donna hushed - we adjourned to thy ever to be praised bottegua!

With what precision didst thou there mete out the many varied ingredients - the exact relative proportions - which can alone embody our conception of the nectar of the Gods, punch à la Romaine!

Whose cigars ever equalled thine, thou prince of Ganymedes? and when were cigars more justly appreciated, than as our puffs kept time with the trolling ditty, resounding through the walls of thy domain?

The luxury of those days!

Then would Sol come peeping in upon us; as unwelcome and unlooked-for a visitant, as to the enamoured Juliet, when she sighing told her lover that

> "'Twas but a meteor that the sun exhaled,
> To be to him that night a torch-bearer,
> And light him on his way to Mantua."

Then, with head dizzy from its gladness, with heart unduly elate, has the Strada Teatro seen us, imperiously calling for the submissive calèche. Arrived in our chamber, how gravely did we close its shutters! With what a feeling of satisfied enjoyment, did we court the downy freshness of the snow-white sheet!

Sweet and deep were our slumbers - for youth's spell was upon us, and our fifth lustre had not *yet* heralded us to serious thoughts and anxious cares.

Awoke by the officious valet, and remorseless friend, deemest though our debauch was felt? No! an effervescent draught of soda calmed us; we ate a blood orange, and smoked a cigar!

We often hear Malta abused. Byron is the stale authority; and every snub-nosed cynic turns up his prominent organ, and talks of "sirocco, sun, and sweat." Byron disliked it - he had cause. He was there at a bad season, and was suffering from an attack of bile. *We* know of no place abroad, where the English eye will meet with so little to offend it, and so much to please and impress.

There is such a blending together of European, Asiatic, and African customs; there is such a variety in the costumes one meets; there is such grandeur in their palaces - such glory in their annals; such novelty in their manners and habits; such devotion in their religious observances; such simplicity and yet such beauty, in the dress of the women; and their wearers possess such fascinations; that we defy the most fastidious of critics, who has really resided there, to deny to Malta many of those attributes, with which he would invest that place, on whose beauty and agrémens, he may prefer of all others to descant.

With the commonplace observer, its superb harbour, studded with gilded boats; its powerful fortifications, where art towers over nature, and where the eye looks up a rock, and catches a bristling battery; the glare of its scenery, with no foliage to cover the white stone; - all these, together with the different way in which the minutiae of life are transacted, - will call forth his attention, and demand his notice.

Art thou a poet, or a fancied warrior? What scene has been more replete with noble exploits? In whose breasts did the flame of chivalry burn brighter, than in those of the knights of St. John of Jerusalem? Not a name meets thee, that has not belonged to a hero! If thou grievest to find all dissimilar *but* the name; yet mayest thou still muse, contemplative, over the tomb and ashes of him, whom thy mind has shadowed forth, as a noble light in a more romantic age.

Art thou a moralist, a thinking Christian? Thou mayest there trace - and the pursuit shall profit thee - the steps of the sainted apostle; he who was so signally called forth, to hear witness to the truth of ONE, whom he had erst reviled. Yon cordelier will show you the bay, where his vessel took refuge in its distress; and will tell you, that yon jagged rock first gave its dangerous welcome, to the bark of his patron saint.

Lovest thou music? hast loved? or been beloved? or both perchance?

Steal forth when night holds her starry court, and the guitars around are tinkling, as more than one rich voice deplores his mistress's cruelty, in hopes she may now relent. But see! *there* is one, who puts in requisition neither music's spell, nor flattery's lay.

See! he approaches. His cloak wrapped around him, he cautiously treads the tranquil street.

He gains the portico - the signal is given. Who but an expectant maiden could hear one so slight?

Hark! a sound! cautiously the lattice opens - above him blushes the fair one! How brightly her dark eye flashes! how silver soft the tones of her voice!

The stern father - the querulous mother - the tricked duenna - all - all are slumbering. She leans forward, and her ear drinks in his honied words; as her head is supported by her snowy arm.

And now he whispers more passionately. She answers not, but hides her face in her hands. She starts! she throws back her hair from her brow; she waves a white fazzolet, and is gone.

Not thus flies the lover. He crouches beneath the Ionic portico, his figure hardly discernible. A bolt - the last bolt is withdrawn. A form is dimly seen within - retiring, timid, repentant.

Sweet the task to calm that throbbing heart, or teach it to throb no more with fear!

But let him of melancholy mood, wander to the deserted village. A more fearful calamity has befallen it, than ever attended the soft shades, of the one conjured up by the poet.

Here the demon Plague, with baneful wing, and pestilential influence, tarried for many days; till not one - no! not one soul of that village train - that did not join his bygone fathers.

Stray along its grass-grown roofless tenements! where *your* echo alone breaks the silence, as it startles from its resting-place the slumbering owl - for who would dwell in abodes so marked for destruction? Stray there! think of the gentle contadina diffusing happiness around her! *then* think of her as she supports the youth she loves - as she clasps his faint form - and drinks in a poisonous contagion from his pallid lip.

Think of her as the disease seizes on its new victim - still attempting to prop up his head - to reach the cup, that may relieve his maddening thirst, - until, giddy and overpowered, she sinks at last; but - beside him!

Think of their dying together! *that* at least is a solace.

Do not the scene and the thought draw a tear?

If your eye be dry, come - come away - *your* step should not sound there!

The wind continued fair during the whole of the first day. Every trace of Valletta was soon lost; and the good barque Boston swept by the rocky coast of the island, where few human habitations meet the eye, swiftly and cheerily. The sea birds sported round the tall masts - the canvas bulged out bravely - the Captain forgot his shore griefs, and commenced a colloquy with Sir Henry. The sailors sung in chorus; whilst poor Acmé, - we grieve to confess the fact, for never was a Mediterranean sea looked down on by brighter sun, or more cloudless sky, - retired to her cabin, supported by George, a prey to that unsentimental malady, sea sickness. The following day, the wind shifted some points; and the Captain judged it most prudent to forego his original intention of steering direct for Palermo; but to take advantage of the breeze, and adopt the passage through the Faro of Messina.

Delmé felt glad of this change; for Scylla and Charybdis to an Englishman, are as familiar as Whittington and his cat. For the first two days Acmé continued unwell; and George, who already appeared improved by the sea air, never left her side.

Delmé had therefore a dull time of it; which he strove to enliven by conversing, one after the other, with the Captain and his two mates. From all of them, he learnt something; but from all he turned away, as they commenced discussing the comparative merits of the United States, and the old country; a subject he had neither the wish to enter on, nor fortitude to prosecute. Not daunted, he attacked mate the third; and was led to infer better things, as the young gentleman commenced expatiating on the "purple sky," and "dark blue sea." This hope did not last long; for this lover of nature turned round to Sir Henry, and asked him in a nasal twang, if he preferred Cooper's or Mr. Scott's novels? Delmè was not naturally a rude man, but as he turned away, he hummed something very like Yankee-doodle.

And then the moon got up; and Sir Henry felt lonely and sentimental. He leant over the vessel's side, and watched it pictured on the ocean, and quivering as the transient billow swept onwards. And he thought of home, and Emily. He thought of his brother, his heir, - if he died, the only male to inherit the ancient honours of his house, - married to a stranger, and - but Acmé was too sweet a being, not to have already enlisted all his sympathies with her. And as if all these thoughts, like rays converged in a burning glass, did but tend to one object, the image of Julia Vernon suddenly rose before him.

He saw her beautiful as ever - gentleness in her eye - fascination in her smile!

And the air got cold - and he went to bed.

CHAPTER XIX

A DREAM AND A GHOST STORY

"Touching this eye-creation;
What is it to surprise us? Here we are
Engendered out of nothing cognisable -
If this were not a wonder, nothing is;
If this be wonderful, then all is so.
Man's grosser attributes can generate
What *is* not, and has never been at all;
What should forbid his fancy to restore
A being pass'd away? The wonder lies
In the mind merely of the wondering man."

It was the fourth evening of the voyage. Hardly a breath fanned the sails, as the vessel slowly glided between the Calabrian and Sicilian coasts, approaching quite close to the former.

The party, seated on chairs placed on the deck, gazed in a spirit of placid enjoyment on one of those scenes, which the enthusiastic traveller often recals, as in his native clime, he pines for foreign lands, and for novel impressions. The sun was setting over the purple peaks of the Calabrian mountains, smiling in sunny gladness on deep ravines, whose echoes few human feet now woke, save those of simple peasant, or lawless bandit. Where the orb of day held its declining course, the sky wore a hue of burnished gold; its rich tint alone varied, by one fleecy violet cloud, whose outline of rounded beauty, was marked by a clear cincture of white,

On their right, beneath the mountain, lay the little village of Capo del Marte, a perfect specimen of Italian scenery.

Its sandy beach, against which the tide beat in dalliance - the chafed spray catching and reflecting the glories of the setting sun - ran smoothly up a slope of some thirty yards; beyond which, the orange trees, in their greenest foliage, chequered with their shade the white cottages scattered above them.

The busy hum of the fishermen on the coast - the splash of the casting net - and the drip of the oar - were appropriate accompaniments to the simple scene.

On the Sicilian side, a different view wooed attention. There, old Etna upreared his encumbered head, around which the smoke clung in dense majesty; and - not contemptible rivals of the declining deity - the moon's silvery crescent, and the evening star's quiet splendour, were bedecking the cloudless blue of the firmament.

Acmé gazed enraptured on the scene - her long tresses hanging back on the chair, across which one hand was languidly thrown.

"Giorgio," said she, "do you see this beautiful bird close to the ship - swimming so steadily - its snowy plumage apparently unwet from its contact with the wave? To what can you compare it?"

"That bright-eyed gull, love!" replied he, "riding on the water as if all regardless that he is on the wide - wide sea - whose billows may so soon be lashed up to madness; - where may I find a resemblance more close, than my Acmé's simplicity, which guides her through a troubled world, unknowing its treacheries, and happily ignorant of its dangers and its woes?"

"Ah!" said the blushing girl, "how poetical you are this evening; will you tell us a story, Giorgio?"

"*I* will tell you one," said Delmé, interrupting her. "Do you recollect old Featherstone, who had been in the civil service in India, and who lived so near Delmé Park, George?"

"Perfectly," said his brother, "I remember I used to think him mad, because he always looked so melancholy, and used to send us word in the morning when he contemplated a visit; in order that all cats might be kept out of his way."

"The very man! I am glad you know so much about him, for it is on this subject I was going to speak. I cannot tell you where he picked up the idea originally - but I believe in a dream - that a cat would occasion his death.

"Well! he was at Ascot one year, when a gipsy woman came up to him on the course - told him his fortune - and, to his utter astonishment, warned him to beware of the wild cat.

"From that moment, I understand his habits changed. From being a tolerably cheerful companion, he became a wretched hypochondriac; all his energies being directed to the avoiding a contact with any of the feline race.

"Featherstone, two or three years ago, embarked in one of the mining speculations - lost great part of his fortune - and found it necessary to try and retrieve his affairs, by a second voyage to India.

"I heard nothing more of him, till just before leaving England, when my old school-fellow, Lockhart, who went as a cadet to the East, called on me - reminded me of our old whimsical friend - and related his tragic death.

"Lockhart says that one day he and some mutual friends, persuaded Featherstone to accompany them into the interior of the country, to enjoy the diversion of a boar hunt.

"They had had good sport, and were returning homewards, when they suddenly came on a party of natives, headed by the Rajah.

"They were mounted on elephants, and surrounding a jungle, in which, as some sepoys had reported, lay a tiger.

"You know Lockhart's manner - animated and enthusiastic - making one see the scene he is describing.

"I will try and clothe the rest of the story in his own words, although I can hardly hope it will make the same impression on you, that its recital did on me.

"'Well, Sir! we all said we would see the sport - all but Featherstone - who said something about coming on.

"'We were engaged to dine with Sir John M - , who was in that part of the world, on some six-and-eightpenny mission about indigo.

"'The beaters went in, firing and shouting - intending to make him break towards the hunting party.

"'We all drew up on one side, to be in view, but out of the way; Featherstone was next me. He suddenly grasped my arm, and pointed to the jungle, his teeth chattering - his face ashy pale. I turned and saw the tiger! - a splendid beast - certainly!

"'He seemed not to notice us, and stalked on with an innocent yep! yep! like a sick hound's, more than anything else.

"'Suddenly his eye caught us, and flashed fire. At the first view, he crouched to the earth, then came on us, bounding like a tost foot-ball. More magnificent leaps I never beheld! We were struck dumb - but fired - and turned our horses' heads! - all but Featherstone.

"'I shall remember the tones of his voice to my dying hour.

"'"The cat! Lockhart! the cat!"

"'I don't know whether his horse refused the spur - or whether the rider's nerve was gone: but neither appeared to make an effort, till the animal was close on them.

"'The horse gave one plunge - and had hardly recovered his feet, when down went horse and rider.

"'Featherstone gave a piercing scream! Some of the sepoys were by this time up - and fired.

"'The tiger trailed off - the blood spouting down his striped side.

"'We came up - it was all over!

"'The first stroke of that terrific paw had laid the unfortunate man's scull bare. On his shoulder, were the marks of the animal's teeth.

"'The horse was still writhing in agony. One of my pistols relieved him.

"'We bore Featherstone to the nearest cantonment, and buried him there.'"

"How terrible!" said Acmé, as she gave a slight shudder. "Englishmen are generally more sceptical on these points than we are; and disbelieve supernatural appearances, which we are accustomed to think are not unfrequent. I could tell you many stories, which, in my native island, were believed by our enemies the Turks, as well as by ourselves: but if you would like it, I will tell you a circumstance that occurred to myself, the reality of which I dare not doubt.

"You have often, Giorgio! heard me revert with pain, to the horrible scene which took place, on the recapture of our little isle by the infidel Turks; when my family were massacred, and only poor Acmé left to tell their tale."

Here the young bride put her handkerchief to her face, and wept bitterly. George put his arm round her and soothed her. She continued her narrative.

"You know my escape, and how I was sent to a kinsman, who had promised to have me sent to my kind friends in Malta. He was a Corfuote, and it was in Corfu I remained for a long - a very long time - and there first met my dear friend, Zöe Scalvo-Forressi. I was then very young. We lived in the Campagna - about four miles from each other.

"We had both our Greek ponies, and used often to pass the evenings together; and at length knew our road so well, that often it was night before we parted.

"One night, we had been singing together at her house, and it was later than usual when I cantered home.

"About four months had elapsed previous to my landing in Corfu, and I had been eight months there; although at the time, I paid little attention to these circumstances.

"My road lay through an olive grove. I had arrived in its centre, where a small knoll stretched away on my right; on whose summit, was a white Greek monastery, backed by some dark cypress trees.

"The moon was shining brightly - dancing on the silver side of the olive trees - and illuminating the green sward.

"This was smooth and verdant.

"My spirits were more than usually buoyant, when suddenly my pony stopped.

"I could not conceive the reason.

"I looked before me. Immediately in front of me, was the shattered trunk of an old olive tree - it had been blasted by lightning - and sitting quietly at its foot - I saw my own mother, Giorgio! as clearly as I see you now. I could not be mistaken. She wore the same embroidered vest and Albanian shawl, as when I had last seen her.

"She conversed with me calmly for many minutes, and - which surprised me much at the time - I felt no dread, and asked her and answered many questions.

"She told me I should die early, in a foreign land; and many - many more things, which I dare not repeat; for I cannot contemplate the possibility of their being true.

"At the time, I told you I felt composed: without any sense of alarm or surprise. For many days afterwards, however, I never left my bed of sickness.

"I told my kinsman all the circumstances, and he discovered beyond a doubt, that it was on that very day, the twelve-month previous, that my poor mother had been murdered."

Sir Henry and George tried to smile at Acmé's story, and account for what she had seen; - but her manner was so impressive, and her ingenious reasonings - delivered in the most earnest tone - seemed to confute so entirely all their speculations, that they were at length content to deem it "wondrous strange."

In the best and wisest of us, there is such a tendency to believe in a mysterious link, connecting the living and the departed; that a story of this nature, in exciting our feelings, serves to paralyse our reasoning faculties, and leaves us half converts, to the doctrines that we faintly combat.

They looked forth again on the scene. The mountains of Calabria were frowning on them. The village was far behind - and not a straggling light marked its situation.

Numberless stars were reflected on the glassy water, whose serenity was no longer ruffled by wing of sea bird, which long ere now had returned to its "wave girded nest."

Our party and the watch were the only lingerers on deck.

George wrapped Acmé's silk cloak around her, and then carefully assisted her in her descent to the cabin.

CHAPTER XX

THE MAD HOUSE

"And see the mind's convulsion leave it weak."

The land breeze continued to freshen, and the first dawn of morning saw our party on deck, scanning with near view, the opposite coasts of Sicily and Italy, as their vessel glided through the Faro of Messina.

Some pilot boats, - how unlike those which greet the homeward-bound voyager, as he first hails Britain's chalky cliffs - crowded around the vessel, offering their services to guide it through the strait.

Avarice - one incentive to language - had endowed these Sicilian mariners with a competent knowledge of English, which they dealt out vociferously.

As the Captain made his selection, the rejected candidates failed not to use that familiar English salâm; half the gusto of which is lost, when used by foreign lip.

On the Calabrian coast, the sea-port town of Reggio wore an unusual air of bustle and animation.

It was a festa day there; and groups of peasants, in many-coloured costumes, paced up and down the mole; emitting that joyous hum, which is the never-failing concomitant of a happy crowd. Passing through the Faro, the vessel's course lay by the northern coast of Sicily. The current and wind were alike favourable, as it swept on by Melazzo and Lascari.

Etna, towering over the lesser mountains, became once more visible; its summit buried in the clouds of heaven.

On the right, a luminous crimson ring revealed Stromboli, whose fitful volcano was more than usually active.

The following day our party arrived at Palermo. So pleasurable had been their voyage, that it was with a feeling akin to regret, that they heard the rumbling chains of the anchor, rush through the hawse-hole, as their vessel took her station in the bay.

After going through those wearisome forms, which a foreign sea-port exacts; and which appear purposely intended, to temper the rapture of the sea-worn voyager, as he congratulates himself on once more treading terra firma; our party found themselves the inmates of the English hotel; and spent the remainder of the day in engaging a cicerone, and in discussing plans for the morrow.

The morrow came - sunny and cloudless - and the cicerone bowed to the ground, as he opened the door of the commodious fiacre.

"Where shall I drive to, Sir?"

"What were our plans, George?" said Sir Henry.

"I think," replied George, "that we only formed one plan to change it for another. Let the cicerone decide for us."

He, nothing loath, accepted the charge; and taking his station on the box of the carriage, directed the driver.

The carriage first stopped before a large stone building. The bell was rung - a veteran porter presented himself - and our party entered the court yard.

"What place is this?" said Delmé.

"This," rejoined his guide, with the true cicerone fluency, "is the famous lunatic asylum, instituted by the illustrious Baron Pisani. This, gentlemen, is the Baron!"

Here a benevolent-looking little man with a large nose, took off his hat.

"So much approved of was his beneficent design, that our noble King, and our paternal Government, have not only adopted it; but have graciously permitted the Baron, to continue to preside over that institution, which he so happily commenced, and which he so refulgently adorns."

During this announcement, the Baron's face flushed with a simple, but honest pride.

These praises did not to him appear exaggerated; for his intentions had been of the purest, and in this institution was his whole soul wrapt up. Acmé became somewhat pale, as she heard where they were, and looked nervously at George; who could not forbear smiling, as he begged they would be under no apprehensions.

"Yes! gentlemen," said the Baron, "circumstances in early life made me regard mental disease as the most fearful of all. I observed its victims struggling between reason and insanity; goaded on by the ignorance of empirics, and the harsh treatment of those about them, until light fled the tortured brain, and madness directed its every impulse. You, gentlemen, are English travellers, I perceive! In *your* happy land, where generosity and wealth go hand in hand, there are, I doubt not, many humane institutions, where those, who - bowed down by misfortunes, or preyed on by disease - have lost the power to take care of themselves, may find a home, where they may be anxiously tended, and carefully provided for.

"Here we knew not of such things.

"I have said, gentlemen, that chance made me feel a deep interest in these unfortunates. I sunk the greater part of my fortune, in constructing this mansion, trusting that the subscriptions of individuals, would enable me to prosecute the good work.

"In this I was disappointed; but our worthy Viceroy, who took an interest in my plans, laid the matter before the Government, which - as Signer Guiseppe observes - has not only undertaken to support my asylum, but also permits me to preside over the establishment. *That*, gentlemen, is my apartment, with the mignionette boxes in front, and without iron bars in the window; though indeed these very bars are painted, at my suggestion, such a delicate green, that you might not have been aware that they were such.

"This is our first chamber - cheerful and snug. Here are the patients first brought. We indulge them in all their caprices, until we are enabled to decide with certainty, on the fantasy the brain has conjured up. From this room, we take them to the adjacent bed-room, where we administer such remedies as we think the best fitted to restore reason.

"If these fail, we apportion the patient a cell, and consider the case as beyond our immediate relief. We cure, on an average, two-thirds of the cases forwarded to us; and there have been instances of the mind's recovering its tone, after a confinement of some years."

"How many inmates have you in the asylum at present?" said Acmé.

"One hundred and thirty-six, eighty-six of whom are males. These are our baths, to which they are daily taken; this the refectory; this the parlatorio, where they see their friends; and now, if the lady is not afraid, we will descend to the court yard, and see my charges."

"There is no fear?" said George.

"Not in the least. Our punishment is so formidable, that few will incur it by being refractory."

"What! then you are obliged to punish them?" said Acmé, with a shudder.

"Sometimes, but not often. I will show you what our punishment consists in. You see this room without furniture! Observe the walls and floor; and even the door as it closes. All these are carefully stuffed; and if you walk across the room, there is no sound.

"We cautiously search violent lunatics; who are then dressed in a plain flannel suit, and left alone. It is seldom we have occasion to retain them longer than twenty-four hours. They soon find they cannot injure themselves; their most violent efforts cannot elicit a sound. Their minds become calmed; and when released, they are perfectly quiet, and generally inclined to melancholy."

They descended to the court yard, set apart for the men. Its inmates were pacing it hurriedly; some jabbering to themselves; others with groups round them, to whom they addressed some quickly delivered jargon. With one or two exceptions, all noticed the entrance of the strangers; and some of them bowed to them, with mock gravity. One man, who wore an old cocked hat with a shabby feather, tapped Sir Henry on the shoulder.

"Vous me reconnaissez - Napoleon! votre Empereur!"

He wheeled round, and called for his Mamelukes.

The next moment, a young and interesting looking person came forward, the tears standing in his, eyes, and extended his hand to Acmé.

"Give me yours," said he, "as a great favour. I was a painter once in Naples - and I went to Rome - and I loved Gianetta Cantieri!"

A more ludicrous incident now occurred. At and since their entrance, our party had heard what seemed the continued bark of a dog. A man on all fours came forward from behind a group, and with unmeaning face, and nostril snuffing up the wind, imitated to perfection the deep bay of a mastiff.

"That man's peculiarity," observed the Baron, "is an extraordinary one. He had a cottage near Catania, and had saved some little wealth. His house was one night robbed of all it contained. This misfortune preyed on the man's reason, and he now conceives himself a watch dog. He knows the step of every inmate of the asylum, and only barks at strangers."

From the male court yard, the Baron ushered them to the female, where insanity assumed a yet more melancholy shape.

A pale-faced maniac, with quivering frame, and glaring eyeballs, continued to cry, in a low and piteous tone, "Murder! murder!! murder!!!"

One woman, reclining on the cold pavement, dandled a straw, and called it her sweet child; while another hugged a misshapen block of wood to her bared breast, and deemed it her true love.

A third was on her knees, and at regular intervals, bent down her shrivelled body, and devoured the gravel beneath her.

Acmé was happy to leave the scene, and move towards the garden; which was extensive, and beautifully laid out.

As they turned down one of the alleys, they encountered five or six men, drawn up in line, and armed with wooden muskets.

In front stood Napoleon, who, with stentorian voice, gave the word to "present arms!" then dropping his stick, and taking off his hat to Delmé, began to converse familiarly with him, as with his friend Emperor Alexander, as to the efficiency of Poniatowski and his Polish lancers.

"Poor fellow!" said the Baron, as they moved on. "Never was insanity more harmless! He was once brigade major to Murat. This is his hour for exercise. Exactly at two, he goes through the scene of Fontainbleau, What will appear to you extraordinary is, that over the five or six men you saw around him, whose madness has been marked by few distinguishing traits, he has gradually assumed a superiority, until they now believe him to be, in reality, the Emperor he so unconsciously personates."

In the garden, which was of considerable size, were placed a number of swings and whirligigs, in full motion and occupancy.

On a stuccoed wall, were represented grotesque figures of animals dancing; opposite to which, one of Terpsichore's votaries, with a paper cap on his head, shaped like a pyramid, was executing agile capers, whose zeal of purpose would have found infinite favour in the eyes of Laporte.

Having explored the garden, Delmé accompanied the Baron to a small room, where the sculls of the deceased maniacs were ranged on shelves, with a small biographical note attached to each; and heard with attention, the old man's energetic reasoning, as to these fully demonstrating the truth of Spurzheim's theory.

Acmé, meantime, remained on George's arm, talking to a girl of thirteen, who had been selected to conduct them to the carriage.

They entered their names in a book at the lodge, and then, turning to the benevolent director, paid him some well deserved compliments, for which he bowed low and often.

The young girl, who had been conversing most rationally with Acmé, moved forward, and made a signal for the carriage to drive up.

She was a fair-haired gentle-looking creature, with quiet eye, and silvery voice. She assisted Acmé to step into the carriage, who dropped a piece of silver into her hand, for which she gave a sweet smile and a curtsey.

She stood a moment motionless. Suddenly her eye lighted up - she darted into the carriage, and clapped her hands together joyfully.

"Viva! viva! we shall soon be home at Trapani!"

The tears sprang to the eyes of the young Greek.

Even the driver and cicerone were moved.

Acmé took some flowers from her zone - kissed her cheek - and tried to change the current of her thoughts; but it was not till the driver promised he would call again, at the same hour the following day, that she consented with a sigh to relinquish her journey home.

From the Lunatic Asylum, our party adjourned to the Duomo, and beheld the coffin, where the revered body of the Palermitan Saint, attracts many a devout Catholic.

Sweet Rosalia! thy story is a pretty one - thy festa beauteous - the fireworks in thy honour most bright. No wonder the fair Sicilians adore thy memory.

In the cool of the evening, our travellers drove to the Marina; where custom - the crowded assemblage - and the grateful sea breeze - nightly attract the gay inhabitants of Palermo.

The carriages, with their epauletted chasseurs, swept on in giddy succession, and made a scene quite as imposing as is witnessed in most European capitals.

Delmé did not think it advisable, to remain too long in the metropolis of Sicily; and the travellers contented themselves, with the sight-seeing of the immediate neighbourhood.

They admired the mosaics of the Chiesa di Monte Reale; and fed the pheasants, at that beautiful royal villa, well styled "the Favourite." They took a boat to witness the tunny fishery; and Sir Henry explored alone the vast catacombs - that city of the dead.

After a few days thus passed - the weather continuing uncommonly fine - they did not hesitate to engage one of the small vessels of the place, to convey them to Naples.

After enjoying their evening drive as usual, they embarked on board the Sparonara, one fine starry night, in order to get the full advantage of the favouring night breeze.

Vol. II

"My thoughts, like swallows, skim the main,
And bear my spirit back again
Over the earth, and through the air,
A wild bird and a wanderer."

CHAPTER I

NAPLES

"And be it mine to muse there, mine to glide
From day-break when the mountain pales his fire,
Yet more and more, and from the mountain top,
Till then invisible, a smoke ascends,
Solemn and slow."

"Vedi Napoli! e poi muori!"

Memory! beloved memory! to us thou art as hope to other men. The present - solitary, unexciting - where are its charms? The future hath no joys in store for us; and may bereave us of some of the few faint pleasures that still are ours.

What then is left us - old before our time - but to banquet on the past?

Memory! thou art in us, as the basil of the enamoured Florentine. [Footnote 1: See Keats' poem taken from Boccaccio.] Thy blossoms, thy leaves, - green, fresh, and fragrant, - draw their nurture, receive their every colouring, from what was dearest to us on earth. And are they not watered by our tears?

The poet tells us -

"Nessun maggior dolore
Che ricordarsi del tempo felice
Nella miseria."

But it is not so. Where is he of the tribe of the unfortunate, who would not gladly barter the contemplation of present wretchedness, for the remembrance, clogged as it is by a thousand woes, of a time when joyous visions flitted across life's path?

Yes! though the contrast, the succeeding moment, should cut him to the soul.

But

"Joy's recollection is no longer joy,
Whilst sorrow's memory is a sorrow still."

Ah! there's the rub! yet, better to think it *was* joy, than gaze unveiled on the cold reality around; than view the wreck - the grievous wreck - a few short years have made.

We care not, - and, alas! to such as we have in our mind's eye, these are the only cases allowed, - we care not! whether rapture has been succeeded by apathy, or whether the feelings continue as deeply enlisted - the thoughts as intensely concentrated; - but - in the servitude of despair!

And again we say - gentle memory! let us dream over our past joys! ay! And brood over our sorrows - undeserved - as in this hour of solitude, we may justly deem them.

Yes! let us again live over our days of suffering, and deem it wiser to steep our soul in tears, than let it freeze with an iced coating of cynic miscalled philosophy.

And shall adversity - that touchstone - softened as our hearts shall thus be - shall it pass over us, and improve us not?

No! it has purifying and cleansing qualities; and for us, it has them not in vain.

We are not dust, to be more defiled by water; nor are we as the turbid stream, which passing over driven snow, becomes more impure by the close contact.

Thee, Mnemosyne! let us still adore; content rather to droop, fade, and die - martyrs to thee! than linger on as beasts of the forest, that know thee not. No hope may be ours to animate the future: let us still cling to thee, though thine influence sadden the past.

Away! we are on the placid sea! and Naples lies before us.

The sun had just risen from ocean's bed, attired in his robe of gold; as our travellers watched from the deck of their Sparonara, to catch the first view of the "garden of the world," as the Neapolitans fondly style their city,

A dim haze was abroad, the mists were slowly stealing up the mountains, as their vessel glided on; a light breeze anon filling its canvas, then dying away, and leaving the sails to flap against the loosened cordage.

On their left, extended the charming heights of Posilipo - -the classic site of Baia - Pozzuoli - Nisida - and Ischia, to be reverenced for its wine.

On their right, Capra's isle and Portici - and Vesuvius - wreathed in vapour, presented themselves.

As their vessel held on her way, Naples became visible - its turrets capt by a solitary cloud, which had not yet acknowledged the supremacy of the rising deity.

The effulgence of the city was dimmed, but it was lovely still, - as a diamond, obscured by a passing breath; or woman's eye, humid from pity's tear.

"And this," said Sir Henry, for it happened that his travels in Italy had not extended so far south, "this is Naples! and this sea view the second finest in the world!"

"Which is the first?" said Acmé, laughing, "not in England, I trust; for we foreigners do not invest your island with beauty's attributes."

"My dear Acmé!" replied Sir Henry, somewhat gravely, "I trust the day may arrive, when you will deem Delmé Park, with its mansion bronzed by time - its many hillocks studded with ancient trees - its glistening brook, and hoary gateways - its wooded avenue, where the rooks have built for generations - its verdant glades, where the deer have long found a home: - when you will consider all these, as forming as fair a prospect, as ever eye reposed on. But I did not allude at the time to England; but to the Turkish capital. George! I remember your glowing description of your trip in Mildmay's frigate, up the Dardanelles. What comparison would you make between the two scenes?"

"I confess to have been much disappointed," replied George, "in my first view of Stamboul; and even the beauty of the passage to the Dardanelles, seemed to me to have been exaggerated. But what really *did* strike me, as being the most varied, the most interesting scenery I had ever witnessed, was that which greeted us, on an excursion we made in a row boat, from the Bosphorus into the Black Sea.

"There all my floating conceptions of Oriental luxury, and of Moslem pomp, were more than realised.

"The elegant kiosks - the ornamented gardens - the pinnacled harems, the entrance to which lofty barriers jealously guarded - the number of the tombs in their silent cities - -gave an intense interest to the Turkish coast; - while sumptuous barges, filled with veiled women, swept by us, and gave a fairy charm to the sea. On our return, we were nearly lost from our ignorance of the current, which is rapid and dangerous."

"Well! I am glad to hear such a smiling account of Stamboul," rejoined Acmé. "My feelings regarding it have been quite Grecian. It has always been to me a sort of Ogre city."

The breeze began to freshen, and the vessel made way fast.

As they neared the termination of their voyage, some church, or casino bedecked with statues, or fertile glen, whose sides blushed with the luscious grape, opened at every instant, and drew forth their admiration.

Their little vessel swung to her anchor.

The busy hum of the restless inhabitants, and the joyous toll of the churches, announcing one of the never-failing Neapolitan processions, was borne on the breeze.

The whole party embarked for the quarantine office, and - once authorised to join the throng of Naples - soon found themselves in the Strada Toledo, moving towards the Santa Lucia.

Their hotel was near the mole; its windows commanding an extensive view of the purple sea, beyond which the eye took in the changeful volcano; and many a vista - sunny, smiling, and beauteous enough, for the exacting fancy of an Englishman, who conjures up for an Italian landscape, marble-like villas - and porticoes, where grapes cluster, in festoons of the vine - heaving mountains - a purple sky - faces bronzed, but oh how fair! - and song, revelry, and grace.

But what struck Acmé, and even Sir Henry, who was more inured to the whirl of cities, as the characteristical feature of Naples, was its moving life. In the streets, there was an incessant bustle from morning until midnight. Each passer by wore an air of importance, almost amounting to a consciousness of happiness. There was fire in the glance - speech in the action - on the lip a ready smile.

In no city of Italy, does care seem more misplaced. The noble rolls on in his vehicle on the Corso, with features gay and self-possessed; while the merry laugh of the beggar - as he feasts on the lengthened honors of his Macaroni - greets the ear at every turn. Stray not there! oh thou with brow furrowed by anguish!

If thy young affections have been blighted - if hope fondly indulged, be replaced by despair - if feelings that lent their roseate hue, to the commonest occurrences of life, now darken every scene - if thou knowest thyself the accessary to this, thy misery, stray not in Naples, all too joyous for thee!

Rather haunt the shrines of the world's ancient mistress! Perchance the sunken pillar - and the marble torso - and the moss-grown edifice - and the sepulchre, with the owl as tenant - and the thought that the great, the good, and the talented, who reared these fading monuments - are silent and mouldering below: mayhap these things will speak to thy heart, and repress the full gush of a sorrow that may not be controlled! And if - the martyr to o'er-sicklied refinement - to sentiment too etherialised for the world, where God hath placed thee - ideal woes have stamped a wrinkle on the brow, and ideal dreams now constitute thy pleasure and thy bane: for such as thou art! living on feeling's excess - soaring to rapture's heights - or sinking to despair's abyss - Naples is not fitting!

Visit the city of the sea! there indulge thy shapeless imaginings - with no sound to break thy day dreams - save the shrill cry of the gondolier, and the splash of his busy oar.

The young Greek, Delmé, and George, were soon immersed in the round of sight seeing.

Visits to the ancient palace of Queen Joanna - to the modern villa of the Margravine - to the Sibyl's Cave, and to Maro's Tomb - to *some* sites that owed their interest to classic associations - to *others* that claimed it from present beauty - wiled away days swiftly and pleasurably.

What with youth, change of scene, and an Italian sky, George was no longer an invalid. His eye wore neither the film of apathy, nor the unnatural flush of delirium; but smiled its happiness on all, and beamed its love on Acmé.

One night they were at the Fondo, and after listening delightedly to Lalande, and following with quick glance, the rapid movements of the agile ballerina, and after George had been honoured by a bow - which greatly amused Acmé - from the beautiful princess; who, poor girl! *then* felt a penchant for Englishmen, which she failed not to avow from her opera box - the party agreed to walk home to the hotel. On their way, they turned into a coffee-room to take ice.

The fluent waiter prattled over his catalogue; and Acmé selected his "sorbetto Maltese," because the name reminded her of the loved island.

Leaving the coffee-room, they were accosted by a driver of one of the public coaches.

"Now, Signore! just in time for Vesuvius! See the sun rise! superb sight! elegant carriage!"

"Do let us go!" said Acmé, clapping her hands with youthful enthusiasm.

"No, no! my dear!" said Sir Henry, "we must not think of it! you would be so tired."

"No, no! you do not know how strong I am; and I intend sleeping on George's shoulder all the way - and we are all in such high spirits - and these improvised excursions you yourself granted were always best - and besides, you know we must always start at this hour, if we expect to see the sunrise from the mountain. What do *you* say, Giorgio?"

The discussion ended, by the driver taking the direction of the hotel; whence, after making arrangements as to provisions and change of dress, the party started for the mountain.

The warm cheek of Acmé was reposing on that of her husband; and the wanton night air was disporting with her wavy tresses, as the loud halloo of the driver, warned them that they were in Portici, and in the act of arousing Salvador, the guide to the mountain. After some short delay, they procured mules. Each brother armed himself with a long staff, and leaving the carriage, they wended their way towards the Hermitage.

It was a clear night. The moon was majestically gliding on her path, vassalled by myriads of stars.

There was something in the hour - and the scene - and the novelty of the excursion - that enjoined silence.

Arrived at the Hermitage, the party dismounted. Acmé clung to the strap, fastened round their guide, and they commenced the ascent. In a short time, they had manifest proofs of their vicinity to the volcano. The ashy lava gave way at each footstep, and it was only by taking short and quick steps, and perseveringly toiling on, that they were enabled to make any progress.

More than once, was Acmé inclined to stop, and take breath, but the guide assured them they were already late, and that they would only just be in time for the sunrise.

As the last of the party reached the summit, the sun became perceptible - and rose in glory indescribable. The scene afar how gorgeous! around them how grand!

Panting from their exertions, they sat on a cloak of Salvador's, and gazed with astonishment at the novelties bursting on the eye.

Each succeeding moment, gusts of flame issued forth from the crater.

They looked down on the bason, above which they were. From a conical pyramid of lava, were emitted volumes of smoke, which rolled up to heaven in rounded and fantastic shapes of beauty. Below, a deep azure - above, of a clear amber hue - the clouds wreathed and ascended majestically, as if in time to the rumbling thunder - the accompaniments of nature's subterraneous throes.

Their fatigues were amply repaid. Sir Henry's curiosity was aroused, and he descended with the guide to the crater. George and Acmé, delighted with the excursion, remained on the summit, partaking of Salvador's provisions.

The descent they found easy and rapid; the lava now assisting, as much as it had formerly impeded them.

At Portici, Salvador introduced them to his apartment, embellished with specimens of lava. They purchased some memorials of their visit - partook of some fruit - and, after rewarding the guide, they returned to Naples.

Another of their excursions, and it is one than which there are few more interesting, was to that city - which, like the fabulous one of the eastern tale, rears its temples, but there are none to worship; its theatres, but there are none to applaud; its marble statues, where are the eyes that should dwell on them with pride? Its mansions are many - its walls and tesselated pavements, show colours of vivid hue, and describe tales familiar from our boyhood. The priest is at his altar - the soldiers in their guard-room - the citizen in his bath. It is indeed difficult, as our step re-echoes through the silent streets, to divest ourselves of the impression, that we are wandering where the enchanter's wand has been all powerful, that he has waved it, and lo! the city sleeps for a season, until some event shall have been fulfilled.

Our party were in the Via Appia of Pompeii, when Acmé turned aside, to remark one tomb more particularly. It was an extensive one, surrounded with a species of iron net work, through which might be seen ranges of red earthen vases. Acme turned to the custode, and asked if this was the burial place of some noble family.

"No! Signora! this is where the ashes of the gladiators are preserved."

From the Appian Way, they entered through the public gate; and passing many shops, whose signs yet draw notice, if they no longer attract custom, they came to the private houses, and entered one - that called Sallust's - for the purpose of a more minute inspection.

"Nothing appears to be more strange," said George, "on looking at these frescoed paintings, and on such mosaics as we have yet seen; than the extraordinary familiarity of their subjects.

"There are many depicted on these walls, and I do not think, Henry, *we* are first rate classics; - and yet it would be difficult to puzzle us, in naming the story whence these frescoes have their birth. Look at this Latona - and Leda - and the Ariadne abbandonata - and this must certainly be the blooming Hebe. Ah! and look at this little niche! This grinning little deity - the facsimile of an Indian idol - must express their idea of the Penates. Strange! is it not?"

"But are you not," rejoined Sir Henry, "somewhat disappointed in the dwelling-houses? This seems one of the most extensive, and yet, how diminutive the rooms! and how little of attraction in the whole arrangement, if we except this classic fountain.

"This I think is a proof, that the ancient Romans must have chiefly passed their day abroad - in the temples - the forum - or the baths - and have left as home tenants none but women, and those unadorned with the toga virilis.

"These habits may have tended to engender a manlier

independence; and to impart to their designs a loftier spirit of enterprise. What say you, Acmé?"

"I might perhaps answer," replied Acmé, "that the happiness gained, is well worth the glory lost. But I must not fail to remind you, that - grand as this nation must have been - my poor fallen one was its precursor - its tutor - and its model."

Hence they wandered to the theatre - the forum - the pantheon - and amphitheatre: - which last, from their converse in the earlier part of the day - fancy failed not to fill with daring combatants. As the guide pointed out the dens for the wild beasts - the passages through which they came - and the arena for the combat - Sir Henry, like most British travellers, recalled the inimitable story of Thraso, and his lion fight. [Footnote: In Valerius.]

The following day was devoted to the Studio, and to the inspection of the relics of Pompeii.

These relics, interesting as they are, yet convey a melancholy lesson to the contemplative mind. Each modern vanity here has its parallel - each luxury its archetype. Here may be found the cameoed ring - and the signet seal - and the bodkin - and paint for the frail one's cheek - a cuirass, that a life guardsman might envy - weights - whose elegance of shape charm the eye. Not an article of modern convenience or of domestic comfort, that has not its representative. They teach us the trite French lesson.

"L'histoire se répète."

With the exception of these two excursions, and one to Poestum; our travellers passed their mornings sight-seeing in Naples, and chiefly at the Studio, whose grand attraction is the thrilling group of the Taureau Farnese.

In the cool of the evening, until twilight's hour was past, they drove into the country, or promenaded in the gardens of the

Villa Reale, to the sound of the military band.

Each night they turned their footsteps towards the Mole; where they embarked on the unruffled bay. To a young and loving heart - the heart of a bride - no pleasure can equal that, of being next the one loved best on earth - at night's still witching hour. The peculiar scenery of Naples, yet more enhances such pleasure.

Elsewhere night may boast its azure vault and its silver stars. Cynthia may ride the heavens in majesty - the water may be serene - and the heart attuned to the night's beauty: - but from the *land*, if discernible - we can rarely expect much addition to the charms of the scene, and can never expect it to form its chief attraction. At Naples it is otherwise.

Our eyes turn to the Volcano, whose flame, crowning the mountain's summit, crimsons the sky.

We watch with undiminished interest, its fitful action - now bursting out brilliantly - now fading, as if about to be extinguished for ever. Seated beside George, and thus gazing, what pleasure was Acmé's! We need not say time flew swiftly. Never did happiness meet with more ardent votary than in that young bride - or find a more ready mirror, on which to reflect her beaming attributes - than on the features of that bride's husband.

Their swimming eyes would fill with tears - and their voices sink to the lowest whisper.

Sir Henry rarely interrupted their converse; but leant his head on the boat's side, and thoughtfully gazed on the placid waters, till he almost deemed he saw reflected on its surface, the face of one, in whose society *he* felt he too might be blest.

But these fancies would not endure long. Delmé would quickly arouse himself; and, warned by the lateness of the hour, and feeling the necessity that existed, for his thinking for the all-engrossed pair, would order the rowers to direct the boat's course homewards.

Returned to their hotel, it may be that orisons more heavenward, have issued from hearts more pure.

Few prayers more full of gratitude, have been whispered by earthly lips, than were breathed by George and his young wife in the solitude of their chamber.

How often is such uncommon happiness as this the precursor of evil!

CHAPTER II

THE DOCTOR

"Son port, son air de suffisance,
Marquent dans son savoir sa noble confiance.
Dans les doctes debats ferme et rempli de coeur,
Même après sa défaite il tient tête an vainqueur.
Voyez, pour gagner temps, quelles lenteurs savantes,
Prolongent de ses mots les syllabes traînantes!
Tout le monde l'admire, et ne peut concevoir
Que dans un cerveau seul loge tant de savoir."

It was soon after the excursion to Poestum, that a packet of letters reached the travellers from Malta. These letters had been forwarded from England, on the intelligence reaching Emily, of George's intended marriage. They had been redirected to Naples, by Colonel Vavasour, and were accompanied by a few lines from himself.

In Sir Henry's communication with his sister, he had prudently thrown a veil, over the distressing part of George's story, and had dwelt warmly, on the beauty and sweetness of temper of Acmé Frascati. He could hardly hope that the proposed marriage, would meet with the entire approval of those, to whom he addressed himself.

The letters in reply, however, only breathed the affectionate overflowings of kind hearts. Mrs. Glenallan sent her motherly blessing to George; and Emily, in addition to a long communication to her brother, wrote to Acmé as to a beloved sister; begging her to hasten George's return to England, that they might meet one, in whom they must henceforward feel the liveliest interest.

"How kind they all are," said George. "I only wish we *were* with them."

"And so do I," said Acmé. "How dearly I shall love them all."

"George!" said Sir Henry, abruptly, "do you know, I think it is quite time we should move farther north. The weather is getting most oppressive; and we have nearly exhausted the lions of Naples."

"With all my heart," replied George. "I am ready to leave it whenever you please."

On Sir Henry's considering the best mode of conveyance, it occurred to him, that some danger might arise from the malaria of the Pontine marshes; and indeed, Rome and its environs were represented, at that time, as being by no means free from this unwelcome visitant.

Sir Henry enquired if there were any English physicians resident in Naples; and having heard a high eulogium passed by the waiter, on a Doctor Pormont, "who attended the noble Consul, and my Lord Rimington," ventured to enclose his card, with a note, stating that he would be glad of five minutes' conversation with that gentleman.

In a short time, Doctor Pormont was introduced.

He was a tall man, with very marked features, and a deeply furrowed brow; whose longitudinal folds, however, seemed rather the result of thought or of study, than of age. The length of his nose was rivalled by the width of his mouth. When he spoke, he displayed two rows of very clean and very regular teeth, but which individually narrowed to a sharp point, and gave his whole features a peculiarly unpleasing expression. His voice was husky - his manners chilling - his converse that of a pedant.

Doctor Pormont was in many respects a singular man. From childhood, he had been remarkable for stoicism of character. He possessed none of the weak frailties, or gentle sympathies, which ordinarily belong to human nature. His blood ran cold, like that of a fish. Never had he been known to lose his equanimity of deportment.

A species of stern principle, however, governed his conduct; and his very absence of feeling, made him an impartial physician, and one of the most successful anatomists of the day.

What brought him to bustling, sunny Naples, was an unfathomed mystery. Once there, he acquired wealth without anxiety, and patients without friends.

Amongst the many anecdotes, current amongst his professional brethren, as to the blunted feelings of Doctor Pormont, was one, - related of him when he was lecturer at a popular London institution. A subject had been placed on the anatomist's table, for the purpose of allowing the lecturer, to elucidate to the young students, the advantages of a post mortem examination, in the determination of diseases. The lecturer dissected as he proceeded, and was particularly clear and luminous. He even threw light on the previous habits of the deceased, and showed at what period of life, the germ of decay was probably forming.

A friend casually enquired, as they left the lecture room, whether the subject had been a patient of his own.

"No!" replied the learned lecturer, "the body is that of my cousin and schoolfellow, Harry Welborne. I attended his funeral, at some little distance from town, a couple of days ago. My servant must have given information to the exhumer. It is clear the body was removed from the vault on the same evening."

Sir Henry Delmé briefly explained to Doctor Pormont, his purpose in sending for him. He stated that he was anxious to take his advice, as to the best mode of proceeding to Rome, and also as to the best sleeping place for the party; - that he had a wholesome dread of the malaria, but that one of his party being a female, and another an invalid, he thought it might be as well to sleep one night on the road. Regarding all this, he deferred to the advice and superior judgment of the physician.

"Judgment," said Doctor Pormont, "is two-fold. It may be defined, either as the faculty of arriving at the knowledge of things, which may be effected by the synthetic or analytic method; or it may be considered as the just perception of them, when they are fully indagated.

"Our problem seems to resolve itself into two cases.

"First: does malaria exist to an unusual and alarming extent, on the route you purpose taking?

"Secondly: the existence conceded - what is the best method to escape the evil effects that might attend its inhibition into the human system?

"Let us apply the synthetic method to our first case."

The Doctor prefaced his arguments, by a long statement, as to the gradual commencement, and progress of malaria; - showed how the atmosphere, polluted by exhalations of water, impregnated with decaying and putrified vegetable matter, gave forth miasmata; which he described as being particles of poison in a volatile state.

He alluded to the opinion held by many, that the disease owed its origin to the ravages of the barbarians, who destroying the

Roman farms and villas, had made *desert* what were *fertile* regions.

He traced it from the time of the late Roman Emperors, to that of the dominion of the Popes, whose legislative enactments to arrest the malady, he failed not to comment on at length.

He explained the uncertainty which continued to exist, as to the boundaries of the tract of country, in which the disease was rife; and then plunged into his argument.

George, at this crisis, quietly took the opportunity of gliding from the room. Sir Henry stretched his legs on an ottoman, and appeared immersed in the study of a print - the Europa of Paul Veronese - which hung over the mantel-piece.

"The Diario di Roma," continued the Doctor, "received this day, decidedly states that malaria is fearfully raging on the Neapolitan road. Pray forgive me, if I occasionally glide into the vulgar error, of confounding the disease itself, with the causes of that disease.

"On the other hand, a young collegian, who arrived in Naples from Rome yesterday evening, states that he smoked and slept the whole journey, and suffered no inconvenience whatever.

"Here two considerations present themselves. While sleep has been considered by the best authorities, as predisposing the human frame to infection, by opening the pores, relaxing the integuments, and retarding the circulation of the blood; I cannot overlook the virtues of tobacco, narcotic - aromatic - disinfecting - as we must grant them to be.

"Here then may I place in juxta-position, the testimony of the Diario, and that of a young gentleman, half of his time asleep - the other half, under the influence of the fumes of tobacco.

"Synthetically, I opine, that we may conclude that malaria does exist, and to a great degree, in the Campagna di Roma. Will you now allow me, to submit the question under dispute, to the analytic process? By many, in the present age, though not by me, it is considered the more philosophical mode of reasoning."

"I am extremely obliged to you, Doctor," said Sir Henry, in a quiet tone of voice, "but you have raised the synthetic structure so admirably, that I think that in this instance we may dispense with your analysis. Pray proceed!"

"Having already shown, then - although your kindness has allowed me to do so but partially - that malaria does indeed exist, it becomes me to show, which is the best mode of avoiding its baneful effects.

"Injurious as are the miasmata in general, and fatal as are the effects of that peculiar form in this country, termed malaria; the diseases they engender, I apprehend to be rather endemic than epidemic.

"It would be difficult to determine, to what part of the Campagna, the disease is at present confined; but I should certainly not advise you, to sleep within the bounds of contagion, for the predisposing effects of sleep I have already hinted at.

"Rapid travelling is, in my opinion, the best prophylactic I can prescribe, as besides a certain exhilarating effect on the spirits, the swift passage through the air, will remove any spiculæ of the marsh miasmata, which may be hovering near your persons. Air, cheerfulness, and exercise, however, predispose to, and are the results of sleep: and to an invalid especially, sleep is indispensable.

"In Mr. Delmé's case, therefore, I would recommend a temporary halt."

Dr. Pormont then gave an account of the length of the stages, the nature of the post-house accommodations, and the probable degree of danger attached to each site.

From all this, Delmé gathered, that malaria existed to some extent, on the line of road they were to travel - that sleep would be necessary for George - and that, on the whole, it would be most desirable to sleep at an inn, situated at a hamlet between Molo di Gaetà and Terracina, somewhat removed from the central point of danger.

But the truth is, that Sir Henry Delmé was disposed to consider Dr. Pormont, with his pomposity, and wordy arguments, as a mere superficial thinker; and he half laughed at himself, for having ever thought it necessary to consult him. This class of men influence less than they ought. Sensible persons are apt to set them down, as either fools or pedants. Their very magniloquence condemns them; for, in the present day, it seems an axiom, that simplicity and genius are invariably allied.

This rule, like most others, has its exceptions; and it would be well for all of us, if we thought less of the manner, in which advice may be delivered, and more of the matter which it may contain.

The Doctor rose to take leave, - Sir Henry witnessed his departure with lively satisfaction; and, with the exception of enjoying a hearty laugh, at his expense, with George and Acmé, ceased to recollect that such a personage existed.

Delmé, however, had cause to remember that Doctor Pormont.

Were it not so, he would not have figured in these pages.

The last evening they were at Naples, they proceeded, as was their custom, to the Mole; and there engaging a boat, directed it to be rowed across the bay.

The volcano was more than usually brilliant, and the villages at its base, appeared as clear as at noonday.

The water's surface was not ruffled by a ripple. A bridal party was following in the wake of their boat - and nuptial music was floating past them in subdued cadence.

A nameless regret filled their minds, as they thought of the journey on the coming morrow. They had been so happy in Naples. Could they hope to be happier elsewhere?

It was midnight, when they returned to the hotel. As they neared its portico, the round cold moon fell on the forms of the lazzaroni, who were lying in groups round the pillars.

One of the party sprang to his feet, alarming the slumberers. The whole of them rose with admirable cheerfulness - took off their hats respectfully - and made way for the forestieri.

During the momentary pause that ensued, Acmé turned to the volcano, and playfully waved her hand in token of farewell.

Her eyes filled with tears, and she clung heavily to George's arm.

She was doomed never to look on that scene again.

CHAPTER III

THE BEGINNING OF THE END

"Thou too, art gone! thou loved and lovely one,
Whom youth and youth's affections bound to me."

At an early hour, rich aureate hues yet streaking the east, our party were duly seated in a roomy carriage of Angrasani's, on their way to Rome.

They had hopes of arriving at the capital, in time to witness that unique sight, the illumination of Saint Peter's; a sight which few can remember, without deeming its anticipation well worthy, to urge on the jaded traveller, to his journey's termination.

Who can forget the play of the fountains in front of the Vatican, the music of whose descending water is most distinctly audible, although crowds throng the wide and noble space.

Breathless - silent all - is the assembled multitude, as the clock of Saint Peter's gives its long expected signal.

Away! darkness is light! a fairy palace springs before us! Its beautiful proportions starting into life, until the giddy brain reels, from the excess of that splendour, on which the eye suddenly and delightedly feasts!

With the exception of a short halt, which afforded the travellers time for an early dinner at the Albergo di Cicerone, which is about half a mile from the Molo di Gaeta, they prosecuted their journey without intermission, till arrived within sight of their resting place.

This bore the aspect of an extensive, but dilapidated mansion, evidently designed for some other purpose.

Its proprietor had erected it, at a period, when malaria was either less prevalent or less dreaded; and his descendants had quitted it, for some more salubrious site.

The albergo itself, occupied but a small portion of the building, immediately on the right and left of the porch.

The other apartments, which formed the wings, were either wholly tenantless, or were fitted up as hay-lofts, granaries, or receptacles for farming utensils.

In the upper rooms, the panes of glass were broken; and the whole aspect of the place betokened desolation and decay.

As they drove to the door, a throng of mendicants and squalid peasants came forth. Their faces had a cadaverous hue, which could not but be remarked. Their eyes, too, seemed heavy, and deep set in the head; while many had their throats bandaged, from the effects of glandular swellings, brought on by the marshy exhalations.

Acmé threw some small pieces of Neapolitan money amongst them; and their gratitude in consequence was boundless.

She sprang from the carriage like a young fawn.

"Come, come, Giorgio! look at that sweet sun-set - and at the blue clouds edged with burnished gold! Would it not be a sin to remain in-doors on such an evening? and besides," added she, in a whisper - "is it not a pleasure to leave behind us these sickly faces, to muse on an Italian landscape, and admire an Italian sky? Driver! will you order supper? We will take a stroll while it is preparing.

"Come! Henry! come away! do not look so grave, or you will make me think of your amusing friend - Dr. Pormont."

"Thompson!" said George, as the smiling bride bore off the brothers in triumph, "do not forget your mistress' guitar case!"

The travellers passed a paved court, in rear of the building; whence a wicket gate admitted them to a kitchen garden, well stocked with the requisites for an Italian salad.

Behind this, enclosed with embankments, was a small vineyard. The vines twined round long poles, these again being connected with thin cords, which the tendrils were already clasping.

Thus far, there was nothing that seemed indicative of an unwholesome situation. As they extended their walk, however, pursuing the continuation of the path, that had led them through the vineyard, they arrived at the edge of a dark sluggish stream, whose surface was nearly on a level with them; and which, gradually becoming broader, at length emptied itself into what might be styled a wide and luxuriant marsh, which abounded with water-fowl. This was studded with small round lakes, and with islets of an emerald verdure.

From the bosom of the marsh itself, rose bulrushes and pollard willows, towered over by gigantic noisy reeds.

The stream was thickly strewn with the pure honours of the water lily.

If - as Eastern poets tell us - these snowy flowers bathe their charms, when the sun is absent, but lift up their virgin heads, when he looks down approvingly: - but that, sometimes deceived, on some peerless damsel's approaching, they mistake her eye for their loved luminary, and pay to her beauty an abrupt and involuntary homage: - *now* might they indeed gaze upward, to greet as fair a face as ever looked down on the water they bedecked.

They approached the edge of the marsh, and discovered a rural arbour of faded boughs - the work of children - placed around a couple of willow trees.

Within it, was a rude seat; and some parasitical plant with a deep red flower, had twined round the withered boughs, and mingled fantastically with the dead leaves.

Below the arbour, was a small stone embankment, which prevented the waters from encroaching, and made the immediate site comparatively free from dampness.

Acme arranged her cloak - took one hand of each of the brothers in hers - and in the exuberance of health and youth - commenced prattling in that charming domestic strain, which only household intimacy can beget or justify. George leant back in silence, but could have clasped her to his heart.

Memory! memory! who that hath a soul, cannot conjure up one such gentle being, - while the blood for one moment responds to thy call, and rolls through the veins with the tide of earlier and of happier days?

At the extremity of the horizon, was a more extensive lake, than any near them. Over this, the sun was setting; tinting its waters with a clear rich amber, save in its centre, where, the lake serving as a halo to its glory, a blood-red sun was vividly reflected.

As the sun descended, one slender ray of light, came quivering and trembling through the leaves of the arbour.

This little incident gave rise to a thousand fanciful illustrations on the part of Acmé. Her spirits were as buoyant as a child's;

and her playful mood soon communicated itself to her travelling companions.

They compared the solitary ray to virtue in loneliness - to the flickering of a lamp in a tomb - to a star reflected on quicksilver - to the flash of a sword cutting through a host of foes - and to the light of genius illuming scenes of poverty and distress.

Thompson made his appearance, and announced the supper as being ready.

"This," said George, good-naturedly, "is an odd place, is it not, Thompson? Is it anything like the Lincolnshire Fens?"

"Not exactly, your honour!" replied the domestic, with perfect gravity, "but there ought to be capital snipe shooting here."

"Ah! che vero Inglese!" said the laughing Acmé.

They retraced their steps to the inn, and were ushered into the supper room, which was neither more nor less than the kitchen, although formerly, perhaps, the show room of the mansion. Around the deep-set fireplace, watching the simmering of the cauldron, were grouped some peasants.

The supper table was laid in one corner of the room; and although neither the accommodation nor the viands were very tempting, there was such a disposition to be happy, that the meal was as much enjoyed as if served up in a palace.

The repast concluded, Acmé rose; and observing a countryman with his arm bound up, enquired if he had met with an accident; and patiently listened to the prosy narrative of age.

An old bronzed husbandman, too, was smoking his short earthen pipe, near the window sill.

"What a study for Lanfranc!" said the happy wife, as she took up a burnt stick, and sketched his dried visage to the life.

The old man regarded his portrait on the wall, with intense satisfaction; and commenced dilating on what he had been in youth.

How different, thought Sir Henry, is all this from the conduct of a well bred English girl! yet how natural and amiable does it appear in Acmé! With what an endearing manner - with what sweet frankness - does this young foreigner wile away - what would otherwise have been - a tedious evening in an uncomfortable inn!

As the night advanced, George brought out the guitar; and Acmé warbled to its accompaniment like a fairy bird.

It was a late hour, before Delmé ventured to remind the songstress, that they must prosecute their journey early on the following morning.

"I will take your hint," said Acmé, as she shook his hand, and tripped out of the room; "buona sera! miei Signori."

"She is a dear creature!" said Delmé,

"She is indeed!" replied his brother, "and I am a fortunate man. Henry! I think I shall be jealous of you, one of these days. I do believe she loves you as well as she does me!"

The brothers retired.

Sir Henry's repose was unbroken, until morning dawned; when George entered his room in the greatest agitation, and with a face as pale as death, told him Acmé was ill.

Delmé arose immediately; and at George's earnest solicitation, entered the room.

Her left cheek, suffused with hectic, rested on one small hand.

The other arm was thrown over the bed-clothes. Her eyes sparkled like diamonds. Her lips murmured indistinctly - the mind was evidently wandering.

A man and horse were sent express to Naples. The whole of that weary day, George Delmé was by Acmé's side, preparing cooling drinks, and vainly endeavouring to be calm.

As the delirium continued, she seemed to be transported to the scenes of her early youth,

As night wore on, the fever, if it were such, gradually increased.

George's state of mind bordered on distraction. Sir Henry became exceedingly alarmed, and anxious for the presence of the medical attendant.

At about four o'clock the following morning, Doctor Pormont was announced,

Cold and forbidding as was his aspect, George hailed him as his tutelary angel, and burst into tears, as he implored him to exert his skill to the uttermost.

The physician approached the invalid, and in a moment saw that the case was a critical one.

His patient was bled twice during the day, and strong opiates administered.

Towards evening, she slept; and awoke with restored consciousness, but with feelings keenly alive to her own danger.

The following night and day she lingered on, speaking but little.

During the whole of that time, even, when she slept, George's hand remained locked in hers. On this, her tears would sometimes fall, but these she strove to restrain.

To the others around her, she spoke gratefully, and with feminine softness; but her whole heart seemed to be with George.

Doctor Pormont, to do him justice, was unremitting in his exertions, and hardly took rest.

All his professional skill was called to her aid; but from the second day, he saw it was in vain.

The strength of the invalid failed her more and more.

Doctor Pormont at length called Sir Henry on one side, and informed him that he entertained no doubt of a fatal result; and recommended his at once procuring such religious consolation as might be in his power.

No Protestant clergyman was near at hand, even had Delmé thought it adviseable to procure one.

But he was well aware, that however Acme might have sympathised with George, her earlier religious impressions would now in all probability be revived.

A Catholic priest was sent for, and arrived quickly. He was habited in the brown garb of his order, his waist girt with a knotted cord. He bore in his hand the sainted pyx, and commenced to shrive the dying girl.

It was the soft hour of sunset, and the prospect in rear of the mansion, presented a wide sea of rich coloured splendour.

Over the window, had been placed a sheet, in order to exclude the light from the invalid's chamber. The priest knelt by her bedside; and folding his hands together, began to pray.

The rays of the setting sun, fitfully flickered on the sheet, over whose surface, light shadows swiftly played, ever and anon glancing on the shorn head of the kneeling friar.

His intelligent face was expressive of firm belief.

His eye turned reverentially to heaven, as in deep and sonorous accents, he implored forgiveness for the sufferer, for the sins committed during her mortal coil.

Acmé sat up in her bed. On her countenance, calm devotion seemed to usurp the place of earthly affections, and earthly passions.

The soul was preparing for its upward flight. Delmé led away the sorrowing husband, and the minister of Christ was left alone, to hear the contrite outpourings of a weak departing sinner.

The priest left the chamber, but spoke not, either to the physician, or the expecting brothers. His impassioned glance belonged to another and a higher world.

He made one low obeisance - his robes swept the passage quickly - and the Franciscan friar sought his lonely cell to reflect on death.

The brothers re-entered. They found Acmé in the attitude in which they had left her - her features wearing an expression at once radiant and resigned.

But - as her eye met George's - as she saw the havoc grief had already made - the feelings of the woman resumed the mastery.

She extended her arms - she brought his lip to hers - as if she would have made *that* its resting place for ever.

Alas! an inward pang told her to be brief. She drew away her face, crimsoned with her passion's flush - tremblingly grasped his hand - and, with voice choked by emotion, gave her last farewell.

"Giorgio, my dearest! my own! I shall soon join my parents. I feel this - and my mother's words, as she met me by the olive tree, ring in my ear.

"She told me I should die thus; but she told me, too, that I should kill the one dearest to me on earth. Thank God! this cannot be - for I know my life to be ebbing fast.

"Dearest I do not mourn for me too much. You may find another Acmé - as true. But, oh! sometimes - yes! even when your hearts cling fondly together, as ours were wont to do - think of your own Acmé - who loved you first - and only - and does it now! oh! how well! Giorgio! dear! dearest! adieu! My feet are *so, so* cold - and ice seems" -

A change shadowed the face, as from some corporeal pang.

She tried to raise an ebony cross hung round her neck.

In the effort, her features became convulsed - and George heard a low gurgling in the throat, as from suffocation.

Ah! that awful precursor of "the first dark hour of nothingness."

George Delmé sprang to his feet, and was supporting her head, when the physician grasped his arm.

"Stop! stop! you are preventing" -

The lower lip quivered - and drooped - slightly! very slightly!

The head fell back.

One long deep drawn sigh shook the exhausted frame.

The face seemed to become fixed.

Doctor Pormont extended his hand, and silently closed those dark fringed lids.

The cold finger, with its harsh touch, once more brought consciousness.

Once more the lid trembled! there was an upward glance that looked reproachful!

Another short sigh! Another!

Lustreless and glaring was that once bright eye!

Again the physician extended his hand.

"Assuredly, gentlemen! vitality hath departed!"

A deep - solemn - awful silence - which not a breath disturbed - came over that chamber of death.

It seemed as if the insects had ceased their hum - that twilight had suddenly turned to night - that an odour, as of clay, was floating around them, and impregnating the very atmosphere.

George took the guitar, whose chords were never more to be woke to harmony by that loved hand, and dashed it to the ground.

Ere Delmé could clasp him, he had staggered to the bedside - and fallen over Acmé's still form.

And did her frame thrill with rapture? did she bound to his caress? did her lip falter from her grateful emotion? - did she bury his cheek in her raven tresses?

No, no! still - still - still were all these! still as death!

CHAPTER IV

ROME

"Woe unto us, not her; for she sleeps well."

* * * * *

"The Niobe of nations! there she stands,
Childless and crownless, in her voiceless woe;
An empty urn within her wither'd hands,
Whose holy dust was scatter'd long ago.
The Scipios' tomb contains no ashes now;
The very sepulchres lie tenantless
Of their heroic dwellers; dost thou flow,
Old Tiber! through a marble wilderness?
Rise, with thy yellow waves, and mantle her distress."

Undertakers! not one word shall henceforth pass our lips in your dispraise!

An useful and meritorious tribe are you!

What! though sleek and rosy cheeked, you seem to have little in common with the wreck of our hopes?

What! if our ears be shocked by profane jests on the weight of your burden, as you bear away from the accustomed mansion, what *was* its light and its load star - but what *is* - pent up in your dark, narrow tenement, but -

"A heap,
To make men tremble, that never weep."

What! if our swimming eye - as we follow those dear - dear remains to their last lone resting place - glance on the heartless myrmidons, who salute the passer by with nods of recognition, and smiles of indifference?

What! if, returning homewards - choked with bitter recollections, which rise fantastic, quick, and ill-defined - the very ghosts of departed scenes and years - what if we start as we then perceive you - lightsome of heart, and glib of speech - clustered and smirking, on that roof of nodding plumes - neath which, one short hour since - lay what was dearest to us on earth?

Let us not heed these things! for - light as is the task to traders in death's dark trappings; painful and soul-subduing are those withering details to the grieving and heart-struck mourner!

We left George lying half insensible by the side of his dead wife.

Sir Henry and Thompson carried him to the apartment of the former, and while Thompson hung over his master, attempting to restore consciousness - Delmé had a short conference with Doctor Pormont as to their ulterior proceedings.

Doctor Pormont - as might be expected - enjoined the greatest promptitude, and recommended that poor Acmé's remains, should be consigned to the burial place of the hamlet.

George's objections to this, however, as soon as he was well enough to comprehend what was going forward, seemed quite insurmountable; and after Sir Henry had sought the place by moonlight, and found it wild and open, with goats browsing on the unpicturesque graves, and with nothing to mark the sanctity of the spot, save a glaring painted picture of the Virgin, his own prejudices became enlisted, and he consented to proceed to Rome.

After this decision was made, he found it utterly impossible, to procure a separate conveyance for the corpse; and was equally unsuccessful in his attempt to procure that - which from being a common want, he had been disposed to consider of every day attainment - a coffin.

While his brother made what arrangements he best might, poor George returned to the chamber of death, and gazed long and fixedly - with the despair of the widower - on those hushed familiar features.

Her hair was now turned back, and was bound with white ribbon, and festooned with some of the very water lilies that Acmé had admired. A snow-white wreath bound her brow. It was formed of the white convolvulus. We have said the features were familiar; but oh! how different! The yellow waxen hue - the heavy stiffened lid - how they affected George Delmé, who had never looked on death before!

First he would gaze with stupid awe - then turn to the window, and attempt to repress his sobs - return again - and refuse to credit his bereavement. Surely the hand moved? No! of its free will shall it never move more! The eye! was there not a slight convulsion in that long dark lash?

No! over it may crawl the busy fly, and creep the destructive worm, without let, and without hindrance!

No finger shall be raised in its behalf - that lid shall remain closed and passive!

The insect and the reptile shall extend their wanderings over the smooth cheek, and revel on the lips, whose red once rivalled that of the Indian shell.

Moveless! moveless shall all be!

The long - long night wore on.

An Italian sunrise was gilding the heavens.

Acmé was never to see a sunrise more; and even this reflection - trite as it may seem, occurring to one, who had watched through the night, by the side of the dead - even this reflection, convulsed again the haggard features of the mourner.

Delmé had made the requisite arrangements during the night, for their early departure.

Just previous to the carriage being announced, he led George out of the room; whilst the physician, aided by the women, took such precautions as the heat of the climate rendered necessary.

Linen cloths, steeped in a solution of chlorate of lime, were closely wound round the body - a rude couch was placed in the inside of the carriage, which was supported by the two seats - and the carriage itself was darkened.

These preparations concluded - and having parted with Doctor Pormont - whose attentions, in spite of his freezing manner, had been very great - the brothers commenced their painful task.

George knelt at the head of the corpse - ejaculated one short fervent prayer - and then, assisted by his brother, bore it in his arms to the vehicle.

The Italian peasants, with rare delicacy, witnessed the scene from the windows of the inn, but did not intrude their presence.

The body was placed crosswise in the carriage. George sat next the corpse. Delmé sat opposite, regarding his brother with anxious eye.

Most distressing was that silent journey! It made an impression on Sir Henry's mind, that no after events could ever efface; and yet it had already been his lot, to witness many scenes of horror, and ride over fields of blood.

We have said it was a silent journey. George's despair was too deep for words.

The first motion of the carriage affected the position of the corpse. George put one arm round it, and kept it immoveable. Sometimes, his scalding tears would fall on that cold face, whose outline yet preserved its beautiful roundness.

It appeared to Sir Henry, that he had never seen life and death, so closely and painfully contrasted. There sat his brother, in the full energies of manhood and despair; his features convulsed - his frame quivering - his sobs frequent - his pulse quick and disturbed.

There lay extended his mistress - cold - colourless - silent - unimpassioned. There was life in the breeze that played on her raven tresses - grim death was enthroned on the face those tresses swept.

Not that decay's finger had yet really assailed it; but one of the peculiar properties of the preservative used by Doctor Pormont, is its pervading sepulchral odour.

They reached Rome; and the consummation of their task drew nigh.

Pass we over the husband's last earthly farewell. Pass we over that subduing scene, in which Henry assisted George to sever long ringlets, and rob the cold finger, of affection's dearest pledge.

Alas! these might be retained as the legacy of love.

They were useless as love's memento. Memory, the faithful mirror, forbade the relic gatherer ever to forget!

Would you know where Acmé reposes?

A beautiful burial ground looks towards Rome. It is on a gentle declivity leaning to the south-east, and situated between Mount Aventine and the Monte Testaccio.

Its avenue is lined with high bushes of marsh roses; and the cemetery itself, is divided into three rude and impressive terraces.

There sleeps - in a modest nook, surmounted by the wall-flower, and by creeping ivy, and by many-coloured shrubs, and by one simple yellow flower, of very peculiar and rare fragrance; a type, as the author of these pages deemed, of the wonderful etherialised genius of the man - *there* sleeps, as posterity will judge him, the first of the poets of the age we live in - Percy Bysshe Shelley! There too, moulders that wonderful boy author - John Keats.

Who can pass his grave, and read that bitter inscription, dictated on his deathbed, by the heart-broken enthusiast, without the liveliest emotion?

> "Here lies one, whose name was writ in water.
> February 4th, 1821."

The ancient wall of Rome, crowns the ridge of the slope we have described. Above it, stands the pyramid of Caius Cæstius, constructed some twenty centuries since.

Immediately beneath it, in a line with a round tower buried with ivy, and near the vault of our beautiful countrywoman, Miss Bathurst, who was thrown from her horse and drowned in the Tiber, may be seen a sarcophagus of rough granite, surmounted by a black marble slab.

Luxuriant with wild flowers, and studded even in the winter season, with daisies and violets, the sides of the tomb are now almost concealed. Over the slab, one rose tree gracefully droops.

When seen in the dew of the morning, when the cups of the roses are full, and crystal drops, distilling from leaves and flowers, are slowly trickling on the dark stone, you might think that inanimate nature was weeping for the doom of beauty.

Only one word is engraved on that slab. Should you visit Rome, and read it, recollect this story.

That word is - "Acmé!"

* * * * *

Sir Henry and his brother remained at Rome nearly a month.

The former, with hopes that the exertion might be useful, in distracting George from the constant contemplation of his loss, plunged at once into the sight-seeing of "the eternal city."

Their days were busily passed - in visiting the classic sites of Rome and its neighbourhood - in wandering through the churches and convents - and loitering through the long galleries of the Vatican.

Delmé, fearfully looking back on the scenes that had occurred in Malta, was apprehensive, that George's despair might lead to some violent outbreak of feeling; and that mind and body might sink simultaneously.

It was not so.

That heavy infliction appeared to bear with it a torpedo-like power. The first blow, abrupt and stunning, had paralysed.

Afterwards, it seemed to carry with it a benumbing faculty, which repressed external display. We say *seemed*; for there were not wanting indications, even to Sir Henry's partial eye, that the wound had sunk very deep,

The mourner *might* sink, although he did not writhe.

In the mornings, George, followed by Thompson, would find his way to the Protestant burial ground; and weep over the spot where his wife lay interred.

During the day, he was Sir Henry's constant and gentle companion; giving vent to no passionate display, and uttering few unavailing complaints. Yet it was now, that a symptom of disease first showed itself, which Delmé could not account for.

George would suddenly lean back, and complain of a spasm on the left side of the chest. This would occasionally, but rarely, affect the circulation. George's sleep too, was disturbed, and he frequently had to rise from his bed, and pace the apartment; but this last circumstance, perhaps, was the mere result of anxiety of mind.

Sir Henry, without informing George, consulted a medical gentleman, who was well known to him, and who happened to be at Rome at the time, regarding these novel symptoms.

He was reassured by being informed, that these pains were probably of a neuralgic character, and not at all likely to proceed from any organic affection.

George Delmé's mind was perfectly clear and collected; with the exception, that he would occasionally allude to his loss, in connection with some scene or subject of interest before them; and in a tone, and with language, that, appeared to his brother eccentric, but inexpressibly touching.

For instance, they were at Tivoli, and in the Syren's grotto, looking up to the foaming fall, which dashes down a rude cleft, formed of fantastically shaped rocks.

Immediately below this, the waters make a semicircular bend.

On their surface, a mimic rainbow was depicted in vivid colours.

"Not for me!" burst forth the mourner, "not for me! does the arc of promise wear those radiant hues. Prismatic rays once gilded my existence. With Acmé they are for ever fled. But look! how the stream dashes on! Thus have the waters of bitterness passed over my soul!"

In the gallery of the Vatican, too, the very statues seemed to speak to him of his loss.

"I like not," would he exclaim, "that disdainful Apollo. Thus cold, callous, and triumphing in the work of destruction, must be the angel of death, who winged the shaft at my bright Acmé.

"May the launching of his arrow, have been but the signal, for her translation to a sphere, more pure than this.

"Let us believe her the habitant of some bright planet, such as she pointed out to us in the Bay of Naples - a seraph with a golden lyre - and shrouded in a white cymar! No, no!" would he continue, turning his footsteps towards the adjacent room, where the suffering pangs of Apollo's high priest are painfully told in marble, "let let me rather contemplate the Laocoon! His agony seems to sympathise with mine - but was his fate as hard? *He* saw his sons dying before him; could a son, or sons, be as the wife of one's bosom? The serpent twines around him, too, awaking exquisite corporeal pangs, but would it not have been luxury to have died with my Acmé?

"Can the body suffer as the mind?"

At night, reposing from the fatigues of the day, might the

brothers frequently be seen at the fountain of Trevi; George listlessly swinging on the chains near it, and steadfastly watching the water, as it gurgled over the fantastic devices beneath - while his mind wandered back to Malta, and to Acmé.

Sir Henry's conduct during this trying period was most exemplary. Like the mother, who lavishes her tenderest endearments on her sickliest child, did he now endeavour to support his brother in his afflictions.

As the bleak night wind came on, he would arouse George from his reverie - would make him lean his tall form on his - would wrap closely the folds of his cloak around him - would speak *so* softly - and soothe *so* tenderly.

And gratefully did George's heart respond to his kindness. He knew that the sorrow which bowed *him* to the earth, was also blanching the cheek of his brother, and he loved him doubly for his solicitude.

Ah! few brothers have thus made sweet the fraternal tie!

CHAPTER V

THE EAST INDIAN

> "Would I not stem
> A tide of suffering, rather than forego
> Such feelings for the hard and worldly phlegm
> Of those whose thoughts are only turn'd below,
> Gazing upon the ground, with thoughts that
> dare not glow?"

From Rome and our care-worn travellers, let us turn to Mrs. Vernon's drawing-room at Leamington.

An unforeseen event suddenly made a considerable change in the hopes and prospects of our fair friend Julia.

One warm summer's morning - it was on the very day, that the brothers, with Acmé, were sailing close to the Calabrian mountains, and the latter was telling her ghost story, within view of the sweet village of Capo del Marte - one balmy summer's morning, the Miss Vernons were seated in a room, furnished like most English drawing-rooms; that is to say, it had tables for trinkets - a superb mirror - a Broadwood piano - an Erard harp - a reclining sofa - and a woolly rug, on which slept, dreamt, and snored, a small Blenheim spaniel.

Julia had a mahogany frame before her, and was thoughtfully working a beaded purse.

The hue of health had left her cheek. Its complexion was akin to that of translucent alabaster. The features wore a more fixed and regular aspect, and their play was less buoyant and quick changing than heretofore.

Deep thought! thus has been thy warfare for ever. First, thou stealest from the rotund face its joyous dimples; then, dost thou gradually imprint remorseless furrows on the anxious brow.

A servant entered the room, and bore on a salver a letter addressed to Miss Vernon.

Its deep black binding - its large coat of arms - bespoke it death's official messenger.

Julia's cheek blanched as she glanced over its first page.

Her sisters laid down their work, and looked towards her with some curiosity.

Julia burst into tears.

"Poor uncle Vernon!"

Her sisters seemed surprised at the announcement, but not to participate in Julia's feelings on the occasion.

One of them took up the letter, which had fallen to the ground, and the two read its contents.

"How very odd!" said they together, "uncle has left you Hornby, and Catesfield, and almost all the property!"

"Has he?" replied Julia, "I could not read it all, for however he may have behaved to mamma, I ever found him good and kind; and had always hoped, that we might have yet seen him with us once more. Poor old man! and the letter says a lingering illness - how sad to think that we were not with him to soothe his pillow, and cheer his death bed!"

"Well!" said one of the sisters reddening, "I must say it was his own fault. He would not live with his nearest relations, who loved him, and tried to make his a happy home - but showed his caprice *then*, as he has *now*. But I will go up stairs, and break it to mamma, and will tell her you are an heiress."

"An heiress!" replied Julia, with heart-broken tone! "an heiress!" The tear quivered in her eye; but before the moisture had formed its liquid bead, to course down her pallid cheek; a thought flashed across her, which had almost the power to recal it to its cell.

That thought comprised the fervency and timidity - the hopes and fears of woman's first love. She thought of her last meeting with Sir Henry Delmé: of the objections which might now be removed.

A new vista of happiness seemed to open before her.

It was but for a moment.

The blush which that thought called up, faded away - the tear trickled on - her features recovered their serenity - and she turned with a sweet smile to her sisters.

"My dear - dear sisters! it is long since we have seen my poor uncle.

"Affection's ties may have been somewhat loosened. They cannot - I am sure - have been dissolved.

"Do not think me selfish enough to retain this generous bequest.

"It may yet be in my power, and it no doubt is, to amend its too partial provisions.

"Let us be sisters still - sisters in equality - sisters in love and affection."

Julia Vernon was a very noble girl. She lived to become of age, and she acted up to this her resolve.

And, now, a few words as to the individual, by whose death the Miss Vernons acquired such an accession of property.

The Miss Vernons' father had an only and a younger brother, who at an early age had embarked for the East, in the civil service. He had acquired great wealth, and, after a residence of twenty-five years in the Bengal Presidency, had returned to England a confirmed bachelor, and a wealthy nabob. His brother died, while Mr. Benjamin Vernon was on his passage home. He arrived in England, and found himself a stranger in his native land.

He shouldered his cane through Regent Street, and wandered in the Quadrant's shade; - and in spite of the novelties that every where met him - in spite of cabs and plated glass - felt perfectly isolated and miserable.

It is true, his Indian friends found him out at the Burlington, and their cards adorned his mantelpiece - for Mr. Benjamin Vernon was said to be worth a plum, and to be on the look out for a vacancy in the Directory.

But although these were indisputably his Indian friends, it appeared to Mr. Vernon, that they were no longer his friends of India. They seemed to him to live in a constant state of unnatural excitement.

Some prided themselves on being stars in fashion's gayest circle - others, whom he had hardly known, *were* fathers - for their families were educating in England - he now found surrounded by children, on whose provision they were wholly intent.

These were off at a tangent, "to see Peter Auber, at the India House," or, "could not wait an instant; they were to meet Josh: Alexander precisely at two."

And then their flippant sons! taking wine with him, forsooth – adjusting their neckcloths - and asking "whether he had met their father at Madras or Calcutta?"

This to a true Bengalee!

Nor was this all!

The young renegades ate their curry with a knife!

Others, from whom he had parted years before, shook hands with him at the Oriental, as if his presence there was a matter of course; and then asked him "what he thought of Stanley's speech?"

Now, there are few men breathing, who have their sympathies so keenly alive - who show and who look for, such warmth of heart - who are so chilled and hurt by indifference - as your bachelor East Indian.

The married one may solace himself for coldness abroad, by sunny smiles at home; - but the friendless bachelor is sick at heart, unless he encounter a hearty pressure of the hand - an eye that sparkles, as it catches his - an interested listener to his thousand and one tales of Oriental scenes, and of Oriental good fellowship.

Mr. Benjamin Vernon soon found this London solitude - it was worse than solitude - quite insupportable.

He determined to visit his brother's widow, and left town for Leamington. The brother-in-law felt more than gratified at the cordial welcome that there met him.

His heart responded to their tones of kindness, and the old

Indian, in the warmth of his gratitude, thought he had at length discovered a congenial home. He plunged into the extreme of dangerous intimacy; and was soon domiciled in Mrs. Vernon's small mansion.

It is absurd what trifles can extinguish friendships, and estrange affection. Mr. Vernon had always had the controul of his hours - loved his hookah, and his after-dinner dose.

His brother's widow was an amiable person, but a great deal too independent, to humour any person's foibles.

She liked activity, and disliked smoking; and was too matter-of-fact in her ideas, to conceive that these indulgences, merely from force of habit, might have now become absolute necessities.

Mrs. Vernon first used arguments; which were listened to very patiently, and as systematically disregarded.

As she thought she knew her ground better, she would occasionally secrete the hookah, and indulge in eloquent discourse, on the injurious effects, and waste of time, that the said hookah entailed.

Nor could the old man enjoy in peace, his evening slumber.

One of his nieces was always ready to shake him by the elbow, and address him with an expostulatory "Oh! dear uncle!" which, though delivered with silvery voice, seemed to him deuced provoking.

For some time, the old Indian good-naturedly acquiesced in these arrangements; and was far too polite at any time to scold, or hazard a scene.

Mrs. Vernon was all complacency, and imagined her triumph assured.

Suddenly the tempest gathered to a head. Bachelor habits regained their ascendancy; and Mrs. Vernon was thunderstruck, when it was one morning duly announced to her, that her brother-in-law had purchased a large estate in Monmouthshire, and that he intended permanently to reside there.

Mrs. Vernon was deeply chagrined.

She thought him ungrateful, and told him so.

At the outset, our East Indian was anxious that his niece Julia, who had been by far the most tolerant of his bachelor vices, should preside over his new establishment; but the feelings of the mother and daughter were alike opposed to this arrangement.

This was the last rock on which he and his brother's widow split; and it was decisive.

From that hour, all correspondence between them ceased.

Arrived in Wales, our nabob endeavoured to attach himself to country pursuits - purchased adjoining estates - employed many labourers - and greatly improved his property. But his rural occupations were quite at variance with his acquired habits.

He pined away - became hypochondriacal - and died, just three years after leaving Mrs. Vernon, for want of an Eastern sun, and something to love.

CHAPTER VI

VEIL

"The seal is set."

On the day fixed for the departure of Sir Henry Delmé and his brother, they together visited once more the sumptuous pile of St. Peter's, and heard the voices of the practised choristers swell through the mighty dome, as the impressive service of the Catholic Church was performed by the Pope and his conclave.

The morning dawn had seen George, as was his daily custom in Rome, kneeling beside the grave of Acmé, and breathing a prayer for their blissful reunion in heaven.

As the widower staggered from that spot, the thought crossed him, and bitterly poignant was that thought, that now might he bid a second earthly farewell, to what had been his pride, and household solace.

Now, indeed, "was the last link broken." Each hour - each traversed league - was to bear him away from even the remains of his heart's treasure.

Their bones must moulder in a different soil.

It was Sir Henry's choice that they should on that day visit Saint Peter's; and well might the travellers leave Rome with so unequalled an object fresh in the mind's eye.

Whether we gaze on its exterior of faultless proportions - or on the internal arrangement, where perfect symmetry reigns; - whether we consider the glowing canvas - or the inspired marble, - or the rich mosaics; - whether with the enthusiasm of the devotee, we bend before those gorgeous shrines; or with the comparative apathy of a cosmopolite, reflect on the historical recollections with which that edifice - the focus of the rays of Catholicism - teems and must teem forever; - we must in truth acknowledge, that *there* alone is the one matchless temple, in strict and perfect harmony with Imperial Rome.

Gazing there - or recalling in after years its unclouded majesty - the delighted pilgrim knows neither shade of disappointment - nor doth he harbour one thought of decay.

Where is the other building in the "eternal city," of which we can say thus much?

Sir Henry Delmé had engaged a vettura, which was to convey them with the same horses as far as Florence.

This arrangement made them masters of their own time, and was perhaps in their case, the best that could be adopted; for slowness of progress, which is its greatest objection, was rather desirable in George's then state of health.

As is customary, Delmé made an advance to the vetturino, who usually binds himself to defray all the expenses at the inns on the road.

The travellers dined early - left Rome in the afternoon - and proposed pushing on to Neppi during the night.

When about four miles on their journey, Delmé observed a mausoleum on the side of the road, which appeared of ancient date, and rather curious construction.

On consulting his guide-book, he found it designated as the tomb of Nero.

On examining its inscription, he saw that it was erected to the memory of a Prefect of Sardinia; and he inwardly determined to distrust his guide-book on all future occasions.

The moon was up as they reached the post-house of Storta.

The inn, or rather tavern, was a small wretched looking building, with a large courtyard attached, but the stables appeared nearly - if not quite - untenanted.

Sir Henry's surprise and anger were great, when the driver, coolly stopping his horses, commenced taking off their harness; - and informed the travellers, that *there* must they remain, until he had received some instructions from his owner, which he expected by a vettura leaving Rome at a later hour.

It was in vain that the brothers expostulated, and reminded him of his agreement to stop when they pleased, expressing their determination to proceed.

The driver was dogged and unmoved; and the travellers had neglected to draw up a written bargain, which is a precaution absolutely necessary in Italy.

They soon found they had no alternative but to submit. It was with a very bad grace they did so, for Englishmen have a due abhorrence of imposition.

They at length stepped from the vehicle - indulged in some vehement remonstrances - smiled at Thompson's voluble execrations, which they found were equally unavailing - and were finally obliged to give up the point.

They were shown into a small room. The chief inmates were some Papal soldiers of ruffianly air, engaged in the clamorous game of moro. Unlike the close shorn Englishmen, their beards and mustachios, were allowed to grow to such length, as to hide the greater part of the face.

Their animated gestures and savage countenances, would have accorded well with a bandit group by Salvator.

The landlord, an obsequious little man, with face pregnant with mischievous cunning, was watching with interest, the turns of the game; and assisting his guests, to quaff his vino ordinario, which Sir Henry afterwards found was ordinary enough.

Delmé's equanimity of temper was already considerably disturbed.

The scanty accommodation afforded them, by no means diminished his choler; which he began to expend on the obstinate driver, who had followed them into the room, and was busily placing chairs round one of the tables.

"See what you can get for supper, you rascal!"

"Signore! there are some excellent fowls, and the very best wine of Velletri."

The wine was produced and proved vinegar.

The host bustled away loud in its praise, and a few seconds afterwards, the dying shriek of a veteran tenant of the poultry yard, warned them that supper was preparing.

"Thompson!" said George, rather languidly, "do, like a good fellow, see that they put no garlic with the fowl!"

"I will, Sir," replied the domestic; "and the wine, Mr. George, seems none of the best. I have a flask of brandy in the rumble."

"Just the thing!" said Sir Henry.

To their surprise, the landlord proffered sugar and lemons.

Sir Henry's countenance somewhat brightened, and he declared he would make punch.

Punch! thou just type of matrimony! thy ingredients of sweets and bitters so artfully blended, that we know not which predominate, - so deceptive, too, that we imbibe long and potent draughts, nor awake to a consciousness of thy power, till awoke by headache.

Hail to thee! all hail!

Thy very name, eked out by thine appropriate receptacle, recals raptures past - bids us appreciate joys present - and enjoins us duly to reverence thee, if we hope for joys in futurity.

A bowl of punch! each merry bacchanal rises at the call!

Moderate bacchanals all! for where is the abandoned sot, who would not rather dole out his filthy lucre, on an increase of the mere alchohol - than expend it on those grateful adjuncts, which, throwing a graceful veil over that spirit's grossness, impart to it its chief and its best attraction.

Up rises then each hearty bacchanal! thrice waving the clear tinkling crystal, ere he emits that joyful burst, fresh from the heart, which from his uncontrolled emotion, meets the ear husky and indistinct.

Delmé squeezed the lemons into not a bad substitute for a bowl, viz. a red earthen vase of rough workmanship, but elegant shape, somewhat resembling a modern wine cooler.

George stood at the inn door, wistfully looking upward; when he remarked an intelligent boy of fourteen, with dark piercing eyes, observing him somewhat earnestly.

On finding he was noticed, he approached with an air of ingenuous embarrassment - pulled off his cap - and said in a tone of enquiry,

"Un Signore Inglese?"

"Yes! my fine fellow! Do you know anything of me or the English?"

"Oh yes!" replied the boy with vivacity, replacing his cap, "I have travelled in England, and like London very much."

George conversed with him for some time; and found him to be one of that class, whose numbers make us unmindful of their wants or their loneliness; who eke out a miserable pittance, by carrying busts of plaster-of-Paris - grinding on an organ - or displaying through Europe, the tricks of some poodle dog, or the eccentricities of a monkey disguised in scarlet.

It is rare that these come from a part of Italy so far south; but it appeared in this instance, that Giuseppe's father being a carrier, had taken him with him to Milan - had there met a friend, rich in an organ and porcupine - and had entrusted the boy to his care, in order that he might see the world, and make his fortune.

Giuseppe gave a narrative of some little events, that had occurred to him during his wanderings, which greatly interested George; and he finally concluded, by saying that his father had now retired to his native place at Barberini, where many strangers came to see the "antichità." George, on referring to the guide book, found that this was indeed the case; and that Isola Barberini is marked as the site of ancient Veii, the rival of young Rome.

"And when do you go there, youngster, and how far is it from this?"

"I am going now, Signore, to be in time for supper. It is only a 'piccolo giro' across the fields; and looks as well by moonlight as at any other time."

"Ah!" replied George, "I would be glad to accompany you. Henry," said he, as he entered the room of the inn, "I am away on a classic excursion to Veii. The night is lovely - I have an excellent guide - and shall be back before you have finished your punch making.

"*Do* let me go!" and he lowered his voice, and the tears swam in his eyes, "I cannot endure these rude sounds of merriment, and a moonlight walk will at least afford nothing that can *thus* pain me."

Sir Henry looked out. The night was perfectly fine. The young peasant, all willingness, had already shouldered his bundle, and was preparing to move forward.

"You must not be late, George," said his brother, assenting to his proposal. "Do not stay too long about the ruins. Remember that you are still delicate, and that I shall wait supper for you."

As the boy led on, George followed him in a foot path, which led through fields of meadow land, corn, and rye.

The fire-flies - mimic meteors - were giddily winging their way from bush to bush, - illuming the atmosphere, and imparting to the scene a glittering beauty, which a summer night in a northern clime cannot boast.

As they approached somewhat nearer to the hamlet, their course was over ground more rugged; and the disjointed fragments of rocks strewed, and at intervals obstructed, the path.

The cottages were soon reached.

The villagers were all in front of their dwellings, taking their last meal for the day, in the open air.

The young guide stopped in front of a cottage, a little apart from the rest. The family party were seated round a rude table, on which were plates and napkins.

Before the master of the house - a wrinkled old man, with long grey hair - was a smoking tureen of bread soup, over which he was in the act of sprinkling some grated Parmesan cheese.

A plate of green figs, and a large water melon - the cocomero - made up the repast.

"Giuseppe! you are late for supper," said the old patriarch, as the boy approached to whisper his introduction of the stranger.

The old man waved his hand courteously - made a short apology for the humble viands - and pointed to a vacant seat.

"Many thanks," said George, "but my supper already awaits me. I will not, however, interfere with my young guide. Show me the ruins, Giuseppe, and I will trouble you no further."

The boy moved on towards what were indeed ruins, or rather the vestige of such.

Here a misshapen stone - there a shattered column - decaying walls, overgrown with nettles - arches and caves, choked up with rank vegetation - bespoke remains unheeded, and but rarely visited.

George threw the boy a piece of silver - heard his repeated cautions as to his way to Storta - and wished him good night, as he hurried back to the cottage.

George Delmé sat on the shaft of a broken pillar, his face almost buried in his hands, as he looked around him on a scene once so famous.

But with him classic feelings were not upper-most. The widowed heart mourned its loneliness; and in that calm hour found the full relief of tears.

The mourner rose, and turned his face homeward, slowly - sadly - but resignedly.

The heavens had become more overcast - and clouds occasionally were hiding the moon.

It was with some difficulty that George avoided the pieces of rock which obstructed the path.

The road seemed longer, and wilder, than he had previously thought it.

Suddenly the loud bay of dogs was borne to his ear; and almost, before he had time to turn from the path, two large hounds brushed past him, followed by a rider - his gun slung before his saddle - and his horse fearlessly clattering over the loose stones.

The horseman seemed a young Roman farmer. He did not salute, and probably did not observe our traveller. As the sound from the horse receded, and the clamour of the dogs died away, a feeling almost akin to alarm crossed George's mind.

George was one, however, who rarely gave way to vague fears.

It so happened that he was armed.

Delancey had made him a present of a brace of pocket pistols, during the days of their friendship; and, very much to Sir Henry's annoyance, George had been in the habit, since leaving Malta, of constantly carrying these about him.

He strode on without adventure, until entering the field of rye.

The pathway became very narrow - so that on either side him, he grazed against the bearded ears.

Suddenly he heard a rustling sound. The moon at the moment broke from a dark cloud, and he fancied he discerned a figure near him half hid by the rye.

Again the moon was shrouded.

A rustling again ensued.

George felt a ponderous blow, which, aimed at the left shoulder, struck his left arm.

The collar of his coat was instantaneously grasped.

For a moment, George Delmé felt irresolute - then drew a pistol from his pocket and fired.

The hold was loosened - a man fell at his feet.

The pistol's flash revealed another figure, which diving into the corn - fled precipitately.

Let us turn to Sir Henry Delmé and to Thompson.

For some time after George's departure, they were busily engaged in preparing supper.

While they were thus occupied, they noticed that the Papal soldiers whispered much together - but this gave rise to no suspicion on their part.

One by one the soldiers strolled out, and the landlord betook himself to the kitchen.

The punch was duly made, and Sir Henry, leaving the room,

paced thoughtfully in front of the inn.

At length it struck him, that it was almost time for his brother to return.

He was entering the inn, for the purpose of making some enquiries; when he saw one of the soldiers cross the road hurriedly, and go into the courtyard, where he was immediately joined by the vetturino.

Delmé turned in to the house, and called for the landlord.

Before the latter could appear, George rushed into the room.

His hat was off - his eyes glared wildly - his long hair streamed back, wet with the dews of night. He dragged with him the body of one of the soldiers; and threw it with supernatural strength into the very centre of the room.

"Supper!" said he, "ha, ha, ha! *I* have brought you supper!"

The man was quite dead.

The bullet had pierced his neck and throat. The blood was yet flowing, and had dabbled the white vest. His beard and hair were clotted with gore.

Shocked as Sir Henry was, the truth flashed on him. He lost not a moment in beckoning to Thompson, and rushing towards the stable. The driver was still there, conversing with the soldier.

As Sir Henry approached, they evinced involuntary confusion; and the vetturino - at once unmanned - fell on his knees, and commenced a confession.

They were dragged into the inn, and the officers of justice were sent for.

Sir Henry Delmé's anxious regards were now directed to his brother.

George had taken a seat near the corpse; and was sternly regarding it with fixed, steady, and unflinching gaze.

It is certainly very fearful to mark the dead - with pallid complexion - glazed eye - limbs fast stiffening - and gouts of blood - standing from out the face, like crimson excrescences on a diseased leaf.

But it is far more fearful than even this, to look on one, who is bound to us by the nearest and most cherished ties - with cheek yet glowing - expression's flush mantling still - and yet to doubt whether the intellect, which adorned that frame - the jewel in the casket - hath not for ever left its earthly tenement.

CHAPTER VII

THE VETTURINI

"Far other scene is Thrasymene now."

* * * * *

"Fair Florence! at thy day's decline
When came the shade from Appennine,
And suddenly on blade and bower
The fire-flies shed the sparkling shower,
As if all heaven to earth had sent
Each star that gems the firmament;
'Twas sweet at that enchanting hour,
To bathe in fragrance of the Italian clime,
By Arno's stream."

The brothers were detained a few days at Storta; while the Roman police, who, to do them justice, were active on the occasion, and showed every anxiety to give the travellers as little trouble as possible - were investigating the occurrences we have described. It appeared that some suspicion had previously attached itself to Vittore Santado, and that the eyes of the police had been on him for some time.

It now became evident, both from his own confession, and subsequent discoveries, that this man had for years trafficked in the lives and property of others; - and that the charge connected with George, was one of the least grave, that would be brought against him.

It was shown that he was an active agent, in aiding the infamous designs of that inn, on the Italian frontier, whose enormities have given rise to more than one thrilling tale of fiction, far out-done by the reality - that inn - where the traveller retired to rest - but rose not refreshed to prosecute his journey: - where - if he slumbered but once, that sleep was his last.

Until now, his career had been more than usually successful.

The crafty vetturino had had the art to glean a fair reputation even from his crimes.

More than once, had he induced a solitary traveller to leave the high road and his carriage, for the purpose of visiting some ruin, or viewing some famous prospect.

On such occasions, Vittore's accomplices were in waiting; and the unsuspecting stranger - pillaged and alarmed, would return to the vettura penniless.

Vittore would be foremost in his commiseration; and with an air of blunt sincerity, would proffer the use of his purse; such conduct ensuring the gratitude, and the after recommendations of his dupe.

It is supposed that the vetturino had contemplated rifling the carriage in the inn yard; but some suspicion as to the servant's not leaving the luggage, and the sort of dog fidelity displayed by Thompson towards the brothers; had induced him rather to sanction an attempt on George during his imprudent excursion to Barberini.

Vittore Santado was executed near the Piazza del Popolo, and to this day, over the chimney-piece of many a Roman peasant, may be seen the tale of his crimes - his confessions - and his death; which perused by casual neighbour guests - calls up many a sign of the cross - and devout look of rustic terror.

After the incident we have related in the last chapter, George Delmé, contrary to Sir Henry's previous misgivings, enjoyed a good night's rest, and arose tolerably calm and refreshed.

The following night he was attacked with palpitation of the heart.

His brother and Thompson felt greatly alarmed; but after an hour's severe suffering, the paroxysm left him.

Nothing further occurred at Storta, to induce them to attach very great importance to the shock George's nerves had experienced; but in after life, Sir Henry always thought, he could date many fatal symptoms from that hour of intense excitement.

Delmé was in Rome two days; during which period, his depositions, as connected with Santado, were taken down; and he was informed that his presence during the trial would not be insisted on.

Delmé took that opportunity again to consult his medical friend; who accompanied him to Storta, to visit George; and prescribed a regimen calculated to invigorate the general system.

He directed Delmé not to be alarmed, should the paroxysm return; and recommended, that during the attack, George should lie down quietly - and take twenty drops of Battley's solution of opium in a wine glass of water.

As his friend did not appear alarmed, Delmé's mind was once more assured; and he prepared to continue their journey to Florence, by the way of Perugia.

Punctual to his time, the new vetturino - as to whose selection

Sir Henry had been very particular - arrived at Storta; and the whole party, with great willingness left the wretched inn, and its suspicious inmates.

There certainly could not be a greater contrast, than between the two Vetturini.

Vittore Santado was a Roman; young - inclined to corpulency - oily faced - plausible - and a most consummate rascal.

Pietro Molini was a Milanese; - elderly - with hardly an ounce of flesh on his body - with face scored and furrowed like the surface of the hedge pippin - rough in his manners - and the most honest of his tribe.

Poor Pietro Molini! never did driver give more cheering halloo to four-footed beast! or with spirit more elate, deliver in the drawling patois of his native paesi, some ditty commemorative of Northern liberty! Honest Pietro! thy wishes were contained within a small compass! Thy little brown cur, snarling and bandy-legged - thy raw-boned steeds - these were thy first care; - the safety of thy conveyance, and its various inmates, the second.

To thee - the most delightful melody in this wide world, was the jingling of thy horses' bells, as all cautiously and slowly they jogged on their way: - the most discordant sound in nature, the short husky cough, emitted from the carcase of one of these, as disease and continued fatigue made their sure inroads.

Poor simple Pietro! his only pride was encased in his breeches pocket, and it lay in a few scraps of paper - remembrances of his passengers.

One and all lavished praise on Pietro!

Yes! we have him again before us as we write - his ill-looking, but easy carriage - his three steeds - the rude harness, eked out with clustering knots of rope - and the happy driver, seated on a narrow bench, jutting over the backs of his wheelers, as he contentedly whiffs from his small red clay pipe - at intervals dropping off in a dose, with his cur on his lap. At such a time, with what perfect nonchalance would he open his large grey eyes, when recalled to the sense of his duties, by the volubly breathed execration of some rival whip - and with what a silent look of ineffable contempt, would he direct his horses to the side of the road, and again steep his senses in quiescent repose.

At night, Pietro's importance would sensibly increase, as after rubbing down the hides of his favourites, and dropping into the capacious manger the variegated oats; he would wait on his passengers to arrange the hour of departure - would accept the proffered glass of wine, and give utterance to his ready joke.

A King might have envied Pietro Molini, as - the straw rustling beneath him - he laid down in his hairy capote, almost between the legs of his favourite horse.

To do so will be to anticipate some years!

Yet we would fain relate the end of the Vetturino.

Crossing from Basle to Strasbourg, in the depth of winter, and descending an undulated valley, Pietro slept as usual.

Implicitly relying on the sure footedness of his horses, a fond dream of German beer, German tobacco, and German sauer-kraut, soothed his slumbers.

A fragment of rock had been loosened from its ancient bed, and lay across the road.

Against this the leader tripped and fell.

The shock threw Pietro and his dog from their exalted station.

The pipe, which - whether he were sleeping or waking - had

long decked the cheek of the honest driver, now fell from it, and was dashed into a thousand pieces.

It was an evil omen.

When the carriage was stopped, Pietro Molini was found quite lifeless. He had received a kick from the ungrateful heel of his friend Bruno, and the wheel of the carriage, it had been his delight to clean, had passed over the body of the hapless vetturino.

Ah! as that news spread! many an ostler of many a nation, shook his head mournfully, and with saddened voice, wondered that the same thing had not occurred years before.

At the time, however, to which we allude - viz., the commencement of the acquaintance between our English travellers, and Pietro; the latter thought of anything rather than of leaving a world for which he had an uncommon affection.

He and Thompson soon became staunch allies; and the want of a common language seemed only to cement their union.

Not Noblet, in her inimitable performance of the Muette, threw more expression into her sweet face - than did Pietro, into the furrowed lines of his bronzed visage, as he endeavoured to explain to his friend some Italian custom, or the reason why he had selected another dish, or other wine; rather than that, to which they had done such justice the previous day.

Thompson's gestures and countenance in reply, partook of a more stoical character; but he was never found wanting, when a companion was needed for a bottle or a pipe.

Their friendship was not an uninstructive one.

It would have edified him, who prides himself on his deep

knowledge of human nature, or who seizes with avidity on the minuter traits of a nation, to note with what attention the English valet, would listen to a Milanese arietta; whose love notes, delivered by the unmusical Pietro, were about as effectively pathetic as the croak of the bull frog in a marsh, or screech of owl sentimentalising in ivied ruin; and to mark with what gravity, the Italian driver would beat his hand against the table; in tune to "Ben Baxter," or "The British Grenadiers," roared out more Anglico.

There are two grand routes from Home to Florence: - the one is by Perugia, the other passes through Sienna. The former, which is the one Sir Henry selected, is the most attractive to the ordinary traveller; who is enabled to visit the fall of Terni, Thrasymene, and th temple of Clitumnuss The first, despite its being artificial, is equal in our opinion, to the vaunted Schaffhausen; - the second is hallowed in story; - and the third has been illustrated by Byron.

"Pass not unblest the genius of the place!
If through the air a zephyr more serene
Win to the brow, 'tis his; and if ye trace
Along the margin a more eloquent green,
If on the heart, the freshness of the scene
Sprinkle its coolness, and from the dry dust
Of weary life a moment lave it clean
With nature's baptism, - 'tis to him ye must
Pay orisons for this suspension of disgust."

Poor George Delmé showed little interest in anything connected with this journey. Sir Henry embarked on the lake above, in order to see the cascade of Terni in every point of view; and afterwards took his station with George, on various ledges of rock below the fall - whence the eye looks upward, on that mystic scene of havoc, turbulence, and mighty rush of water.

But the cataract fell in snowy sheet - the waves hissed round the sable rocks - and the rainbow played on the torrent's foam;

- but these possessed not a charm, to rouse to a sense of their beauty, the sad heart of the invalid.

Near the lake of Thrasymene, they passed some hours; allowing Pietro to put up his horses at Casa di Piano. Sir Henry, with a Livy in his hand, first proceeded to the small eminence, looking down on the round tower of Borghetto; and on that insidious pass, which his fancy peopled once more, with the advancing troops of the Consul.

The soldier felt much interested, and attempted to impart that interest to George; but the widowed husband shook his head mournfully; and it was evident, that his thoughts were not with Flaminius and his entrapped soldiers, but with the gentle Acmé, mouldering in her lonely grave.

From Borghetto, they proceeded to the village of Torre, where Delmé was glad to accept the hospitable offer of its Priest, and procure seats for himself and George, in the balcony of his little cottage. From this point, they looked down on the arena of war.

There it lay, serene and basking in the rays of the meridian sun.

On either side, were the purple summits of the Gualandra hills.

Beneath flowed the little rivulet, once choked by the bodies of the combatants; but which now sparkled gaily through the valley, although at intervals, almost dried up by the fierce heat of summer.

The lake was tranquil and unruffled - all on its margin, hushed and moveless. What a contrast to that exciting hour, which Sir Henry was conjuring up again; when the clang of arms, and crash of squadrons, commingled with the exulting shout, that bespoke the confident hope of the wily Carthaginian; and with that sterner response, which hurled back the indomitable spirit of the unyielding, but despairing Roman!

Our travellers quitted the Papal territories; and entering Tuscany, passed through Arezzo, the birth-place of Petrarch; arriving at Florence just previous to sunset.

As they reached the Lung' Arno, Pietro put his horses to a fast trot, and rattling over the flagged road, drew up in front of Schneidorff's with an air of greater importance, than his sorry vehicle seemed to warrant.

The following morning, George Delmé was taken by his brother, to visit the English physician resident at Florence; and again was Delmé informed, that change of scene, quiet, and peace of mind, were what his brother most required.

George was thinner perhaps, than when at Rome, and his lip had lost its lustrous red; but he concealed his physical sufferings, and always met Henry with the same soft undeviating smile.

On their first visit to the Tribune, George was struck with the Samian Sibyl of Guercino.

In the glowing lip - the silken cheek - the ivory temple - the eye of inspiration - the bereaved mourner thought he could trace, some faint resemblance to the lost Acmé. Henceforward, it was his greatest pleasure, to remain with eyes fixed on that masterpiece of art.

Sir Henry Delmé, accompanied by the custode, would make himself acquainted with the wonders of the Florentine gallery; and every now and then, return to whisper some sentence, in the soothing tones of brotherly kindness. At night, their usual haunt was the public square - where the loggio of Andrea Orcagna presents so much, that may claim attention.

There stands the David! in the freshness of his youth! proudly regarding his adversary - ere he overthrow, with the weapon of the herdsman, the haughty giant.

The inimitable Perseus, too! the idol of that versatile genius, Benvenuto Cellini: - an author! a goldsmith! a cunning artificer in jewels! a founder in bronze! a sculptor in marble! the prince of good fellows! the favored of princes! the warm friend and daring lover! as we gaze on his glorious performance, and see beside it the Hercules, and Cacus of his rival Baccio Bandanelli, - we seem to live again in those days, with which Cellini has made us so familiar: - and almost naturally regard the back of the bending figure, to note if its muscles warrant the stinging sarcasm of Cellini, which we are told at once dispelled the pride of the aspiring artist - "that they resembled cucumbers!"

The rape of the Sabines, too! the white marble glistening in the obscurity, until the rounded shape of the maiden seems to elude the strong grasp of the Roman!

Will she ever fly from him thus? will the home of her childhood be ever as dear? No! the husband's love shall replace the father's blessing; and the affections of the daughter, shall yield to the tender yearnings of the mother's bosom.

We marvel not that George's footsteps lingered there!

How often have *we* - martyrs to a hopeless nympholepsy - strayed through that piazza, at the self same hour - there deemed that the heart would break - but never thought that it might slowly wither.

How often have *we* gleaned from those beauteous objects around, but aliment to our morbid griefs; - and turning towards the gurgling fountain of Ammonati, and gazing on its trickling waters, have vainly tried to arrest our trickling tears!

CHAPTER VIII

ARGUÀ

"There is a tomb in Arquà: rear'd in air,
Pillar'd in their sarcophagus, repose
The bones of Laura's lover."

* * * * *

"I stood in Venice on the Bridge of Sighs."

How glorious is the thrill, which shoots through our frame, as we first wake to the consciousness of our intellectual power; as we feel the spirit - the undying spirit - ready to burst the gross bonds of flesh, and soar triumphant, over the sneers of others, and our own mistrust.

How does each thought seem to swell in our bosom, as if impatient of the confined tenement - how do the floating ideas congregate - how does each impassioned feeling subdue us in turn, and long for a worthy utterance!

This is a very bright moment in the history of our lives. It is one in which we feel - indubitably feel - that we are of the fashioning of God; - that the light which intellect darts around us, is not the result of education - of maxims inculcated - or of principles instilled; - but that it is a ray caught from the brightness of eternity - that when our wavering pulse has ceased to beat, and the etherialised elements have left the baser and the useless dust - that ray shall not be quenched; but shall again be absorbed in the full effulgence from which it emanated.

Surely then, if such a glorious moment as this, be accorded to even the inferior votaries of knowledge - to the meaner pilgrims, struggling on towards the resplendent shrines of science: - how must *he* - the divine Petrarch, who could so exquisitely delineate love's hopes and story, as to clothe an earthly passion, with half the attributes of an immortal affection: - how must *he* have revelled in the proud sensations called forth at such a moment!

It is the curse of the poet, that he must perforce leave the golden atmosphere of loftiest aspirations - step from the magic circle, where all is pure and etherial - and find himself the impotent denizen, of a sombre and an earthly world,

It was in the early part of September, that the brothers turned their backs on the Etrurian Athens. Their destination was Venice, and their route lay through Bologna and Arquà.

They had been so satisfied, under the guidance of their old vetturino, that Sir Henry made an arrangement, which induced him to be at Florence, at the time of their departure; - and Pietro and Thompson were once more seated beside each other.

Before commencing the ascent of the Appennines, our travellers visited the country seat of the Archduke; saw the gigantic statue executed by John of Bologna, which frowns over the lake; and at Fonte-buona, cast a farewell glance on Florence, and the ancient Fiesole.

As they advanced towards Caravigliojo, the mountains began to be more formidable, and the scenery to lose its smiling character.

Each step seemed to add to the barrenness of the landscape.

The wind came howling down from the black volcanic looking ridges - then swept tempestuously through some deep ravine.

On either side the road, tall red poles presented themselves, a guide to the traveller during winter's snows; while, in one exposed gully, were built large stone embankments for his protection - as a Latin inscription intimated - from the violence of the gales.

Few signs of life appeared.

Here and there, her white kerchief shading a sun-burnt face, a young Bolognese shepherd girl might be seen on some grassy ledge, waving her hand coquettishly; while her neglected flock, with tinkling bell, browsed on the edge of the precipice. As they neared Bologna, however, the scenery changed.

Festoons of grapes, trained to leafy elms, began to appear - white villas chequered the suburbs - and it was with a pleasurable feeling, that they neared the peculiar looking city, with its leaning towers, and old façades. It is the only one, where the Englishman recals Mrs, Ratcliffe's harrowing tales; and half expects to see a Schedoni, advancing from some covered portico.

The next day found them in the Bolognese gallery, which is the first which duly impresses the traveller, coming from the north, with the full powers of the art.

The soul of music seems to dwell in the face of the St. Cecilia; and the cup of maternal anguish to be filled to the brim, as in Guide's Murder of the Innocents, the mother clasps to her arms the terrified babe, and strives to flee from the ruthless destroyer.

It was on the fourth morning from their arrival in Bologna, that they approached the poet's "mansion and his sepulchre."

As they threaded the green windings of vine covered hills, these gradually assumed a bolder outline, and, rising in separate cones, formed a sylvan amphitheatre round the lovely village of Arquà.

The road made an abrupt ascent to the Fontana Petrarca. A large ruined arch spanned a fine spring, that rushes down the green slope.

In the church-yard, on the right, is the tomb of Petrarch.

Its peculiarly bold elevation - the numberless thrilling associations connected with the poet - gave a tone and character to the whole scene. The chiaro-scuro of the landscape, was from the light of his genius - the shade of his tomb.

The day was lovely - warm, but not oppressive. The soft green of the hills and foliage, checked the glare of the flaunting sunbeams.

The brothers left the carriage to gaze on the sarcophagus of red marble, raised on pilasters; and could not help deeming even the indifferent bronze bust of Petrarch, which surmounts this, to be a superfluous ornament in such a scene.

The surrounding landscape - the dwelling place of the poet - his tomb facing the heavens, and disdaining even the shadow of trees - the half-effaced inscription of that hallowed shrine - all these seemed appropriate, and melted the gazer's heart.

How useless! how intrusive! are the superfluous decorations of art, amid the simpler scenes of nature.

Ornament is here misplaced. The feeling heart regrets its presence at the time, and attempts, albeit in vain, to banish it from after recollections.

George could not restrain his tears, for he thought of the dead; and they silently followed their guide to Petrarch's house, now partly used as a granary. Passing through two or three unfinished rooms, whose walls were adorned with rude frescoes of the lover and his mistress, they were shown into Petrarch's chamber, damp and untenanted.

In the closet adjoining, were the chair and table consecrated by the poet.

There did he sit - and write - and muse - and die!

George turned to a tall narrow window, and looked out on a scene, fair and luxuriant as the garden of Eden.

The rich fig trees, with their peculiar small, high scented fruit, mixed with the vines that clustered round the lattice.

The round heads of the full bearing peach trees, dipped down in a leafy slope beneath a grassy walk; - and this thicket of fruit was charmingly enlivened, by bunches of the scarlet pomegranate, now in the pride of their blossom.

The poet's garden alone was neglected - rank herbage choking up its uncultivated flowers.

A thousand thoughts filled the mind of George Delmé.

He thought of Laura! of his own Acmé!

With swimming glance, he looked round the chamber.

It was almost without furniture, and without ornament. In a niche, and within a glass case, was placed the skeleton of a dumb favourite of Petrarch's.

Suddenly George Delmé felt a faintness stealing over him: - and he turned to bare his forehead, to catch the slight breeze from below redolent of sweets.

This did not relieve him.

A sharp pain across the chest, and a fluttering at the heart, as of a bird struggling to be free, succeeded this faintness.

Another rush of blood to the head: - and a snap, as of some tendon, was distinctly felt by the sufferer.

His mouth filled with blood.

A small blood-vessel had burst, and temporary insensibility ensued.

Sir Henry was wholly unprepared for this scene.

Assisted by Thompson, he bore him to the carriage - sprinkled his face with water - and administered cordials.

George's recovery was speedy; and it almost seemed, as if the rupture of the vessel had been caused by the irregular circulation, for no further bad effects were felt at the time.

The loss of blood, however, evidently weakened him; and his spasms henceforward were more frequent.

He became less able to undergo fatigue; and his mind, probably in connection with the nervous system, became more than ordinarily excited.

There was no longer wildness in his actions; but in his thoughts and language, was developed a poetical eccentricity - a morbid sympathy with surrounding scenes and impressions, which kept Sir Henry Delmé in a constant state of alarm, - and which was very remarkable.

* * * * *

"What! at Mestré already, Pietro?" said Sir Henry.

"Even so, Signore! and here is the gondola to take you on to Venice."

"Well, Pietro! you must not fail to come and see us at the inn."

The vetturino touched his hat, with the air of a man who would be very sorry *not* to see them.

It was not long ere the glittering prow of the gondola pointed to Venice.

Before the travellers, rose ocean's Cybele; springing from the waters, like some fairy city, described to youthful ear by aged lip.

The fantastic dome of St. Mark - the Palladian churches - the columned palaces - the sable gondolas shooting through the canals - made its aspect, as is its reality, unique in the world.

"Beautiful, beautiful city!" said George, his eye lighting up as he spoke, "thou dost indeed look a city of the heart - a resting place for a wearied spirit. And our gondola, Henry, should be of burnished silver; and those afar - so noiselessly cutting their way through the glassy surface - those should be angels with golden wings; and, instead of an oar flashing freely, a snowy wand of mercy should beat back the kissing billows.

"And Acmé, with her George, should sit on the crystal cushion of glory - and we would wait expectant for you a long long time - and then you should join us, Henry, with dear Emily.

"And Thompson should be with us, too, and recline on the steps of our bark as he does now.

"And together we would sail loving and happy through an amethystine sea."

During their stay in Venice, George, in spite of his increasing languor, continued to accompany his brother, in his visits to the various objects of interest which the city can boast.

The motion of the gondola appeared to have a soothing

influence on the mind of the invalid.

He would recline on the cushions, and the fast flowing tears would course down his wan cheeks.

These, however, were far from being a proof of suffering; - they were evidently a relief to the surcharged spirit.

One evening, a little before sunset, they found themselves in the crowded piazza of Saint Mark. The cafés were thronged with noble Venetians, come to witness the evening parade of an Austrian regiment. The sounds of martial music, swelled above the hum of the multitude; and few could listen to those strains, without participating in some degree, in the military enthusiasm of the hour.

But the brothers turned from the pageantry of war, as their eyes fell on the emblems of Venice free - the minarets of St. Mark, with the horses of Lysippus, a spoil from Byzantium - the flagless poles that once bore the banners of three tributary states - the highly adorned azure clock - the palaces of the proud Doges - where Faliero reigned - where Faliero suffered: - these were before them.

Their steps mechanically turned to the beautiful Campanile.

George, leaning heavily on Sir Henry's arm, succeeded in gaining the summit: and they looked down from thence, on that wonderful city.

They saw the parade dismissed - they heard the bugle's fitful blast proclaim the hour of sunset. The richest hues of crimson and of gold, tinted the opposite heavens; while on those waters, over which the gondolas were swiftly gliding, quivered another city, the magic reflection of the one beneath them.

They gazed on the scene in silence, till the grey twilight came on.

"Now, George! it is getting late," said Sir Henry. "I wonder whether we could find some old mariner, who could give us a chaunt from Tasso?"

Descending from the Campanile, Sir Henry made enquiries on the quay, and with some difficulty found gondoliers, who could still recite from their favourite bard.

Engaging a couple of boats, and placing a singer in each, the brothers were rowed down the Canale Giudecca - skirted many of the small islands, studding the lagoons; and proceeded towards the Adriatic.

Gradually the boats parted company, and just as Sir Henry was about to speak, thinking there might be a mistake as to the directions; the gondolier in the other boat commenced his song, - its deep bass mellowed by distance, and the intervening waves. The sound was electric.

It was so exquisitely appropriate to the scene, and harmonised so admirably, with the associations which Venice is apt to awaken, that one longed to be able to embody that fleeting sound - to renew its magic influence in after years. The pen may depict man's stormy feelings: the sensitive caprice of woman: - the most vivid tints may be imitated on the glowing canvas: - the inspired marble may realise our every idea of the beauty of form: - a scroll may give us at will, the divine inspiration, of Handel: - but there are sounds, as there are subtle thoughts, which, away from the scenes, where they have charmed us, can never delight us more.

It was not until the second boatman answered the song, that the brothers felt how little the charm lay, in the voice of the gondolier, and that, heard nearer, the sounds were harsh and inharmonious.

They recited the death of Clorinda; the one renewing the stanza, whenever there was a momentary forgetfulness on the part of the other.

The clock of St. Mark had struck twelve, before the travellers had reached the hotel. George had not complained of fatigue, during a day which even Sir Henry thought a trying one; and the latter was willing to hope that his strength was now increasing.

Their first design had been to proceed though Switzerland, resting for some time at Geneva. Their plans were now changed, and Sir Henry Belme determined, that their homeward route should be through the Tyrol and Bavaria, and eventually down the Rhine.

He considered that the water carriage, and the very scenes themselves, might prove beneficial to the invalid.

Thompson was sent over to Mestré, to inform Pietro; and they prepared to take their departure.

"You have been better in Venice," said Sir Henry, as they entered the gondola, that was to bear them from the city. "God grant that you may long remain so!"

George shook his head doubtingly.

"My illness, Henry, is not of the frame alone, although that is fragile and shattered.

"The body lingers on without suffering; but the mind - a very bright sword in a worthless sheath - is forcing its way through. Some feelings must remain to the last - gratitude to you - love to dear Emily! Acmé, wife of my bosom! when may I join you?"

CHAPTER IX

INSPRUCK

> "Oh there is sweetness in the mountain air,
> And life, that bloated ease can never hope to share."

Inspruck! a thousand recollections flash across us, as we pronounce the word!

We were there at a memorable period; when the body of the hero of the Tyrol - the brave, the simple-minded Anderl Hofer - was removed from Mantua, where he so nobly met a patriot's death, to the capital of the country, which he had so gallantly defended.

The event was one, that could not fail to be impressive; and to us it was doubly so, for that very period formed an epoch in our lives.

We had lost! we had suffered! we had mourned! Our mind's strength was shook. Ordinary remedies were worse than futile.

We threw ourselves into the heart of the Tyrol, and became resigned if not happy.

Romantic country! did not duty whisper otherwise, how would we fly to thy rugged mountains, and find in the kindly virtues of thine inhabitants, wherewithal to banish misanthropy, and it may be purchase oblivion.

Noble land! where the chief in his hall - the peasant in his hut - alike open their arms with sheltering hospitality, to welcome the stranger - where kindness springs from the heart, and dreams not of sordid gain - where courtesy attends superior rank, without question, but without debasement - where the men are valiant, the women virtuous - where it needed but a few home-spun heroes - an innkeeper and a friar - to rouse up to arms an entire population, and in a brief space to drive back the Gallic foeman! Oh! how do we revert with choking sense of gratitude, to the years we have spent in thy bosom!

Oh! would that we were again treading the mountain's summit - the rifle our comrade - and a rude countryman, our guide and our companion.

In vain! in vain! the net of circumstance is over us!

We may struggle! but cannot escape from its close meshes.

We have said that we were at Inspruck at this period.

It was our purpose, on the following morning, to take our departure.

With renewed health, and nerves rebraced, we hoped to combat successfully, a world that had already stung us.

There was a group near the golden-roofed palace, that attracted our attention. It consisted of a father and his five sons.

They were dressed in the costume of the country; wearing a tapering hat, with black ribbons and feather - a short green jerkin - a red vest surmounted by broad green braces - and short boots tightly laced to the ancle.

They formed a picture of free mountaineers.

We left our lodging, and passed them irresolutely twice or thrice.

The old man took off his hat to the stranger.

"Sir! I am of Sand, in Passeyer.

"Anderl Hofer was my schoolfellow; and these are my boys, whom I have brought to see all that remains of him. Oh! Sir! they did not conquer him, although the murderers shot him on the bastion; but, as he wrote to Pulher - *his* friend and mine - it was indeed 'in the name, and by the help of the Lord, that he undertook the voyage,'"

We paced through the city sorrowfully. It was night, as we passed by the church of the Holy Cross.

Solemn music there arrested our footsteps; and we remembered, that high mass would that night be performed, for the soul of the deceased patriot.

We entered, and drew near the mausoleum of Maximilian the First: - leaning against a colossal statue in bronze, and fixing our eyes on a bas relief on the tomb: one of twenty-four tablets, wrought from Carrara's whitest marble, by the unrivalled hand of Colin of Malines!

One blaze of glory enveloped the grand altar: - vapours of incense floated above: - and the music! oh it went to the soul!

Down! down knelt the assembled throng!

Our mind had been previously attuned to melancholy; it now reeled under its oppression.

We looked around with tearful eye. Old Theodoric of the Goths seemed to frown from his pedestal.

We turned to the statue against which we had leant.

It was that of a youthful and sinewy warrior.

We read its inscription.

Artur, Konig Von England

"Ah! hast *thou* too thy representative, my country?"

We looked around once more.

The congregation were prostrate before the mysterious Host; and we alone stood up, gazing with profound awe and reverence on the mystic rite.

The rough caps of the women almost hid their fair brows. In the upturned features of the men, what a manly, yet what a devout expression reigned!

Melodiously did the strains proceed from the brazen-balustraded orchestra; while sweet young girls smiled in the chapel of silver, as they turned to Heaven their deeply-fringed eyes, and invoked pardon for their sins.

Alas! alas! that such as these *should* err, even in thought! that our feelings should so often mislead us, - that our very refinement, should bring temptation in its train, - and our fervent enthusiasm, but too frequently terminate in vice and crime!

Our whole soul was unmanned! and well do we remember the morbid prayer, that we that night offered to the throne of mercy.

"Pity us! pity us! Creator of all!

"With thousands around, who love - who reverence - whose hearts, in unison with ours, tremble at death, yet sigh for eternity; - who gaze with eye aspiring, although dazzled - as, the curtain of futurity uplifted, fancy revels in the glorious visions of beatitude: - even here, oh God! hear our prayer and pity us!

"We are moulded, though faintly, in an angel's form. Endow us with an angel's principles. For ever hush the impure swellings of passion! Lull the stormy tide of contending emotions! let not circumstances overwhelm!

"Receive our past griefs: the griefs of manhood, engrafted on youth; accept these tears, falling fast and bitterly! take them as past atonement, - as mute witnesses that we feel: - that reason slumbers not, although passion may mislead: - that gilded temptation may overcome, and gorgeous pleasure intoxicate: - but that sincere repentance, and bitter remorse, are visitants too.

"Oh guide and pity us!"

A cheerless dawn was breaking, and a thick damp mist was lazily hanging on the water's surface, as our travellers waved the hand to Venice.

"Fare thee well!" said George, as he rose in the gondola to catch a last glimpse of the Piazzetta, "sea girt city! decayed memorial of patrician splendour, and plebeian debasement! of national glory, blended with individual degradation! - fallen art thou, but fair! It was not with freshness of heart, I reached thee: - I dwelt not in thee, with that jocund spirit, whose every working or gives the lip a smile, or moistens the eye of feeling with a tear.

"Sad were my emotions! but sadder still, as I recede from thy shores, bound on a distant pilgrimage. Acmé! dear Acmé! would I were with thee!"

Passing through Treviso, they stopped at Castel Franco, which presents one of the best specimens of an Italian town, and Italian peasantry, that a stranger can meet with.

At Bassano, they failed not to visit the Municipal Hall, where are the principal pictures of Giacomo da Ponte, called after his native town.

His style is peculiar.

His pictures are dark to an excess, with here and there a vivid light, introduced with wonderful effect.

From this town, the ascent of the mountains towards Ospedale is commenced; and the route is one full of interest.

On the right, lay a low range of country, adorned with vineyards; beyond which, the mountains rose in a precipitous ridge, and closed the scene magnificently.

The Brenta was then reached, and continued to flow parallel with the road, as far as eye could extend.

Farther advanced, the mountains presented a landscape more varied: - *here* chequered with hamlets, whose church hells re-echoed in mellow harmony: there - the only break to their majesty, being the rush of the river, as it formed rolling cascades in its rapid route; or beat in sparkling foam, against the large jagged rocks, which opposed its progress.

At one while, came shooting down the stream, some large raft of timber, manned by adventurous navigators, who, with graceful dexterity, guided their rough bark, clear of the steep banks, and frequent fragments of rock; - at another - as if to mark a road little frequented, a sharp turn would bring them on some sandalled damsel, sitting by the road side, adjusting her ringlets. Detected in her toilet, there was a mixture of frankness and modesty, in the way in which she would turn away a blushing face, yet neglect not, with native courtesy, to incline the head, and wave the sun-burnt hand.

From Ospedale, nearing the bold castle of Pergini, which effectually commands the pass; the travellers descended through regions of beauty, to the ancient Tridentum of Council celebrity.

The metal roof of its Duomo was glittering in the sunshine; and the Adige was swiftly sweeping by its fortified walls.

Leaving Trent, they reached San Michele, nominally the last Italian town on the frontier; but the German language had already prepared them for a change of country.

The road continued to wind by the Adige, and passing through Lavis, and Bronzoli, the brothers halted for the night at Botzen, a clean German town, watered by the Eisach.

The following day's journey, was one that few can take, and deem their time misspent.

Mossy cliffs - flowing cascades - "chiefless castles breaking stern farewells" - all these were met, and met again, as through Brixen, they reached the village of Mülks.

They had intended to have continued their route; but on drawing up at the post-house, were so struck with the gaiety of the scene, that they determined to remain for the night.

Immediately in rear of the small garden of the inn, and with a gentle slope upwards, a wide piece of meadow land extended. On its brow, was pitched a tent, or rather, a many-coloured awning; and, beside it, a pole adorned with flags. This was the station for expert riflemen, who aimed in succession at a fluttering bird, held by a silken cord.

The sloping bank of the hill was covered with spectators.

Age looked on with sadness, and mourned for departed manhood - youth with envy, and sighed for its arrival.

After seeing their bedrooms, George leant on Henry's arm, and, crossing the garden, they took a by-path, which led towards the tent.

The strangers were received with respect and cordiality.

Seats were brought, and placed near the scene of contest.

The trial of skill over, the victor took advantage, of his right, and selected his partner from the fairest of the peasant girls.

Shrill pipes struck up a waltz - a little blind boy accompanied these on a mandolin - and in a brief space, the hill's flat summit was swarming with laughing dancers.

Nor was youth alone enlisted in Terpsichore's service.

The mother joined in the same dance with the daughter; and not unfrequently tripped with foot as light.

Twilight came on, and the patriarchs of the village, and with them our travellers, adjourned to the inn.

The matrons led away their reluctant charges, and the youth of the village alone protracted the revels.

The brothers seated themselves at a separate table, and watched the village supper party, with some interest.

Bowls of thick soup, with fish swimming in butter, and fruit floating in cream, were successively placed in the middle of the table.

Each old man produced his family spoon, and helped himself with primitive simplicity: - then lighted his pipe, and told his long tale, till he had exhausted himself and his hearers.

Nor must we forget the comely waiter.

A bunch of keys hanging on one side, - a large leathern purse on the other - with a long boddice, and something like a hoop

- she really resembled, save that her costume was more homely, one of the portraits of Vandyke.

The brothers left Mülks by sunrise, and were not long, ere they reached the summit of the Brenner, the loftiest point of the Tyrol.

From the beautiful town of Gries, embosomed in the deep valley, until they trod the steep Steinach, the mountain scenery at each step become more interesting. The road was cut on the face of a mountain. On one side, frowned the mountain's dark slope; on the other, lay a deep precipice, down which the eye fearfully gazed, and saw naught but the dark fir trees far far beneath. Dividing that dense wood, a small stream, entangled in the dark ravine, glided on in graceful windings, and looked more silvery from its contrast with the sombre forest.

At the Steinach Pietro pulled up, to show the travellers the capital of the Tyrol, and to point in the distance to Hall, famous for its salt works.

Casting a hasty glance, on the romantic vale beneath them: - the fairest and most extensive in the northern recesses of the Alps, Sir Henry desired his driver to continue his journey.

They rapidly descended, and passing by the column, commemorative of the repulse of the French and Bavarian armies, soon found themselves the inmates of an hotel in Inspruck.

CHAPTER X

THE STUDENTS' STORIES

"The lilacs, where the robins built,
And where my brother set
The laburnum on his birth-day -
The tree is living yet."

At Inspruck, Delmé had the advantage of a zealous, if not an appropriate guide, in the red-faced landlord of the hotel, whose youth had been passed in stirring times, which had more than once, required the aid of his arm, and which promised to tax his tongue, to the last day of his life.

He knew all the heroes of the Tyrolese revolution - if revolution it can be called - and had his tale to tell of each.

He had got drunk with Hofer, - had visited Joseph Speckbacker, when hid in his own stable, - and had confessed more than once to Haspinger, the fighting Capuchin.

His stories were very characteristic; and, if they did not breathe all the poetry of patriotism, were at least honest versions, of exploits performed in as pure and disinterested a spirit, as any that have ever graced the sacred name of Liberty.

After seeing all its sights, and making an excursion to some glaciers in its neighbourhood, Delmé and George left the capital of the Tyrol, to proceed by easy stages to Munich.

In the first day's route, they made the passage of the Zirl, which has justly been lauded; and Pietro failed not to point to a crucifix, placed on a jutting rock, which serves to mark the site of Maximilian's cave.

The travellers took a somewhat late breakfast, at the guitar-making Mittelwald, where chance detained them later than usual. They were still at some distance from their sleeping place, the hamlet of Wallensee, when the rich hues of sunset warned Pietro, that if he would not be benighted, he must urge on his jaded horses.

The sun's decline was glorious. For a time, vivid streaks of crimson and of gold, crowned the summits of the heaving purple mountains. Gradually, these streaks became fainter, and died away, and rolling, slate-coloured clouds, hung heavily in the west.

The scene and the air seemed to turn on a sudden, both cold and grey; and, as the road wound through umbrageous forests of pine, night came abruptly upon them; and it was a relief to the eye, to note the many bright stars, as they shone above the tops of the lofty trees.

A boding stillness reigned, on which the sound of their carriage wheels ungratefully broke. The rustling of each individual bough had an intonation of its own; and the deep notes of the woodman, endeavouring to forget the thrilling legends of his land, mingled fitfully with the hollow gusts, which came moaning through the leafless branches below.

Hist! can it be the boisterous revel of the *forst geister*, that meets his ear? or is it but the chirp of insects, replying from brake to underwood?

Woodman! stay not thy carol!

Yon sound *may* be the wild laugh of the Holz König! Better for thee, to deem it the whine of thine own dog, looking from the cottage door, and awaiting but thy presence, to share in the homely meal.

Arrived on the summit of the hill, the lights of the hamlet at length glistened beneath them. The tired steeds, as if aware of the near termination of their labours, shook their rough manes, and jingled their bells in gladness.

An abrupt descent - and they halted, at the inn facing the lake.

And here may we notice, that it has been a source of wonder to us, that English tourists, whose ubiquity is great, have not oftener been seen straying, by the side of the lake of Wallensee.

A sweeter spot exists not; - whether we rove by its margin, and perpetrate a sonnet; limn some graceful tree, hanging over its waters; or gaze on its unruffled surface, and, noting its aspect so serene, preach from that placid text, peace to the wearied breast.

They were shown into a room in the inn, already thronged with strangers. These were students on their way to Heidelberg.

They were sitting round a table, almost enveloped in smoke; and were hymning praises to their loved companion - beer.

As being in harmony with the moustaches, beard, and bandit propensities - which true bürschen delight to cultivate - they received the strangers with an unfriendly stare, and continued to vociferate their chorus.

Sir Henry, a little dismayed at the prospect before them, called for the landlord and his bill of fare; and had the pleasure of discovering, that the provisions had been consumed, and that two hours would elapse, before more could be procured.

At this announcement, Delmé looked somewhat blank. One of the students, observing this, approached, and apologising, in English, for their voracity, commenced conversing with the landlord, as to the best course to be pursued towards obtaining supper.

His comrades, seeing one of their number speaking with the travellers, threw off some part of their reserve, and made way for them at the table.

George and Henry accepted the proffered seats, although they declined joining the drinking party.

The students, however, did not appear at ease. As if to relieve their embarrassment, one of them addressed the young man, with whom Sir Henry had conversed.

"Carl! it is your turn now! if you have not a song, we must have an original story."

Carl at once complied, and related the following.

The First Story

Perhaps some of you remember Fritz Hartmann and his friend Leichtberg. They were the founders of the last new liberty club, and were famous at *renowning*.

These patriots became officers of the Imperial Guard, and at Vienna were soon known for their friendship and their gallantries.

Fritz had much sentiment and imagination; but some how or other, this did not preserve him from inconstancy.

If he was always kind and gentle, he was not always faithful.

His old college chums had the privilege of joking him on these subjects; and we always did so without mercy. Fritz would sometimes combat our assertions, but they ordinarily made him laugh so much, that a stranger would have deemed he assented to their truth.

One night after the opera, the friends supped together at Fritz's.

I was of the party, and brought for my share a few bottles of Johannisberg, that had been sent me by my uncle from the last vintage. Over these we got more than usually merry, and sang all the songs and choruses of Mother Heidelberg, till the small hours arrived. The sitting room we were in, communicated on one side with the bedroom; - on the other, with a little closet, containing nothing but some old trunks.

This last was closed, but there was a small aperture in the door, over which was a slight iron lattice work.

The officer who had last tenanted Fritz's quarters, had kept pheasants there, and had had this made on purpose.

After one of our songs, Leichtberg attacked Fritz on the old score.

"Fritz! you very Werter of sentiment! I was amazed to see you with no loves to-night at the opera. Where is the widow with sandy hair? or the actress who gave your *kirschenwasser* such a benefit? where our sallow-faced friend? or more than all, where may the fair Pole be who sells such charming fruit? Fritz! Fritz! your sudden attachment to grapes is too ominous."

"Come, Leichtberg!" said Hartmann, laughing, "this is really not fair. Do you know I think myself very constant, and as to the Pole, I have thought of little else for these three months."

"Not so fast! not so fast! Master Hartmann. Was it not on Wednesday week I met you arm in arm with the actress? Were you not waltzing with the widow at the Tivoli? have you not" -

"Come, come!" said Fritz, reddening, "let us say no more. I confess to having made a fool of myself with the actress, but she begged and prayed to see me once more, ere we parted for ever. With this exception - "

"Yes, yes!" interrupted Leichtberg, "I know you, Master Fritz, and allyour evil doings. Have you heard of our Polish affaire de coeur, Carl?", and he turned to me.

"No!" replied I, "let me hear it."

"Well, you must know that a certain friend of ours is very economical, and markets for himself. He bargains for fruit and flowers with the peasant girls, and the prettiest always get his orders, and bring up their baskets, and - we will say no more. Well! our friend meets a foreign face, dark eye - Greek contour - and figure indescribable. She brings him home her well arranged bouquets. He swears her lips are redder than her roses - her brow whiter than lilies - and her breath - which he stoops to inhale - far sweeter than her jasmines. To his amazement, the young flower girl sees no such great attractions in the Imperial Guardsman; leaves her nosegays, - throws his Napoleon, which he had asked her to change, in his face, - and makes her indignant exit. Our sentimental friend finds out her home, and half her history; - renews his flattering tales - piques her pride, - rouses her jealousy; - and makes her love him, bon gré - mal gré, better than either fruit or flowers.

"Fritz swears eternal constancy, and keeps it, as I have already told you, with the actress and the sandy haired widow."

Leichtberg told this story inimitably, and Fritz laughed as much as I did. At length we rose to wish him good night, and saw him turn to his bedroom door, followed by a Swiss dog, which always slept under his bed. The rest of the story we heard from his dying lips.

It was as near as he could guess, between two and three in the morning, that he awoke with the impression that some one was near him. For a time he lay restless and ill at ease; with the vague helpless feeling, that often attacks one, after a good supper.

Fritz had just made up his mind to ascribe to this cause, all his nervousness; when something seemed to drop in the adjoining room; and his dog, starting to its feet, commenced barking furiously.

Again all was still.

He got up for a moment, but fancying he heard a footstep on the stair, concluded that the noise proceeded from one of the inmates of the house, who was come home later than usual.

But Fritz could not sleep; and his dog seemed to share his feelings; for he turned on his side restlessly, and occasionally gave a quick solitary bark.

Suddenly a conviction flashed across Hartmann, that there was indeed some one in the chamber.

His curtain stirred.

He sprang from his bed, and reached his tinder box. As the steel struck sparks from the flint, these revealed the face of the intruder.

It was the young Polish girl.

A fur cloak was closely folded around her; - her face was deadly pale; - with one hand she drew back her long dark hair, while she silently uplifted the other.

Our friend's last impression was his falling back, at the moment his dog made a spring at the girl.

The inmates of the house were alarmed. His friends were all sent for.

I arrived among the earliest. What a sight met me!

The members of the household were so stupefied that they had done nothing. Fritz Hartmann lay on the floor insensible: - his night shirt steeped in blood, still flowing from a mortal wound in his breast.

At his feet, moaning bitterly, its fangs and mouth filled with mingled fur and gore, lay the Swiss dog, with two or three deep gashes across the throat. In the adjoining room, thrown near the door, was the instrument of Fritz's death - one of the knives we had used the evening before.

Beside it, lay a woman's cloak, the fur literally dripping with blood.

Fritz lingered for five hours. Before death, he was sensible, and told us what I have stated: - and acknowledged that he had loved the girl, more than her station in life might seem to warrant.

Of course, the young Pole had been concealed in the closet, and heard Leichtberg's sallies. Love and jealousy effected the rest.

We never caught her, although we had all the Vienna police at our beck; and accurate descriptions of her person were forwarded to the frontiers.

We were not quite certain as to her fate, but we rather suppose her to have escaped by a back garden; in which case she must have made a most dangerous leap; and then to have passed as a courier, riding as such into Livonia.

Where she obtained the money or means to effect this, God knows. She must have been a heroine in her way, for this dog is not easily overpowered, and yet - look here! these scars were given him by that young girl.

The student whistled to a dog at his feet, which came and licked his hand, while he showed the wounds in his throat.

"I call him Hartmann," continued he, "after my old friend. His father sent him to me just after the funeral, and Leichtberg has got his meershaum."

* * * * *

The students listened attentively to the story, refilling their pipes during its progress, with becoming gravity. Carl turned towards his right hand neighbour. "Wilhelm! I call on you!"

The student, whom he addressed, passed his hand through his long heard, and thus commenced.

The Second Story

My father's brother married at Lausanne, in the Canton de Vaud, and resided there. He died early, and left one son; who, as you may suppose, was half a Frenchman. In spite of that, I thought Caspar von Hazenfeldt a very handsome fellow. His chestnut hair knotted in curls over his shoulders. His eyes, the veins of his temples, and I would almost say, his very teeth, had a blueish tint, that I have noticed in few men; and which must, I think, be the peculiar characteristic of his complexion. When engaged in pleasure parties, either pic-nicing at the signal, or promenading in the evening on Mont Benon, or sitting tête-à-tête at Languedoc, he had no eyes or ears but for Caroline de Werner.

He waltzed with her - he talked with her - and he walked with her - until he had fairly talked, walked, and waltzed himself into love.

She was the daughter of a rich old colonel of the Empire: - he was the poor son of a poorer widow. What could he do? Caspar von Hazenfeldt could gaze on the house of the old soldier; but the avenue of elms, the waving corn-fields, and the luxuriant gardens, told him that the heiress of Beau-Séjour could never he his.

He was one evening sitting on a stone, in a little ruined chapel, near the house of his beloved; ruminating as usual on his ill fate, and considering which would be the better plan, to mend his fortunes by travel, or mar them by suicide; - when an elderly gentleman, dressed in a plain suit of black, appeared hat in hand before him.

After the usual compliments, they entered into conversation, and at last, having walked for some distance, towards Hazenfeldt's house, agreed to meet again at the chapel on the next evening.

Suffice it to say that they often met, and as often parted, on the margin of the little stream, that ran before the door of Caspar's mother's house: - that they became great friends; - and that the young man confided the tale of his love, hopes, and miseries, to the sympathising senior.

At last *the old gentleman*, for such he really was, told Caspar that he would help him in a trice, through all his difficulties.

"There is one condition, Caspar!" said he, "but that is a mere trifle. You are young, and would be quite happy, were it not for this love affair of yours: - you sleep soundly, you seek and quit your bed early, and you care not for night-roving. Henceforth, lend me your body from ten at night, until two in the morning, and I promise that Caroline de Werner shall be yours. Here she is!" continued he, as he opened his snuff box, and showed the lid to Caspar, "here she is!"

And sure enough, there she was on the inside of the lid, apparently reading to the gouty old colonel, as he sat in his easy chair in the petit salon of Beau-Sejour.

One evening, the old gentleman delighted Caspar, by telling him that he had authority from Colonel de Werner, to bring a guest to a ball at Beau-Séjour, and by begging Caspar to be his shade - to use our Continental expression - on the occasion.

Caspar von Hazenfeldt and he became greater friends than ever, since their singular contract had been made; for made it was in a thoughtless unguarded moment.

Hazenfeldt was introduced to Caroline in due form, and engaged her for the first dance.

Before the quadrille began, his friend in black came to present his compliments, and to say that he had never seen a more beautiful pair.

"Caspar!" continued he, "when your dance is over, give me a few minutes in the next room. We will chat together, and sip our negus."

Caspar *did* so, and *did* sip his negus. The little gentleman in black, was very facetious, and very affable.

"Are you not going to dance again, Caspar? Look at all those pretty girls, waiting for partners! Why do you not lead one to the country dance?"

As he ended speaking, a sylph-like figure, with long golden ringlets, floated past them.

"I can, and I will," replied Caspar, laughing, as he took the fair-haired girl by the hand, and led her to the dance.

He turned to address his friend in triumph, but he had disappeared.

The dance was over, and Caspar led the stranger towards a

silken ottoman.

"Will you not try one waltz?" said the beautiful girl, as she shook her ringlets, over his flushed cheek; "but I must not ask you, if you are tired."

"How can I refuse?" rejoined Caspar.

Caroline was forgotten, as his partner's golden hair floated on his shoulders, and her soft white arms were twined around him, as they danced the mazy coquettish waltz, which was then the fashion in Lausanne.

"How warm these rooms are!" she exclaimed at last. "The moon is up: let us walk in the avenue."

Caspar assented; for he grew fonder of his new partner, and more forgetful of Caroline. She pressed closer and closer to his side. A distant clock struck ten. Entwined in her tresses, encircled in her arms, he sunk senseless to the ground.

When Caspar recovered from the trance, into which he had fallen, the cold morning breeze, that precedes the dawn, was freshening his cheek; a few faint streaks on the horizon, reflected the colours of the coming sun; and the night birds were returning tired to the woods, as the day birds were merrily preparing for their flight. He was not where he had fallen: he was sitting on a rustic bench, beneath a moss-grown rock.

Caroline de Werner was beside him.

Her white frock was torn; her hair was hanging in Bacchante curls, twined with the ivy that had wreathed it; her eyes glared wildly, and blood bubbled from her mouth. Her hand was fast locked in that of Hazenfeldt.

"Caroline!" he exclaimed, in a tone of wonderment, as one who awakes from a deep sleep, "Caroline! why are we here?

what means this disorder?"

"You now speak," said she, "as did my Caspar,"

Caroline de Werner is in a mad-house near Vevay: - the man in black has not been seen since he disappeared from the ball room of Beau-Séjour: - my cousin, Caspar von Hazenfeldt, took to wandering alone over the Swiss mountains; and before three months had elapsed, from the time he met *the old gentleman*, was buried in the fall of an avalanche, near the pass of the Gemmi.

* * * * *

Supper was not ready as the student finished this story; and George proposed a stroll. The change from the heated room to the margin of the lake, was a most refreshing one. As the brothers silently gazed upwards, a young lad approached, and accosted them.

"Gentlemen! I have seen the horses fed, and they are now lying down."

"Have you?" said Delmé, drily.

"A very fine night! gentlemen! Perhaps you have heard of the famous echo, on the other side of the lake. It will be a good hour, I am sure, before your supper is ready. My boat lies under that old tree. If you like it, I will loose the chain, and row you over."

The brothers acquiesced. They were just in the frame of mind for an unforeseen excursion. The motion of the boat, too, would be easy for George, and he might there unrestrainedly give way to his excited feelings, or commune ungazed on, with the current of his thoughts.

A thin crescent of a moon had risen. It was silvering the tops of the overhanging boughs, and was quiveringly mirrored on the light ripple. George leant against the side of the boat, and listened to the liquid music, as the broad paddle threw back the resisting waters.

How soothing is the hour of night to the wounded spirit!

The obscurity which shrouds nature, seems to veil even man's woes - the harsh outline of his sufferings is discerned no more. Grief takes the place of despair - pensive melancholy of sorrow.

As we gaze around, and feel the chill air damp each ringlet on the palid brow; know that *that* hour hath cast a shade on each inanimate thing around us; we feel resigned to our bereavements, and confess, in our heart's humility, that no changes *should* overwhelm, and that no grief *should* awaken repinings.

To many a bruised and stricken spirit, night imparts a grateful balm.

In the morning, the feelings are too fresh; - oblivion is exchanged for conscious suffering; - the merriment of the feathered songsters seems to us as a taunt; - our sympathies are not with waking nature. The glare and splendour of noon, bid us recal *our* hopes, and their signal overthrow. The zenith of day's lustre meets us as a wilful mockery.

Eve may bring rest, but on her breast is memory. But at night! when the mental and bodily energies are alike worn out by the internal struggle; - when hushed is each sound - softened each feature - dimmed each glaring hue; - a calm which is not deceptive, steals over us, and we regard our woes as the exacted penalty of our erring humanity.

Calumniated night! to one revelling in the full noon-tide of hope and gladness: - to the one, to whom a guilty conscience incessantly whispers, "Think! but sleep not!" - to such as these, horrors may appear to bound thy reign! - but to him who hath loved, and who hath lost, - to many a gentle but tried spirit, thou comest in the guise of a sober, and true friend.

The boat for some time, kept by the steep bank, under the shadows of the trees. As it emerged from this, towards where the moon-beams cast their light on the water, the night breeze rustled through the foliage, and swept a yet green leaf from one of the drooping boughs.

It fell on the surface of the lake, and George's eye quickly followed it.

"Look at that unfaded leaf! Henry. What a gentle breeze it was, that parted it from its fellows! To me it resembles a youthful soul, cut off in its prime, and wandering mateless in eternity."

Sir Henry only sighed.

The young rower silently pursued his course across the lake; running his boat aground, on a small pebbly strand near a white cottage.

Jumping nimbly from his seat, and fastening the boat to a large stone, the guide, followed by the brothers, shouted to the inmates of the cottage, and violently kicked at its frail door.

An upper window was opened, and the guardian of the echo - a valorous divine in a black night-cap - demanded their business. This was soon told. The priest descended - struck a light - unbarred the door - and with the prospect of gain before him, fairly forgot that he had been aroused from a deep slumber.

They were soon ushered into the kitchen. An aged crone descended, and raking the charcoal embers, kindled a flame, by which the rower was enabled to light his pipe.

The young gentleman threw himself into an arm chair, and puffed away with true German phlegm. The old man bustled about, in order to obtain the necessary materials for loading an ancient cannon; and occupied himself for some minutes, in driving the charge into the barrel.

This business arranged, he led the way towards the beach; and aided by the old woman, pointed his warlike weapon. A short pause - it was fired! Rebounding from hill to hill, the echo took its course, startling the peasant from his couch, and the wolf from his lair.

Again all was still; - then came its distant reverberation - a tone deep and subdued - dying away mournfully on the ear.

"How wonderfully fine!" said George, "but let us embark, for I feel quite chilled."

"I will run for the youngster," replied his brother. As he moved towards the cottage, the priest seized him by the collar of the coat, and held up the torch, by which he had fired the cannon.

"This echo is indeed a wonderful one! It has nineteen distinct repetitions; the first twelve being heard from *this* side of a valley, which, were it day, I would point out; the other seven, on the opposite side. Tradition tells us, that nineteen castles in ancient times, stood near the spot; that each of these laid claim to the echo; and that, as it passes the ruin, where once dwelt Sigismund of the Bloody Hand, the chief springs from the round ivied tower - waves his sword thrice, the drops of blood falling from its hilt as he does so - and proclaims aloud, that whosoever dare gainsay" -

"I am sorry to leave you," interrupted Sir Henry, as he shook him off, "particularly at this interesting part of the story; but it is late, and my brother feels unwell, and I wish to go to the cottage to call our guide."

Delmé was pursued by the echo's elucidator, who being duly remunerated, allowed Sir Henry to accompany the guide towards the boat. George was not standing where he had left him. Delmé stepped forward, and nearly fell ver a prostrate body.

It was the motionless one of his brother.

He gave a shriek of anguish; flew towards the house, and in a moment, was again on the spot, bearing the priest's torch. He raised his brother's head. One hand was extended over the body, and fell to the earth like a clod of clay as it was.

He gazed on that loved face. In that gaze, how much was there to arrest his attention.

On those features, death had stamped his seal.

But there was a thought, which bore the ascendancy over this in Delmé's mind. It was a thought which rose involuntarily, - one for which he could not *then* account, and cannot now. For some seconds, it swayed his every emotion. He felt the conviction - deep, undefinable - that there was indeed a soul, to "shame the doctrine of the Sadducee."

He deemed that on those lineaments, this was the language forcibly engraven! The features were still and fixed: - the brow alone revealed a dying sense of pain.

The lips! how purple were they! and the eye, that erst flashed so freely: - the yellow film of death had dimmed its lustre.

The legs were apart, and one of the feet was in the lake. Henry tried to chafe his brother's forehead.

In vain! in vain! he knew it was in vain!

He let the head fall, and buried his face in his hands.

He turned reproachfully, to gaze on that cloudless Heaven, where the moon, and the brilliant stars, and the falling meteor, seemed to hold a bright and giddy festival.

He clasped his hands in mute agony. For a brief moment - his dark eye seeming to invite His wrath - he dared to arraign the mercy of God, who had taken what he had made.

It was but for a moment he thus thought.

He had watched that light of life, until its existence was almost identified with his own. He had seen it flicker - had viewed it reillumed - blaze with increased brilliancy - fade - glimmer - and fade. Now! where was it?

A bitter cry escaped! his limbs trembled convulsively, and could no longer support him.

He fell senseless beside his brother.

CHAPTER XI

THE STUDENT

"What is my being? *thou* hast ceased to be."

Carl Obers was as enthusiastic a being as ever Germany sent forth. Brought up in a lone recess in the Hartz mountains, with neither superiors nor equals to commune with, he first entered the miniature world, as a student at Heidelberg.

His education had been miserably neglected. He had read much; but his reading had been without order and without system.

The deepest metaphysics, and the wildest romances had been devoured in succession; until the young man hardly knew which was the real, or which was the visionary world: - the one he actually lived in, or the one he was always brooding over: - where souls are bound together by mysterious and hidden links, and where men sell themselves to Satan; - the penalty merely being: - to walk through life, and throw no shadow.

Enrolled amongst a select corps of brüschen, warm and true; his ear was caught by the imposing jargon of patriotism; and his imagination dwelt on those high sounding words, "the rights of man;" - until he became the staunch advocate and unflinching votary of a state of things, which, for aught we know, *may* exist in one of the planets, but which never can, and which never will exist on this earth of ours.

"What!" would exclaim our enthusiast, "have we not all our bodily and our mental, energies? Doth not dame Nature, in our birth, as in our death, deal out impartial justice? She may endow me with stronger limbs, than another: - our feelings as we grow up, may not be chained down to one servile monotony; - the lip of the precocious cynic" - this was addressed to a young matter of fact Englishman - "who sneers at my present animation, may not curl with a smile as often as my own; but let our powers of acting be equal, - our prerogatives the same."

Carl Obers, with his youth and his vivacity, carried his auditors - a little knot of beer drinking liberty-mongers - *with* him, and *for* him, in all he said; and the orator would look round, with conscious power, and considerable satisfaction; and flatter himself, that his specious arguments were as unanswerable, as they were then unanswered.

Many of our generation may remember the unparalleled enthusiasm, which, like an electric flash, spread over the civilised world; as Greece armed herself, to shake off her Moslem ruler.

It was one that few could help sharing.

To almost all, is Greece a magic word. Her romantic history - the legacies she has left us - our early recollections, identifying with her existence as a nation, all that is good and glorious; - no wonder these things should have shed a bright halo around her, - and have made each breast deeply sympathise with her in her unwonted struggle for freedom.

Carl Obers did not hear of this struggle with indifference. He at once determined to give Greece the benefit of his co-operation, and the aid of his slender means. He immediately commenced an active canvass amongst his personal friends, in order to form a band of volunteers, who might be efficient, and worthy of the cause on which his heart was set.

He now first read an useful lesson from life's unrolled volume.

Many a voice, that had rung triumphantly the changes on liberty, was silent now, or deprecated the active attempt to establish it.

The hands that waved freely in the debating room, were not the readiest to grasp the sword's hilt. Many who had poetically expatiated on the splendours of modern Greece; on reflection preferred the sunny views of the Neckar, to the prospect of eating honey on Hymettus.

Youth, however, is the season for enterprise; and Carl, with twenty-three comrades, was at length on his way to Trieste.

He had been offered the command of the little band, but had declined it, with the sage remark, that "as they were about to fight for equality, it was their business to preserve it amongst themselves."

A slight delay in procuring a vessel, took place at Trieste. This delay caused a defection of eight of the party.

The remaining students embarked in a miserable Greek brigantine, and after encountering some storms in the Adriatic, thought themselves amply repaid, as the purple hills of Greece rose before them.

On their landing, they felt disappointed.

No plaudits met them; no vivas rung in the air: but a Greek soldier filched Carl's valise, and on repairing to the commandant of the town, they were told that no redress could be afforded them.

Willing to hope that the scum of the irregular troops was left behind, and that better feeling, and stricter discipline, existed nearer the main body; our students left on the morrow; - placed themselves under the command of one of the noted leaders of the Revolution: - and had shortly the satisfaction of crossing swords with the Turk.

For some months, the party went through extraordinary hardships; - engaged in a series of desultory but sanguinary expeditions; - and gradually learnt to despise the nation, in whose behalf they were zealously combating.

At the end of these few months, what a change in the hopes and prospects of the little band! Some had rotted in battle field, food for vultures; others had died of malaria in Greek hamlets, without one friend to close their eyes, or one hand to proffer the cooling draught to quench the dying thirst; - two were missing - had perhaps been murdered by the peasants; - and five only remained, greatly disheartened, cursing the nation, and their own individual folly.

Four of the five turned homewards.

Carl was left alone, but fought on.

Now there was a Greek, Achilles Metaxà by name, who had attached himself to Carl's fortunes. In person, he was the very model of an ancient hero. He had the capacious brow, the eye of fire, and the full black beard, descending in wavy curls to his chest.

The man was brave, too, for Carl and he had fought together.

It so happened, that they slept one night in a retired convent. Their hardships latterly had been great, and the complaints of Achilles had been unceasing in consequence. In the morning Carl rose, and found that his clothes and arms had vanished, and that his friend was absent also.

Carl remained long enough to satisfy himself, that his friend was the culprit; and then turned towards the sea coast, determined at all hazards to leave Greece.

He succeeded in reaching Missolonghi, in the early part of 1823, shortly after the death of Marco Botzaris - being then in a state of perfect destitution, and his mental sufferings greatly aggravated by the consciousness, that he had induced so many of his comrades to sacrifice their lives and prospects in an unworthy cause.

At Missolonghi, where Mavrocordato reigned supreme, he was grudged the paltry ration of a Suliote soldier, and might have died of starvation, had it not been for the timely interposition of a stranger.

Moved by that stranger's persuasion, Carl consented to form one of a contemplated expedition against Lepanto; and, had his illustrious benefactor lived, might have found a steady friend.

As it was, he waited not to hear the funeral oration, delivered by Spiridion Tricoupi; but was on the deck of the vessel that was to bear him homewards, and shed tears of mingled grief, admiration, and gratitude, as thirty-seven minute guns, fired from the battery, told Greece and Carl Obers, that they had lost Byron, their best friend.

Carl reached Germany, a wiser man than when he left it.

He found his father dead, and he came into possession of his small patrimony; but felt greatly, as all men do who are suddenly removed from active pursuits, the want of regular and constant employment.

He was glad to renew his intercourse with his old University; and found himself greatly looked up to by the students, who were never wearied with listening to his accounts of the Morea, and of the privations he had there encountered.

We need hardly inform our readers, that Carl Obers was one

of the pedestrian students at Wallensee, and was indeed the identical narrator of the Vienna story.

We left George and his brother, on the shore below the priest's cottage. The one was laid cold and motionless - the other wished that *he* also were so.

Immediately on Delmé's falling, the young guide alarmed the priest - brought him down to the spot - pointed to the brothers - threw himself into the boat - and paddled swiftly across the lake, to alarm the guests at the inn.

It was with feelings of deep commiseration, that Carl looked on the two brothers. He was the only person present, whose time was comparatively his own; he spoke English, although imperfectly; and he owed a deep debt of gratitude to an Englishman.

These circumstances seemed to point him out, as the proper person to attend to the wants of the unfortunate traveller; and Carl Obers mentally determined, that he would not leave Delmé, as long as he had it in his power to befriend him, Sir Henry Delmé was completely unmanned by his bereavement. He had been little prepared for such a severe loss; although it is more than probable, that George's life had long been hanging on a thread, which a single moment might snap.

The medical men had been singularly sanguine in his case, for it is rarely that disease of the heart attacks one so young; but it now seemed evident, that even had not anxiety of mind, and great constitutional irritability, hastened the fatal result, that poor George could never have hoped to have survived to a ripe old age.

There was much in his character at any time, to endear him to an only brother. As it was, Delmé had seen George under such trying circumstances - had entered so fully into his feelings and sufferings - that this abrupt termination to his brother's sorrows, appeared to Sir Henry Delmé, to bring with it a sable pall, that enveloped in darkness his own future life and prospects.

The remains of poor George were placed in a small room, communicating with one intended for Sir Henry.

Here Delmé shut himself up, brooding over his loss, and permitting no one to intrude on his privacy.

Carl had offered his services, which were gratefully accepted, in making the necessary arrangements for his brother's obsequies; and Sir Henry, in the solitude of the dead man's chamber, could give free scope to a flood of bitter recollections.

It may be, that those silent hours of agony, when the brother looked fixedly on that moveless face, and implored the departed spirit to breathe its dread and awful secret, were not without their improving tendency; for haggard and wan as was the mourner's aspect, there was no outward sign of quivering, even as he saw the rude coffin lowered, and as fell on his ear, the creaking of cords, and that harsh jarring sound, to which there is nothing parallel on earth, the heavy clods falling on the coffin lid.

The general arrangements had been simple; but Carl's directions had been given in such a sympathising spirit, that they could not be otherwise than acceptable.

About the church-yard itself, there is nothing very striking. It is formed round a small knoll, on the summit of which stands a sarcophagus literally buried in ivy.

Beneath this, is the vault of the baronial family, that for centuries swayed the destinies of the little hamlet; but which family has been extinct for some years.

Round it are grouped the humbler osiered graves; over which, in lieu of tomb stones, are placed large black iron crosses, ornamented with brass, and bearing the simple initials of the bygone dead.

Even Delmé, with all his ancestral pride, felt that George "slept well."

It is true no leaden coffin enclosed his relics, nor did the murky vault of his ancestors, open with creaking hinge to receive another of the race. No escutcheon darkened the porch whence they bore him; and no long train of mourners followed his remains to their last home.

But there was something in the quiet of the spot, that seemed to Delmé in harmony with his history; and to promise, that a sorrowless world had already opened, on one who had loved so truly, and felt so deeply in this.

Sir Henry returned to the inn, and darkened his chamber.

He had not the heart to prosecute his journey, nor to leave the spot, which held what was to him so dear.

Carl Obers attempted to combat his despondency; but observing how useless were his arguments, wisely allowed his grief to take its course.

There was one point, in which Delmé was decidedly wrong.

He could not bring himself, to communicate their loss to his sister.

Carl pressed this duty frequently on him, but was always met by the same reply.

"No! no! how can I inflict such a pang?"

It is possible the intelligence might have been very long in reaching England, had it not been for a providential circumstance, that occurred shortly after George's funeral.

A carriage, whose style and appointments bespoke it English, changed horses at the inn at Wallensee. The courier, while ordering the relays, had heard George's story; and touching his hat to the inmates of the vehicle, retailed it with natural pathos.

On hearing the name of Delmé, the lady was visibly affected. She was an old friend of the family; and as Melicent Dashwood, had known George as a boy.

It was not without emotion, that she heard of one so young, and to her so familiar, being thus prematurely called to his last account.

The lady and her husband alighted, and sending up their cards, begged to see the mourner.

The message was delivered; but Delmé, without comment or enquiry, at once declined the offer; and it was thought better not to persist. They were too deeply interested, however, not to attempt to be of use. They saw Carl and Thompson, - satisfied themselves that Sir Henry was in friendly hands; and thanking the student with warmth and sincerity, for his attention to the sufferer, exacted a promise, that he would not leave him, as long as he could in any way be useful.

The husband and wife prepared to continue their journey; but not before the former had left his address in Florence, with directions to Carl to write immediately, in case he required the assistance of a friend; and the latter had written a long letter to Mrs. Glenallan, in which she broke as delicately as she could, the melancholy and unlooked-for tidings.

CHAPTER XII

THE LETTER

> "And from a foreign shore
> Well to that heart might *hers* these absent greetings pour."

Three weeks had elapsed since George's death.

It would be difficult to depict satisfactorily, the state of Sir Henry Delmé's mind during that period. The pride of life appeared crushed within him. He rarely took exercise, and when he did, his step was slow, and his gait tottering.

That one terrible loss was ever present to his mind; and yet his imagination, as if disconnected with his feelings, or his memory, was constantly running riot over varying scenes of death, and conjuring up revolting pictures of putrescence and decay.

A black pall, and an odour of corruption, seemed to commingle with each quick-springing fantasy; and Delmé would start with affright from his own morbid conceptions, as he found himself involuntarily dwelling on the waxen rigidity of death, - following the white worm in its unseemly wanderings, - and finally stripping the frail and disgusting coat from the disjointed skeleton.

Sir Henry Delmé had in truth gone through arduous and trying scenes.

The very circumstance that he had to conceal his own feelings, and support George through his deeper trials, made the present reaction the more to be dreaded.

Certain are we, that trials such as his, are frequently the prevailing causes, of moral and intellectual insanity. Fortunately, Sir Henry was endued with a firm mind, and with nerves of great power of endurance.

One morning, at an early hour, Thompson brought in a letter.

It was from Emily Delmé; and as Sir Henry noted the familiar address, and the broad black edge, which told that the news of his brother's death had reached his sister, he cast it from him with a feeling akin to pain.

The next moment, however, he sprang from the bed, threw open the shutters, and commenced reading its contents.

EMILY'S LETTER

> My own dear brother,
>
> My heart bleeds for you! But yesterday, we received the sad, sad letter. To-day, although blinded with tears, I implore you to remember, that you have not lost your all! Our bereavement has been great! our loss heavy indeed. But if a link in the family love-chain be broken - shall not the remaining ones cling to each other the closer?
>
> My aunt is heart-broken. Clarendon, kind as he is, did not know our George! Alas! that he should be ours no more!
>
> My only brother! dwell not with strangers! A sister's

arms are ready to clasp you: - a sister's sympathy must lighten the load of your sufferings.

Think of your conduct! your devotedness! Should not these comfort you?

Did you not love and cherish him? did you not - happier than I - soothe his last days? were you not present to the end?

From this moment, I shall count each hour that divides us.

On my knees both night and morning, will I pray the Almighty God, who has chastened us, to protect my brother in his travels by sea and land.

May we be spared, my dearest Henry, to pray together, that HE may bestow on us present resignation, and make us duly thankful for blessings which still are ours.

Your affectionate sister,

EMILY.

Delmé read the letter with tearless eye. For some time he leant his head on his hand, and thought of his sister, and of the dead.

He shook, and laughed wildly, as he beat his hand convulsively against the wall.

Carl Obers and Thompson held him down, while this strong paroxysm lasted.

His sobs became fainter, and he sunk into a placid slumber. The student watched anxiously by his side. He awoke; called for Emily's letter; and as he read it once more, the tears coursed down his sunken cheeks.

Ah! what a relief to the excited man, is the fall of tears.

It would seem as if the very feelings, benumbed and congealed as they may hitherto have been, were suddenly dissolving under some happier influence, and that, - with the external sign - the weakness and pliability of childhood - we were magically regaining its singleness of feeling, and its gentleness of heart.

Sir Henry swerved no more from the path of manly duty. He saw the vetturino, and arranged his departure for the morrow. On that evening, he took Carl's arm, and sauntered through the village church-yard.

Already seemed it, that the sods had taken root over George's grave.

The interstices of the turf were hidden; - a white paper basket, which still held some flowers, had been suspended by some kind stranger hand over the grave; - from it had dropped a wreath of yellow amaranths.

There was great repose in the scene. The birds appeared to chirp softly and cautiously; - the tufts of grass, as they bowed their heads against the monumental crosses, seemed careful not to rustle too drearily.

Sir Henry's sleep was more placid, on *that*, his last night at Wallensee, than it had been for many a night before.

* * * * *

Acting up to his original design, Delmé passed through the capitals of Bavaria and Wurtemburg; and quickly traversing the picturesque country round Heilbron, reached the romantic Heidelberg, washed by the Neckar.

The student, as might be expected, did not arrive at his old University, with feelings of indifference; but he insisted, previous to visiting his college companions, on showing Sir Henry the objects of interest.

The two friends, for such they might now be styled, walked towards the castle, arm in arm; and stood on the terrace, adorned with headless statues, and backed by a part of the mouldering ruin, half hid by the thick ivy.

They looked down on the many winding river, murmuringly gliding through its vine covered banks.

Beyond this, stretched a wide expanse of country; while beneath them lay the town of Heidelberg - the blue smoke hanging over it like a magic diadem.

"Here, here!" said Carl Obers, as he gazed on the scene, with mournful sensations, "*here* were my youthful visions conceived and embodied - *here* did I form vows, to break the bonds of enslaved mankind - *here* did I dream of grateful thousands, standing erect for the first time as free men - *here* did I brood over, the possible happiness of my fellow men, and in attempting to realise it, have wrecked my own."

"My kind friend!" replied Delmé, "your error, if it be such, has been of the head, and not the heart. It is one, natural to your age and your country. Far from being irreparable, it is possible it may have taught you a lesson, that may ultimately greatly benefit you. This is the first time we have conversed regarding your prospects. What are your present views?"

"I have none. My friends regard me as one, who has improvidently thrown away his chance of advancement. My knowledge of any *one* branch of science is so superficial, that this precludes my ever hoping to succeed in a learned profession. I cannot enter the military service in my own country, without commencing in the lowest grade. This I can hardly bring my mind to."

"What would you say to the Hanoverian army?" replied Delmé.

"I would say," rejoined Carl: "for I see through your kind motive in asking, that I esteem myself fortunate, if I have been in any way useful to you; but that I cannot, and ought not, to think, of accepting a favour at your hands."

Sir Henry said no more at that time: and they reached the inn in silence.

Delmé retired for the night. Carl Obers sought his old chums; and, exhilarated by his meershaum, and the excellent beer - rivalling the famous Lubeck beer, sent to Martin Luther, during his trial, by the Elector of Saxony - triumphantly placed "young Germany" at the head of nations.

Early the following morning, they were again en route.

They passed through Manheim, where the Rhine and Neckar meet, - through Erpach, - through Darmstadt, that cleanest of Continental towns, - and finally reached Frankfort-on-the-Maine, where it was agreed that Sir Henry and Thompson were to part from their travelling companions.

Sir Henry in his distress of mind, felt that theirs was not a casual farewell. On reaching the quay, he pressed the student's hand with grateful warmth, but dared not trust to words.

On the deck of the steamer, assisting Thompson to arrange the portmanteaux, stood Pietro Molini.

The natural gaiety of the old driver had received a considerable check at George's death.

He could not now meet Sir Henry, without an embarrassment of manner; and even in his intercourse with Thompson, his former jocularity seemed to have deserted him.

"Good bye, Pietro!" said Delmé, extending his hand. "I trust we may one day or other meet again."

The vetturino grasped it, - his colour went and came, - he looked down at his whip, - then felt in his vest for his pipe, As he saw Delmé turn towards the poop, and as Thompson warned him it was time to leave the vessel, - his feelings fairly gave way.

He threw his arms round the Englishman's neck and blubbered like a child.

We have elsewhere detailed the luckless end of the vetturino.

As for Carl Obers, that zealous patriot; the last we heard of him, was that he was holding a commission in the Hanoverian Jägers, obtained for him by Sir Henry's intervention. He was at that period, in high favour with that liberal monarch, King Ernest.

CHAPTER XIII

HOME

"'Tis sweet to hear the watchdog's honest bark
Bay deep-mouth'd welcome as we draw near home,
'Tis sweet to know there is an eye will mark
Our coming, and look brighter when we come."

Embarking on its tributary stream, Delmé reached the Rhine - passed through the land of snug Treckschut, and wooden-shoed housemaid - and arrived at Rotterdam, whence he purposed sailing for England.

To that river, pay we no passing tribute! The Rhine - with breast of pride - laving fertile vineyards, cities of picturesque beauty, beetling crags, and majestic ruins; hath found its bard to hymn an eulogy, in matchless strains, which will be co-existent, with the language they adorn.

Sir Henry was once more on the wide sea. Where were they who were his companions when his vessel last rode it? where the young bride breathing her devotion? where the youthful husband whispering his love?

The sea yet glistened like a chrysolite; the waves yet laughed in the playful sunbeams - the bright-eyed gull yet dipped his wing in the billow, fearless as heretofore; - where was the one, who from that text had deduced so fair a moral?

Sir Henry wished not to dwell on the thought, but as it flashed across him, his features quivered, and his brow darkened.

He threw himself into the chaise which was to bear him to his home, with alternate emotions of bitterness and despair!

Hurrah for merry England! Click, clack! click, clack! thus cheerily let us roll!

Great are the joys of an English valet, freshly emancipated from sauerkraut, and the horrors of silence!

Sweet is purl, and sonorous is an English oath. Bright is the steel, arming each clattering hoof! Leather strap and shining buckle, replace musty rope and ponderous knot! The carriage is easier than a Landgravine's, - the horses more sleek, - the driver as civil, - the road is like a bowling green, - the axletree and under-spring, of Collinge's latest patent. But the heart! the heart! *that* may be sad still.

Delmé's voyage and journey were alike a blank. On the ocean, breeze followed calm; - on the river, ship succeeded ship; - on the road, house and tree were passed, and house and tree again presented themselves. He drew his cap over his eyes, and his arms continued folded.

His first moment of full consciousness, was as a sharp turn, followed by a sudden pause, brought him in front of the lodge at Delmé.

On the two moss-grown pillars, reposed the well known crest of his family. The porter's daughter, George's friend, issued from the lodge, and threw open the iron gates.

She was dressed in black. How this recalled his loss.

"My dear - dear - dear brother!"

Emily bounded to his embrace, and her cheek fell on his

shoulder. He felt the warm tear trickle on his cheek. He clasped her waist, - gazed on her pallid brow, - and held her lip to his.

How it trembled from her emotion!

"My own brother! how pale - how ill you look!"

"Emily! my sister! I have something yet left me on earth! and my worthy kind aunt, too!"

He kissed Mrs. Glenallan's forehead, and tried to soothe her. She pressed her handkerchief to her eyes, and checked her tears; but continued to sob, with the deep measured sob of age.

How mournful, yet how consoling, is the first family meeting, after death has swept away one of its members! How the presence of each, calls up sorrow, and yet assists to repress it, - awakes remembrances full of grief, yet brings to life indefinable hopes, that rob that grief of its most poignant sting! The very garb of woe, whose mournful effect is felt to the full, only when each one sees it worn by the other - the very garb paralyses, and brings impressively before us, the awful truth, that for our loss, in this world, there is no remedy. How holy, how chaste is the affection, which we feel disposed to lavish, on those who are left us.

Surely if there be a guardian spirit, which deigns to flit through this wayward world, to cheer the stricken breast, and purify feelings, whose every chord vibrates to the touch of woe; surely such presides, and throws a sunny halo, on the group, that blood has united - on which family love has shed its genial influence - and of which, each member, albeit bowed down by sympathetic grief, attempts to lift his drooping head, and to others open some source of comfort, which to the kind speaker, is inefficient and valueless indeed!

For many months, Sir Henry continued to reside with his family. Clarendon Gage was a constant visitor, and companion to the brother and sister in their daily walks and rides.

He had never met poor George, but loved Emily so well, that he could not but sympathise in their heavy loss; and as Delmé noted this quiet sympathy, he felt deeply thankful to Providence, for the fair prospect of the happiness, that awaited his sister.

Winter passed away. The fragile snowdrop, offspring of a night - the mute herald of a coming and welcome guest - might be seen peering beneath the gnarled oak, or enlivening the emerald circle beneath the wide-spreading elm.

Spring too glided by, and another messenger came. The migratory swallow, returned from foreign travel, sought the ancient gable, and rejoicing in safety, commenced building a home. At twilight's hour might she be seen, unscared by the truant's stone, repairing to the placid pool - skimming over its glassy surface, in rapid circle and with humid wing - and returning in triumph, bearing wherewithal to build her nest.

Summer too went by; and as the leaves of Autumn rustled at his feet, Delmé started, as he felt that the sting and poignancy of his grief was gone. It was with something like reproach, that he did so. There is a dignity in grief - a pride in perpetuating it - and his had been no common affliction.

It is a trite, but true remark, that time scatters our sorrows, as it scatters our joys.

The heat of fever and the delirium of love, have their gradations; and so has grief. The impetuous throbbing of the pulse abates; - the influence of years makes us remember the extravagance of passion, with something approaching to a smile; - and Time - mysterious Time - wounding, but healing all, leads us to look at past bereavements, as through a darkened glass.

We do not forget; but our memory is as a dream, which awoke

us in terror, but over which we have slept. The outline is still present, but the fearful details, which in the darkness of the hour, and the freshness of conception, so scared and alarmed us, - these have vanished with the night.

Emily's wedding day drew nigh, and the faces of the household once more looked bright and cheerful.

CHAPTER XIV

A WEDDING

"'Tis time this heart should be unmoved,
Since others it has ceased to move,
But though I may not be beloved,
Still let me love!"

"I saw her but a moment,
Yet methinks I see her now,
With a wreath of orange blossoms
Upon her beauteous brow."

Spring of life! whither art thou flown?

A few hot sighs - and scalding tears - fleeting raptures and still fading hopes - and then - thou art gone for ever. Lovelorn we look on beauty: no blush now answers to our glance; for cold is our gaze, as the deadened emotions of our heart.

Fresh garlands bedeck the lap of Spring. Faded as the shrivelled flowers, that withering sink beneath her rosy feet: yet we exclaim: - Spring of life! how and whither art thou flown?

Clarendon Gage was a happy man. He had entered upon the world with very bright prospects. The glorious visions of his youth were still unclouded, and his heart beat as high with hope as ever.

Experience had not yet instilled that sober truth, that Time will darken the sunniest, as well as the least inviting anticipations; and that the visions of his youth were unclouded, because they were undimmed by the reflections of age.

Clarendon Gage was happy and grateful; and so might he well be! Few of us are there, who, on our first loving, have met with a love, fervent, confiding, and unsuspecting as our own, - fewer are there, who in reflection's calm hour, have recognised in the form that has captivated the eye, the mind on which their own can fully and unhesitatingly rely, - and fewest of all are they, who having encountered such a treasure, can control adverse circumstances - can overcome obstacles that oppose – and finally call it their own.

Passionate, imaginative, and fickle as man may be, this is a living treasure beyond a price: than which this world has none more pure - none as enduring, to offer.

Ah! say and act as we may - money-making - worldly - ambitious as we may become - who among us that will not allow, that in the success of his honest suit - that in his possession of the one first loved - and which first truly loved him - a kind ray from heaven, seems lent to this changeful world. Such affection as this, lends a new charm to man's existence. It lulls him in his anger - it soothes him in his sorrow - calms him in his fears - cheers him in his hopes - it deadens his grief - it enlivens his joy.

It was a lovely morning in May - the first of the month. Not a cloud veiled the sun's splendour - the birds strained their throats in praise of day - and the rural May-pole, which was in the broad avenue of walnut trees, immediately at the foot of the lawn, was already encircled with flowers. Half way up this, was the station of the rustic orchestra - a green bower, which effectually concealed them from the view of the dancers.

On the lawn itself, tents were pitched in a line facing the house. Behind these, between the tents and the May-pole, extended a long range of tables, for the coming village feast.

Emily Delmé looked out on the fair sunrise, and noted the gay preparations with some dismay. Her eye fell on her favourite bed of roses, the rarest and most costly that wealth and extreme care could produce; and she mournfully thought, that ere those buds were blown, a very great change would have taken place in her future prospects. She thought of all she was to leave.

Will *he* be this, and more to me?

How many a poor girl, when it is all too late, has fearfully asked herself the same question, and how deeply must the answer which time alone can give, affect the happiness of after years!

Emily took her mother's miniature, and gazing on that face, of which her own appeared a beautiful transcript; she prayed to God to support him who was still present to her every thought.

The family chapel of the Delmés was a beautiful and picturesque place of worship. With the exception of one massive door-way, whose circular arch and peculiar zig-zag ornament bespoke it co-eval with, or of an earlier date than, the reign of Stephen - and said to have belonged to a ruin apart from the chapel, whose foundations an antiquary could hardly trace - Delmé chapel might be considered a well preserved specimen of the florid Gothic, of the fifteenth and sixteenth centuries.

The progress of the edifice, had been greatly retarded during the wars of the Roses; but it was fortunately completed, before, the doctrine of the Cinquecentists - who saw no beauty save in the revived dogmas of Vitruvius - had so far gained ground, as to make obsolete and unfashionable, the most captivating and harmonious style of Architecture, that has yet flourished in England.

Its outer appearance was comparatively simple - it had neither spire, lantern, or transepts - and its ivy-hidden belfry was a detached tower.

The walls of the aisles were supported by massive buttresses, and surmounted by carved pinnacles; and from them sprung flying buttresses, ornamented with traced machicolations, to bear the weight of the embattled roof of the nave.

The interior was more striking. As the stranger entered by the western door, and proceeded up the nave, each step was re-echoed from the crypt below: - as he trod on strange images, and inscriptions in brass; commemorative of the dead, whose bones were mouldering in the subterranean chapel. On them, many coloured tints fantastically played, through gorgeously stained panes - the workmanship of the Middle Ages.

The richly carved oaken confessional - now a reading desk - first attracted the attention.

In the very centre of the chapel, stood a white marble font, whose chaplet of the flower of the Tudors, encircled by a fillet, sufficiently bespoke its date. Between the altar and this font was a tomb, which merits special attention. It was the chantry of Sir Reginald Delmé, the chief of his house in the reign of Harry Monmouth. It was a mimic chapel, raised on three massive steps of grey stone. The clustered columns, that bore the light and fretted roof, were divided by mullions, rosettes, and trefoils in open work; except where the interstices were filled up below, to bear the sculptured, and once emblazoned shields of the Delmés, and their cognate families. The entrance to the chantry, was through a little turret at its north-eastern corner, the oaken door of which, studded with quarrel-headed nails, was at one time never opened, but when the priests ascended the six steep and spiral steps, and stood around the tomb to chant masses for the dead.

The diminutive font, and the sarcophagus itself, had once been painted. On this, lay the figure of Sir Reginald Delmé.

On a stone cushion - once red - supported by figures of angels in the attitude of prayer, veiling their eyes with their wings, reposed the unarmed head of the warrior: - his feet uncrossed rested on the image of a dog, crouching on a broken horn, seeming faithfully to gaze at the face of his master.

The arms were not crossed - the hands were not clasped; but were joined as in prayer. Sir Reginald had not died in battle. Above the head of the sleeping warrior, hung his gorget, and his helmet, with its beaver, and vizor open; and the banner he himself had won, on the field of Shrewsbury, heavily shook its thick folds in the air. The fading colours on the surcoat of the recumbent knight, still faintly showed the lilies and leopards of England; - and Sir Henry himself was willing to believe, that the jagged marks made in that banner by the tooth of Time, were but cuts, left by the sword of the Herald, as at the royal Henry's command, he curtailed the pennon of the knight; and again restored it to Sir Reginald Delmé - a banner.

The altar, which extended the whole width of the chapel, was enclosed by a marble screen, and was still flanked by the hallowed niche, built to receive the drainings of the sacred cup.

The aisles were divided from the nave, by lancet arches, springing from clustered columns. But how describe the expansive windows, with their rich mullions, and richer rosettes - their deeply moulded labels, following the form of the arch, and resting for support on the quaintest masks - how describe the matchless hues of the glass - valued mementoes of a bygone age, and of an art that has perished?

The walls of the chapel were profusely ornamented with the richest carving; and the oaken panels of the chancel, were adorned with those exquisite festoons of fruit and flowers, so peculiarly English. The very ceiling exacted admiration. It closed no lantern - it obstructed no view - and its light ribs, springing from voluted corbels, bore at each intersection, an emblazoned escutcheon, or painted heraldic device. The intricate fan-like tracery of the roof - the enriched bosses at each meeting of the gilded ribs - gave an airy charm and lightness to the whole, which well accorded with the florid Architecture, and with the chivalrous associations, with which it is identified.

And here, beneath this spangled canopy, in this ancient shrine, whose every ornament was as a memory of her ancestors; stood Emily Delmé, as fair as the fairest of her race, changeful and trembling, a faint smile on her lip, and a quivering tear in her eye.

Clarendon Gage took her hand in his, and placed on her finger the golden pledge of truth, and as he did so, an approving sunbeam burst through the crimson-stained pane, and before lightening the tomb of Sir Reginald, fell on her silvery veil - her snowy robe - her beautiful face.

There was a very gay scene on the lawn, as they returned from the chapel.

The dancing had already commenced - strains of music were heard from on high - the ever moving circle became one moment contracted, then expanded to the full length of the arms of the dancers, as they actively footed it round the garlanded May-pole.

At the first sight of the leading carriage, however, a signal was given - the music suddenly ceased - and the whole party below, with the exception of one individual, proceeded in great state towards an arch, composed of flowers and white thorn, which o'ercanopied the road.

The carriage stopped to greet the procession.

On came the blushing May-Queen, and Maid Marian - both armed with wands wreathed with cowslips - followed by a jovial retinue of morrice dancers with drawn swords - guisers in many-coloured ribbons - and a full train of simple peasants, in white smock-frocks.

The May Queen advanced to the carriage, followed by the peasant girls, and timidly dropped a choice wreath into the lap of the bride. Loud hurras rung in the air, as Sir Henry gave his steward some welcome instructions as to the village feast; and the cavalcade continued its route.

We have said that one individual lingered near the May-pole. As he was especially active, we may describe him and his employment. He was apparently about fifteen. He had coarse straight white hair - a face that denoted stupidity - but with a cunning leer, which seemed to belie his other features.

He was taking advantage of the cessation of dancing, to supply the aspiring musicians with sundry articles of good cheer. A rope, armed with a hook, was dropped from their lofty aërie, and promptly drawn up, on the youngster's obtaining from the neighbouring tents, wherewithal to fill satisfactorily the basket which he attached.

Sir Henry Delmé and George had been so much abroad, and Emily's attachment to Clarendon was of so early a date, that it happened that the members of the Delmé family had mixed little in the festivities of the county in which they resided; and were not intimately known, nor perhaps fully appreciated, in the neighbourhood.

But the family was one of high standing, and had ever been remarkable for its kind-heartedness; and what *was* known of its individuals, was so much to their credit, that it kept alive the respect and consideration that these circumstances might of themselves warrant.

Sir Henry, on the other hand, regarded his sister's marriage as an event, at which it might be proper to show, that neither hauteur nor want of sociability, had precluded their friendly intercourse with the neighbouring magnates; and consequently, most of the principal families were present at Emily's wedding.

While this large assemblage increased the gaiety of the scene, it was somewhat wearisome to Delmé, who was too truly attached to his sister, to be otherwise than thoughtful during the ceremony, and the breakfast that succeeded it.

At length the time came when Emily could escape from the gay throng; and endeavour, in the quiet of her own room, to be once more calm, before she prepared to leave her much-loved home.

The preparations made, a note was despatched to her brother, begging him to meet her in the library. As he did so, a fresh pang shot through Delmé's heart.

As he looked on Emily's flushed face - her dewy cheek - and noted her agitated manner; he for the first time perceived, her very strong resemblance to poor George, and wondered that he had never observed this before.

Clarendon announced the carriage.

"God bless you! dear Henry!"

"God bless and preserve you! my sweet! Clarendon! good bye! I am sure you will take every care of her!"

In another moment, the carriage was whirling past the library window; and Sir Henry felt little inclined, to join the formal party in the drawing-room. Sending therefore a brief message to Mrs. Glenallan, he threw open the library window, and with hurried steps reached a summer-house, half hidden in the shrubbery. He there fell into a deep reverie, which was by no means a pleasurable one.

He thought of Emily - of George - of Acmé, - and felt that he was becoming an isolated being.

And had *he* not loved too? As this thought crossed him, his ambitious dreams were almost forgotten.

Sir Henry Delmé was aroused by the sound of voices. A loving couple, too much engaged to observe *him*, passed close to the summer-house.

It was the "Queen of the May," the prettiest and one of the poorest girls in the parish, walking arm in arm with her rural swain. They had left the "roasted beeves," and the "broached casks," for one half-hour's delicious converse.

There was some little coquettish resistance on the part of the girl, as they sat down together at the foot of a fir tree.

Her lover put his arm round her waist.

"Oh! Mary! if father would but give us a cow or so!"

This little incident decided the matter. Delmé at once resolved that Mary Smith *should* have a cow or so; and also that his own health would be greatly benefited, by a short sojourn at Leamington.

CHAPTER XV

THE MEETING

"Oh ever loving, lovely, and beloved!
How selfish sorrow ponders on the past,
And clings to thoughts now better far removed,
But Time shall tear thy shadow from me last."

We know not whether our readers have followed us with due attention, as we have incidentally, and at various intervals, made our brief allusion to the gradual change of character, wrought on Delmé, by the eventful scenes in which he so lately played a prominent part.

When we first introduced him to our reader's notice, we endeavoured to depict him as he then really was, - a man of strong principles, warm heart, and many noble qualities; but one, prone to over-estimate the value of birth and fortune - with a large proportion of pride and reserve - and with ideas greatly tinctured with the absurd fallacies of the mere man of the world.

But there was much in the family events we have described, to shake Delmé's previous convictions, and to induce him to recal many of his former opinions.

He had seen his brother form a connection, which set at naught all those convenances, which *he* had been accustomed to regard as essential to, and as indeed forming the very ingredient of, domestic happiness.

And yet Sir Henry Delmé could not disguise from himself, that if, in George's short-lived career, there had been much of pain and sorrow, they were chiefly engendered by George's mental struggle, to uphold those very opinions to which he himself was wedded; and that to this alone, might be traced much of the suffering he had undergone. This was it that had so weakened mind and body, as to render change of scene necessary; - this was it that exposed Acmé to the air of the pestiferous marshes, and which left George himself - a broken hearted man - totally incapable of bearing his bereavement.

On the other hand, the sunny happiness his brother had basked in, - and it was very great, - had sprung from the natural out-pourings of an affection, which, - unfettered as it had been by prudential considerations, - had yet the power to make earth a heaven while Acmé shared it with him, and the dark grave an object of bright promise, when hailed as the portal, through which *he* must pass, ere he gazed once more on the load-star of his hopes.

In the case, too, of Emily and Clarendon, although their union was far more in accordance with his earlier theories, yet he could not but note, how little their happiness seemed to rest on their position in society, and how greatly was it based on their love for each other.

These considerations were strengthened, by a growing feeling of isolation, which the death of George and of Acmé, - the marriage of his sister, - and probably the time of life he had arrived at, were all calculated to awaken.

With the knowledge of his disease, sprung up the hope of an antidote; and it may be, that the little episode of the May Queen in our last chapter, came but as a running comment, to reflections that had long been cherished and indulged.

The thoughts of Sir Henry Delmé anxiously centred in Julia Vernon; and as he recalled her graceful emotion when they last parted, the unfrequent blush, - it might be of shame, it might be of consciousness, - coloured his sun-burnt cheek.

At length, - the guests being dismissed, Delmé was at leisure to renew an acquaintance, which had already proved an eventful one to him. He had heard little of Miss Vernon since his return to England. His sister had thought it better to let matters take their own course; and Julia, who knew that in the eyes of the world, her circumstances were very different to what they had been previous to her uncle's death; had from motives of delicacy, shunned any intercourse that might lead to a renewed intimacy with the family.

Her health, too, had been precarious, and her elasticity of mind was gone. Slowly wasting from day to day, she had sought to banish all thoughts that were not of a world less vain than this - and her very languor of body - while it gave her an apology for declining all gaieties, induced a resigned spirit, and a quiet frame of mind.

When Sir Henry Delmé was announced, Julia was alone in the drawing-room. At that name, she attempted to rise from the sofa; but she was weak, and her head fell back on the white pillow.

Delmé stood for a moment irresolute, - a prey to the deepest pangs of remorse.

Well might he be shocked at that altered form!

Her figure was greatly attenuated, - her cheeks sunken, - her eyes bright and large; while over the forehead and drooping eyelid branched the sapphire veins, with their intricate windings so clearly marked, that Delmé almost thought, that he could trace the motion of the blood beneath. That momentary pause, and the one mutual glance of recognition, told a more accurate tale than words could convey.

As Sir Henry pressed that small transparent hand, Julia's thin lip quivered convulsively. She attempted to speak, but the exertion of utterance was too great, and she burst into a flood of tears.

"Julia! my own Julia! forgive me! we will never part more!"

After this interview, it is needless to say that there was little else to be explained. Mrs. Vernon was delighted at Julia's happy prospects, and it was settled that their marriage should take place in the ensuing August. Such arrangements as could be made on the spot to facilitate this, were at once entered on.

At the end of two months, it became necessary that Delmé should proceed to town, for the purpose of seeing the Commander-in-Chief, in order to withdraw a previous application to be employed on active service. He was anxious also to consult a friend, whom he proposed appointing one of the trustees for his marriage settlement; and Clarendon and Emily had exacted a promise, that he would pay them a visit on his way to Delmé Park; which he had determined to take on his route to town, that he might personally inspect some alterations he had lately planned there.

It was with bright prospects before him, that Delmé kissed off the big tear that coursed down Julia's cheek; as she bade him farewell, with as much earnestness, as if years, instead of a short fortnight, were to elapse before they met again.

Miss Vernon's health had decidedly improved. She was capable of much greater exertion; and her spirits were sometimes as buoyant as in other days.

When Sir Henry first reached Leamington, the only exercise that Julia could take was in a wheel chair; and great was her delight at seeing a hand present itself over its side, and know that it was *his*. Latterly, however, she had been able to lean on his arm, and take a few turns on the lawn, and had on one occasion even reached the public gardens.

Mrs. Vernon, with the deceptive hope common to those, who watch day by day by the side of an invalid's couch, and in the very gradual loss of strength, lose sight of the real extent of danger, had never been desponding as to her daughter's ultimate recovery; and was now quite satisfied that a few weeks more would restore her completely to health.

Sir Henry Delmé, with the gaze of a lover, would note each flush of animation, and mistake it for the hue of health; while Julia herself *felt her love, and thought it strength.*

There was only one person who looked somewhat grave at these joyous preparations. This was Dr. Jephson, who noticed that Julia's voice continued very weak, and that she could not get rid of a low hollow cough, that had long distressed her.

Clarendon and his wife were resident at a beautiful cottage near Malvern, on the road to Eastnor Castle. The cottage itself was small, and half hidden with fragrant honey-suckles, but had well appointed extensive grounds behind it. *They* were not of the very many, who after the first fortnight of a forced seclusion, - the treacle moon, as some one has called it, - find their own society, both wearisome and unprofitable. *Theirs* was a lover felt but by superior and congenial minds - a love, neither sensual nor transient - a love on which affection and reflection shed their glow, - which could bear the test of scrutiny, - and which owed its chief charm to the presence of truth.

Delmé passed a week at Malvern, and then proceeded towards town, with the pleasing conviction that his sister's happiness was assured.

Twenty-four hours at Delmé sufficed to inspect the alterations, and to give orders as to Lady Delmé's rooms.

Sir Henry had received two letters from Julia, while at Malvern, and both were written in great spirits. At his club in London another awaited him, which stated that she had not been quite so well, and that she was writing from her room. A postscript from Mrs. Vernon quite did away with any alarm that Sir Henry might otherwise have felt.

Delmé attended Lord Hill's levee; and immediately afterwards proceeded to his friend's office. To his disappointment, he was informed that his friend had left for Bath; and thinking it essential that he should see him; he went thither at an early hour the following day.

At Bath he was again doomed to be disappointed, for his friend had gone to Clifton. Sir Henry dined that day with Mr. Belliston Græme; and on returning to the hotel, had the interview with Oliver Delancey, that has been described in the thirteenth chapter of our first volume.

On the succeeding morning, Delmé was with the future trustee; and finally arranged the affair to his entire satisfaction. His absence from Leamington, had been a day or two more protracted than he had anticipated, and his not finding his friend in London, had prevented his hearing from Miss Vernon so lately as he could have wished.

Sir Henry had posted all night, and it was ten in the morning when he reached Leamington. He directed the postilion to drive to his hotel, but it happened that on his way he had to pass Mrs. Vernon's door.

As the carriage turned a corner, which was distant some hundred yards from Mrs. Vernon's house, Sir Henry was surprised by a momentary check on the part of his driver.

It had rained heavily during the early part of the day. The glasses were up, and so bespattered with the mud and rain, that it was impossible to see through them. Sir Henry let them down; saw a confused mass of carriages; and could clearly discern a mourning coach.

He did not give himself time to breathe his misgivings; but

flung the door open, and sprang from his seat into the road. It was still three or four doors from Mrs. Vernon's house, and he prayed to God that his fears might be groundless.

As he approached nearer, it was evident that there was unusual bustle about *that* house. Delmé grasped the iron railing, and clung to it for support; but with every sense keenly alive to aught that might dispel, or confirm that horrible suspicion.

Two old women, dressed in the characteristic red cloak of the English peasant, were earnestly conversing together - their baskets of eggs and flowers being laid on a step of one of the adjacent houses.

"So you knowed her, Betsy Farmer?"

"Lord a mercy!" responded the other, "I ha' knowed Miss July since she wa' the height of my basket. Ay! and many's the bunch of flowers she ha' had from me. That was afore the family went to the sea side. Well! it's a matter o' five year, sin' she comed up to me one morning - so grown as I'd never ha' known her. But she knowed me, and asked all about me. And I just told her all my troubles, and how I had lost my good man. And sure enough sin' that day she ha' stood my friend, and gived me soup and flannels for the little uns, and put my Bess to service, and took me through all the bad Christmas'. Poor dear soul! she ha' gone now! and may the Lord bless her and all as good as she!"

The poor woman, who felt the loss of her benefactress, put the corner of her apron to her eyes.

Sir Henry strode forward.

Mutes were on each side of the front step. A servant threw open the door of the breakfast room, and Delmé mechanically entered it. It was filled with strangers; on some of these the spruce undertaker was fitting silk scarfs; while others were busy at the breakfast table.

An ominous whisper ran through the apartment.

"Sir Henry Delmé?" said the rosy-cheeked clergyman, enquiringly, as he laid down his egg spoon, and turned towards him.

"I trust you received my letter. Women are so utterly helpless in these matters; and poor Mrs. Vernon was quite overpowered."

Delmé turned away to master his emotion.

At this moment, a friendly hand was laid on his shoulder, and Mrs. Vernon's maid, with her eyes red from weeping, beckoned him up stairs.

He mechanically obeyed her - reeled into an inner drawing room - and stood in the presence of the bereaved mother.

Mrs. Vernon was ordinarily the very picture of neatness. *Now* she sat with her feet on a footstool - her head almost touching her lap - her silver hair all loose and dishevelled. It seemed to Delmé as if age had suddenly come upon her.

She rose as he entered, and with wild hysterical sobs, threw herself into his arms.

"My son I my son! that *should* have been. Our angel is gone - gone!"

Delmé tried to speak, but his tongue clove to his mouth, and the hysteric globe rose to his throat.

Suddenly he heard the sound of wheels, and of heavy footsteps on the stairs.

He imprinted a kiss on the old woman's forehead - it was his farewell for ever! - gave her to the care of the maid servant - and rushed from the room.

He was stopped on the landing of the staircase by the coffin of her he loved so well. The bearers stopped for an instant; they felt that this was no common greeting. Part of the pall was already turned back. Delmé removed its head with trembling hand.

"Julia Vernon. ætate 22."

He dropped the velvet with a groan, and was only saved from falling by the timely aid of the old butler, whose face was as sorrowful as his own.

But there was a duty yet to be performed, and Delmé followed the corpse.

The first mourning coach was just drawn up. An intended occupant had already his foot on the step.

"This place is mine!" said Sir Henry in a hollow voice.

The cortege proceeded; and Delmé, giddy and confused, heard solemn words spoken over his affianced one, and he waited, till even the coffin could he discerned no more.

Thompson, who had followed his master, assisted him into his carriage, placed himself beside him, and ordered the driver to proceed to the hotel. But Delmé gave a quick impetuous motion of the hand, which the domestic understood well; and the horses' heads were turned towards the metropolis.

The mourner tarried not, even to bid his sister farewell; but sought once more his brother's grave. Some friendly hand had kept its turf smooth; no footsteps, save the innocent ones of children, had pressed its grassy mound. It was clothed with soft daisies and drooping harebells. The sun seemed to shine on that spot, to bid the wanderer be contented and at rest.

But as yet there was no rest for Delmé. And he stood beside the marble slab, beneath which lay Acmé Frascati. The downy moss - soft as herself - was luxuriating there; and the cry of the cicalas was pleasant to the ear; and the image of the young Greek girl, as in a vivid picture, rose to his mind's eye. She was not attired in her white cymar; nor was her head wreathed with monumental amaranths; - health was on her cheek, fond smiles on her pouting lip, and tender love swimming in her melting glance.

His own griefs came back on Delmé; he groaned aloud. He traversed the deserts, he crossed lofty mountains, he knew thirst and privations. He was scoffed at and spat upon in an infidel country - he was tossed on the ocean - he shook hands with danger.

He visited our wide Oriental possessions; and sojourned amid the spicy islands of the Indian Archipelago, where vegetation attains a magnificence unknown elsewhere, and animal life partakes of this unexampled exuberance, - where flowers of the most exquisite colours and fragrance charm the senses by day, and delicious plants saturate the air with their odours by night.

Delmé extended his wanderings to the rarely visited "many isles," which stud the vast Pacific, and found that there too were fruitful and smiling regions.

But not on the desert - nor on the mountains - nor in the land of the Moslem - -nor on tempestuous seas - nor in those verdant islets, which seem to breathe of Paradise, to greet the wearied traveller; could Delmé's restless spirit find an abiding place, his thirst for foreign travel be slaked, or his heart know peace.

He madly sought oblivion, which could not be accorded him.

CHAPTER XVI

THE WANDERER

"Then I consider'd life in all its forms,
Of vegetables first, next zoophytes,
The tribe that dwells upon the confine strange
'Twixt plants and fish; some are there from their mouth
Spit out their progeny, and some that breed,
By suckers from their base or tubercles,
Sea-hedgehog, madrepore, sea-ruff, or pad,
Fungus, or sponge, or that gelatinous fish,
That taken from its element at once
Stinks, melts, and dies a fluid; so from these,
Through many a tribe of less equivocal life,
Dividual or insect, up I ranged,
From sentient to percipient, small advance,
Next to intelligent, to rational next,
So to half spiritual human kind,
And what is more, is more than man may know.
Last came the troublesome question - What am I?"

* * * * *

"And vain were the hat, the staff, and stole,
And all outward signs were a snare,
Unless the pilgrim's endanger'd soul
Were inwardly clothed with prayer.

"But the pilgrim prays - and then trials are light -

For prayer to him on his way,
Resembles the pillar of fire by night,
And the guiding cloud by day.

"And salvation's helm the pilgrim wears,
Or vain were all other dress;
And the shield of faith the pilgrim bears,
With the breastplate of righteousness.

"At length his tears all wiped away;
He enters the City of Light;
And how gladly he changes his gown of grey,
For Zion's robe of white."

It was on the 22nd of October, 1836, that an emissary from his sister, sought Sir Henry Delmé. It was at the antipodes to his ancestral home; in Australia, that wonderful country, which - belied and calumniated, as she has hitherto been - presents some anomalous and creditable features.

For her population, she is the wealthiest, the most enterprising, the most orderly and loyal, of our British possessions. There, is the aristocracy of wealth, to an unprecedented degree, subservient to the aristocracy of virtue. While she is stigmatised as the cloacæ of Britain, the philosopher looks into the future, and already beholds a nation, perpetuating the language of the brave and free; when the parent stock has perhaps ceased to be an empire; or is lingering on, like modern Greece, in the hopeless languor of decay and decrepitude.

This agent had arrived from England, a very short period before; and, accredited with a packet, containing various communications from Emily and Clarendon, accompanied by the miniatures of their children, with little silky curls attached to each, proceeded an expectant guest, to Sir Henry Delmé's temporary residence. Early dawn saw him pacing the deck of a steam vessel; and regarding with great surprise, the opposite banks of Hunter's River, up which the vessel was gliding.

A rich dark soil, of great depth, bespoke uncommon fertility; while the varieties of the gum tree - then quite new to him - with their bark of every diversity of colour, gave a primeval grandeur to the scene.

Each moment brought in sight the location of some enterprising settler, which, ever varying in appearance, in importance, and in extent yet told the same tale of difficulties overcome, and success ensuing.

On his reaching the township, near the head of the navigation, this agent found horses waiting for him: - he was addressed by a well-appointed groom - our old friend Thompson - who touched his hat respectfully, and mentioned the name, he was already prepared for by his Sydney advices.

Suffice it, that Sir Henry was no longer the Baronet, and that the name of Delmé was a strange one in his household.

Their route skirted the banks of one of those rivers, which, diverging from that mine of wealth, the Hunter, wind into the bowels of the land, like a vein of gold.

That emissary will not soon forget his lovely ride. His eye, wearied with gazing on the wide expanse of ocean, feasted on the rich and novel landscape. They rode alternately, through cleared lands, studded with rich farms, waving with luxuriant crops of wheat and rye; and again, through regions, where the axe had never resounded, but where eucalypti, and bastard box, and forest oak with its rough acorn, towered above beauteous wild flowers, whose forms and varieties were associated in the mind of the stranger, with some of the most precious and valued flowers which adorn British conservatories.

The russet Certhia, with outspread fluttering wing, pecked at the smooth bark, and preying on some destructive insect, really preserved what it seemed to injure. The larger parrots, travelling in pairs, screamed their passing salutation, as they displayed their bright plumage to the sun; while hundreds, of a smaller kind, with crimson shoulder, were concealed amid the green leaves; and, as they rode beneath them, babbled - like frolicsome children of the forest - a rude, but to themselves a not unmeaning dialogue.

The superb warblers, ornaments alike to the bush or the garden, flitted cheerily from bough to bough. Strangely mated are they! The male, in suit of black velvet, trimmed with sky blue, looks like a knight, attired for a palace festival: - while his lady-love - she resembles some peasant girl, silent and grateful, clothed in modest kirtle of sober brown.

As he reined in his horse, to examine these at leisure, how melodiously came on his ear, the clear, ceaseless, silver tinkle of the bell-bird; this sound ever and anon chequered by the bold chock-ee-chock! of the bald-headed friar. They had proceeded very leisurely, and the sun was already declining, when Thompson, pointing to an abrupt path, motioned him to descend, and at the same time, gave the peculiar cry, known in the colony as the cooï; a cry which was as promptly answered. It was not until he was close to the edge of the river, that the stranger understood its purport.

A punt was rapidly approaching from the opposite bank. An athletic aboriginal native, in an attitude that seemed studiedly graceful, was bending to the stout rope, which, attached to either side of the river, served to propel the punt. He had been spearing fish; for his wife, or gin, or queen - for she was born such, and contradicted in her person the old adage,

> "There's a difference between
> A beggar and a queen" -

was drawing the barb of a spear from the bleeding side of a struggling mullet. She sat at the bottom of the boat, with a blanket closely wound round her. She was young, and her looks were not unpleasing. Her thickly-matted hair was ornamented with kangaroo teeth; and to her shoulder, closely clung a native tailless bear, whose appearance could not do otherwise than excite a smile. With convex staring eyes – hairless nose - and white ruff of fur round his face - he very closely resembled in physiognomy, some grey-whiskered guzzling citizen. The well-trained horses gave no trouble, as they entered the punt; and the smiling boatman, displaying his teeth to Thompson, but without speaking, commenced warping the punt to the opposite side of the river. They were half way across, ere the guest observed the mansion of the friend he sought. It stood on the summit of the hill, on the left; beneath which the river made a very abrupt bend. The house itself resembled the common weather-boarded cottage of the early settler, - wide verandah was over the front entrance, - and two small rooms, the exact width of this, jutted out on either side of it.

Its site however was commanding. The house stood on an eminence, and from the windows, a long reach of the river was visible. At the top of the brow of the hill, extended a range of English rose trees, in full flower. The bank, which might be about thirty yards in front of these, was clothed with foliage to the water's edge.

There might be seen the fragrant mimosa - the abundant acacia - the swamp oak, which would have been styled a fir, had not the first exiles to Australia found twined round its boughs, the misletoe, with its many home associations - the elegant cedar - the close-growing mangrove - and strange parasitical plants, pushing through huge fungi, and clasping with the remorseless strength of the wrestler, and with the round crunching folds of the boa, the trees they were gradually to supplant and destroy.

Suddenly, the quick finger of the black pointed to an object close beside the punt. A bill, as of a bird, and apparently of the duck tribe, protruded above the surface of the water. For an instant, small, black, piercing eyes peered towards them: but as the quadruped, for such it was, prepared to dive in affright, the unerring shot of a rifle splashed the water on the cheek of the stranger - the body rolled slowly over - the legs stiffened - a sluggish stream of dark blood tainted the surrounding wave - and the ferryman, extending his careless hand, threw the victim to his companion, at the same time addressing a few words to her in their native language.

The guest had little difficulty, in recognising the uncouth form of the ornithorhynchus, or water-mole; but he turned with yet more eagerness, towards the spot, whence that shot had proceeded. On the summit of the steep bank, leaning on his rifle, stood Sir Henry Delmé.

His form was still commanding - there was something in the air with which the cap was worn - and in the strap round his Swiss blouse - that bespoke the soldier and the gentleman: but his face was sadly attenuated - the lower jaw appeared to have fallen in - and his hair was very grey.

He received his guest with a cordial and sincere welcome. While the latter delivered his packet the native who had warped the punt over, came up with the dead platypus,

"Well, Boomeroo! is it a female?"

"No, massa! full grown - with large spur!"

Sir Henry saw that his guest was puzzled by this dialogue, and good-naturedly showed him the distinguishing characteristic of the male ornithorhynchus - the spur on the hinder foot, which is hollow, and transmits an envenomed liquid, secreted by a gland on the inner surface of the thigh.

In November, of the year preceding, a burrow of the animal had been opened on the bank of the river, which contained the dam, and three live young ones; - there were many points, yet to be determined relative to its interior organization; and it was on this account, that Sir Henry was anxious to obtain a female specimen at this particular period. As he spoke, Delmé introduced the stranger to his study, which might more aptly be styled a museum; - applied some spirits of wine to the platypus, and placing it under a bell-glass for the morrow's examination, left him turning over his collection of birds, while he perused his valued home letters.

It was with unmixed pleasure, knowing as he did his melancholy history, that the stranger found Sir Henry Delmé engaged in pursuits, which it was evident he was following up with no common enthusiasm. In truth, a mere accidental circumstance, - the difficulty of obtaining a vessel at one of the Indian Islands for any port, - had at first brought him to Australia, a country regarding which he had felt little curiosity. The strange varieties, however, of its animal kingdom, had interested him; - he was struck with the rapid strides that that country has made in half a century - and he continued from month to month to occupy the house where his friend had now found him.

To the stranger's eye, the eye of a novice, the well arranged specimens of birds of the most beautiful plumage - of animals, chiefly marsupial, of the most singular developement - of glittering insects - and of deep coloured shells; were attractive wonders enough; but from the skeletons beside these, it was quite clear, that Delmé had acquired considerable knowledge as to the internal construction of the animals themselves - that he had studied the subsisting relations, between the mechanism and the movements - the structure, and its varied functions.

After dinner, Sir Henry Delmé, who appeared to think that the bearer of his despatches had conferred on him a lasting favour, threw off his habitual reserve, and delighted and interested him with his tales of foreign travel.

As the night wore on, the conversation reverted to his sister and his home. It was evident, that what remained for the living of that crushed heart, was with Emily and Clarendon, and their children; perhaps more than all, with his young heir and god-son, Henry Delmé Gage. The very colour of that sunny lock of hair, gave rise to much speculation: and it seemed as if he would never be wearied, of listening to the minutest description of the dawning of intellect, in a precocious little fellow of barely five years of age.

Encouraged by his evident feeling, and observing many more comforts about him, than he had been led to expect from his previous errant habits; his guest ventured to express his hope, that Sir Henry might yet return to England.

"My good friend!" replied he, "for I must call you such now, for I know not when I have experienced such unalloyed satisfaction, as you have conferred on me this night, by conversing so freely of those I love; I certainly never can forget that I am the last male of an ancient race, and that those who are nearest and dearest to me, are divided from me by a wide waste of waters. I have learnt to suffer with more patience than I had ever hoped for; and, it may be, - although I have hardly breathed the thought to myself - it may yet be accorded me to revisit that ancient chapel, and to dwell once more in that familiar mansion."

His guest was overcome by his emotion, and pressed his hand with warmth, as he made his day's journey the excuse for an early retirement.

Sleep soon visited his eyelids, for the ride, to one fresh from a sea voyage, had brought with it a wholesome weariness. He was aroused from his slumbers, by the deep sonorous accents as of a man reading Spanish.

The light streamed from an adjacent room, through the chinks of a partition. He started up alike forgetful of Delmé, his ride, and his arrival in Australia; conceiving that he was again at the mercy of the waves, in his narrow comfortless cabin.

That light, however, brought the stranger back to the wanderer, and his griefs.

Beside a small table, strewn with his lately received English letters, knelt Sir Henry Delmé. The stranger had seen condemned criminals pray with becoming fervour; and devotees of many a creed lift up their hearts to heaven; but never had he witnessed a more contrite or a humbler spirit imprinted on the features of mortal man, than then shed its radiance on that sorrowful, but noble face.

Strange as it may appear, he knew not whether the words themselves really caught his ear, or whether the motion of the lips expressed them - but this he *did* know, that every syllable seemed to reach his heart, and impress him with a mystic thrill,

"OR EVER THE SILVER CORD BE LOOSED, OR THE GOLDEN BOWL BE BROKEN, OR THE PITCHER BE BROKEN AT THE FOUNTAIN, OR THE WHEEL BROKEN AT THE CISTERN. THEN SHALL THE DUST RETURN TO THE EARTH AS IT WAS: AND THE SPIRIT SHALL RETURN UNTO GOD WHO GAVE IT."

CHAPTER XVII

THE WANDERER'S RETURN

"And he had learn'd to love - I know not why,
For this in such as him seems strange of mood, -
The helpless looks of blooming infancy,
Even in its earliest nurture; what subdued,
To change like this, a mind so far imbued
With scorn of man, it little boots to know;
But thus it was; and though in solitude
Small power the nipp'd affections have to grow,
In him this glow'd when all beside had ceased to glow."

Within a period of two months, from the interview we have described, the stranger found that his arguments had not been thrown away; as he shook Sir Henry's hand on the deck of a vessel bound for Valparaiso. His love of travel and of excitement, had induced such an habitual restlessness, that Delmé was not prepared at once to embark for England. He crossed the Cordillera de los Andes - traversed the Pampas of Buenos Ayres - and finally embarked for his native land.

It was the height of summer, when the carriage which bore the long absent owner to his ancestral home, neared the ancient moss-grown lodge.

Fanny Porter, who was now married, and had a thriving babe at her breast, started with surprise; as, throwing open the gate, she recognised in the care-worn man with bronzed face and silver hair, her well known and beloved master. As the carriage neared the chapel, it struck Sir Henry, that it would be but prudent, to inform Clarendon of his near approach; in order that he might prepare Emily for the meeting. He ordered the postilion to pull up - tore a leaf from his memorandum book - and wrote a few lines to Clarendon, despatching Thompson in advance. He turned into the chapel, and as he approached its altar, the bridal scene, enacted there nearly seven years back, seemed to rise palpably before him.

But the tomb of Sir Reginald Delmé, with its velvet dusty banner - the marble monument of his mother, with the bust above it, whose naked eye seemed turned towards him - his withered heart and hopes soon darkened his recollections of that bright hour. With agitated emotions, Sir Henry left the chapel; and in a spirit of impatience, strode towards the mansion, intending to meet the returning domestic. His feelings were strange, various, and not easily defined.

He was awakened from his day-dream by the sound of children's voices, which sound he instinctively followed, until he reached the old orchard. It was such an orchard, as might be planted by an old Delmé, ere any Linnean or Loudonean horticulturist had decided that slopes are best for the sun, that terraces are an economical saving of ground, that valleys must be swamps, and that blights are vulgar errors. The orchard at Delmé was strikingly unscientific; but the old stock contrived to bear good fruit. The pippins, golden and russet - the pears, jargonelle and good-christian - the cherries, both black and white heart - still thrived; while under their shade, grew hips, haws, crabs, sloes, and blackberries, happy to be shaded from rain, dews, and fierce sun-shine, and unenvious of roses, cherries, apples, damsons, and mulberries; their self-defended, and more aristocratic cousins.

Sir Henry stopped unseen at the gate of the orchard, and for some minutes looked on the almost fairy group, whose voices had led him thither.

Lying on the bank, which enclosed the orchard, was a blue-eyed rosy-cheeked little girl; - the ground ashes had been cut down; and her laughing face was pillowed on the violets and oxlips, that burst from between the roots. She was preparing to take another roll into the clayey ditch below. Another little girl was gazing at the child from within the orchard; half doubtful whether she should encourage or check her. One pale-blue slipper and her little sock were half sunk in the clay, while the veiny and pink-soled foot, the large lids half closed over her deep blue eyes, the finger thrust between her red and pouting lips, her bonnet thrown back and hanging by the strings round her swelling throat, her hair dishevelled and stuck with oxlips, primroses, cowslips, violets, and daisies; and wreathed with the spring-holly, or butcher's-broom - made her a perfect picture of English beauty, and of childish anxiety and indecision.

Beside her stood a boy older than herself, and evidently as perplexed. There was Julia perched cock-horse on the bank - there was Emily, her hair undone, her bonnet crashed, with one shoe and stocking lost - and yet he had promised Mamma, that if she would but once trust his sisters to him, that he would bring them home, "with such a pretty basket of spring-flowers."

The beautiful blossoms of the cherry hung around the boy - the bees buzzed in its bells - the apple and pear blossoms shook their fragrance in the warm air - and the shadows of the flying clouds hurried like wings over the bright green grass. The boy had dropped his basket of fresh-blown flowers at his feet - tears were trembling in his eye-lids, as he gazed on his sisters. His look was that of George.

"Childhood too has its sorrows," said Sir Henry, half aloud, "even when seeking joy on a bank of primroses. Why should *I* then repine?"

The boy started as he heard and saw the stranger: - he involuntarily put one foot forward in an attitude of childish defiance: but children are keen physiognomists, and there was nothing but affection beaming from that mournful face.

"My boy!" said Delmé, and his eyes were moist, "did you ever hear of your Uncle Henry?"

"Emily! Emily! Julia!" exclaimed the little fellow, as he rushed into Sir Henry's arms, "here is Uncle Henry, my god-papa, and he will help us to reach the blackberries."

We need follow the wanderer no further. It is true that in his youth he had not known sympathy; in his manhood he had experienced sorrow; but it is a pleasure to us to reflect, that despair is not the companion of his old age.

Choose from Thousands of 1stWorldLibrary Classics By

George Eliot
George Gissing
George MacDonald
George Meredith
George Orwell
George Sylvester Viereck
George Tucker
George W. Cable
George Wharton James
Gertrude Atherton
Gordon Casserly
Grace E. King
Grace Gallatin
Grace Greenwood
Grant Allen
Guillermo A. Sherwell
Gulielma Zollinger
Gustav Flaubert
H. A. Cody
H. B. Irving
H.C. Bailey
H. G. Wells
H. H. Munro
H. Irving Hancock
H. Rider Haggard
H. W. C. Davis
Haldeman Julius
Hall Caine
Hamilton Wright Mabie
Hans Christian Andersen
Harold Avery
Harold McGrath
Harriet Beecher Stowe
Harry Castlemon
Harry Coghill
Harry Houidini
Hayden Carruth
Helent Hunt Jackson
Helen Nicolay
Hendrik Conscience
Hendy David Thoreau
Henri Barbusse
Henrik Ibsen
Henry Adams
Henry Ford
Henry Frost
Henry James
Henry Jones Ford
Henry Seton Merriman
Henry W Longfellow
Herbert A. Giles
Herbert Carter
Herbert N. Casson
Herman Hesse
Hildegard G. Frey
Homer
Honore De Balzac
Horace B. Day
Horace Walpole
Horatio Alger Jr.
Howard Pyle
Howard R. Garis
Hugh Lofting
Hugh Walpole
Humphry Ward
Ian Maclaren
Inez Haynes Gillmore
Irving Bacheller
Isabel Hornibrook
Israel Abrahams
Ivan Turgenev
J.G.Austin
J. Henri Fabre
J. M. Barrie
J. Macdonald Oxley
J. S. Fletcher
J. S. Knowles
J. Storer Clouston
Jack London
Jacob Abbott
James Allen
James Andrews
James Baldwin
James Branch Cabell
James DeMille
James Joyce
James Lane Allen
James Lane Allen
James Oliver Curwood
James Oppenheim
James Otis
James R. Driscoll
Jane Austen
Jane L. Stewart
Janet Aldridge
Jens Peter Jacobsen
Jerome K. Jerome
John Burroughs
John Cournos
John F. Kennedy
John Gay
John Glasworthy
John Habberton
John Joy Bell
John Kendrick Bangs
John Milton
John Philip Sousa
Jonas Lauritz Idemil Lie
Jonathan Swift
Joseph A. Altsheler
Joseph Carey
Joseph Conrad
Joseph E. Badger Jr
Joseph Hergesheimer
Joseph Jacobs
Jules Vernes
Julian Hawthrone
Julie A Lippmann
Justin Huntly McCarthy
Kakuzo Okakura
Kenneth Grahame
Kenneth McGaffey
Kate Langley Bosher
Kate Langley Bosher
Katherine Cecil Thurston
Katherine Stokes
L. A. Abbot
L. T. Meade
L. Frank Baum
Latta Griswold
Laura Dent Crane
Laura Lee Hope
Laurence Housman
Lawrence Beasley
Leo Tolstoy
Leonid Andreyev
Lewis Carroll
Lewis Sperry Chafer
Lilian Bell
Lloyd Osbourne
Louis Hughes
Louis Tracy
Louisa May Alcott
Lucy Fitch Perkins
Lucy Maud Montgomery
Luther Benson
Lydia Miller Middleton
Lyndon Orr
M. Corvus
M. H. Adams
Margaret E. Sangster
Margret Howth
Margaret Vandercook

Margret Penrose
Maria Edgeworth
Maria Thompson Daviess
Mariano Azuela
Marion Polk Angellotti
Mark Overton
Mark Twain
Mary Austin
Mary Catherine Crowley
Mary Cole
Mary Hastings Bradley
Mary Roberts Rinehart
Mary Rowlandson
M. Wollstonecraft Shelley
Maud Lindsay
Max Beerbohm
Myra Kelly
Nathaniel Hawthrone
Nicolo Machiavelli
O. F. Walton
Oscar Wilde
Owen Johnson
P.G. Wodehouse
Paul and Mabel Thorne
Paul G. Tomlinson
Paul Severing
Percy Brebner
Peter B. Kyne
Plato
R. Derby Holmes
R. L. Stevenson
R. S. Ball
Rabindranath Tagore
Rahul Alvares
Ralph Bonehill
Ralph Henry Barbour
Ralph Victor
Ralph Waldo Emmerson
Rene Descartes
Rex Beach
Rex E. Beach
Richard Harding Davis
Richard Jefferies
Richard Le Gallienne
Robert Barr
Robert Frost
Robert Gordon Anderson
Robert L. Drake
Robert Lansing
Robert Lynd
Robert Michael Ballantyne
Robert W. Chambers
Rosa Nouchette Carey
Rudyard Kipling
Samuel B. Allison
Samuel Hopkins Adams
Sarah Bernhardt
Sarah C. Hallowell
Selma Lagerlof
Sherwood Anderson
Sigmund Freud
Standish O'Grady
Stanley Weyman
Stella Benson
Stella M. Francis
Stephen Crane
Stewart Edward White
Stijn Streuvels
Swami Abhedananda
Swami Parmananda
T. S. Ackland
T. S. Arthur
The Princess Der Ling
Thomas A. Janvier
Thomas A Kempis
Thomas Anderton
Thomas Bailey Aldrich
Thomas Bulfinch
Thomas De Quincey
Thomas Dixon
Thomas H. Huxley
Thomas Hardy
Thomas More
Thornton W. Burgess
U. S. Grant
Valentine Williams
Various Authors
Vaughan Kester
Victor Appleton
Victoria Cross
Virginia Woolf
Wadsworth Camp
Walter Camp
Walter Scott
Washington Irving
Wilbur Lawton
Wilkie Collins
Willa Cather
Willard F. Baker
William Dean Howells
William le Queux
W. Makepeace Thackeray
William W. Walter
William Shakespeare
Winston Churchill
Yei Theodora Ozaki
Yogi Ramacharaka
Young E. Allison
Zane Grey

www.ingramcontent.com/pod-product-compliance
Lightning Source LLC
Chambersburg PA
CBHW020555310726
48979CB00008B/1220/J

9781421823140